D0640708

BOSWELL'S POLITICAL CAREER

Yale Studies in English

Benjamin Christie Nangle, Editor

Volume 155

BOSWELL'S POLITICAL CAREER

by FRANK BRADY

New Haven and London, Yale University Press, 1965

Designed by John O. C. McCrillis,
set in Linotype Garamond,
and printed in the United States of America by
The Carl Purington Rollins Printing-Office of
the Yale University Press, New Haven, Connecticut.

Library of Congress catalog card number: 65–11175

Published with assistance from the Kingsley Trust
Association Publication Fund established by the
Scroll and Key Society of Yale College.

To Frederick A. Pottle

Preface

In its original form, this study was my Yale doctoral dissertation; it has been revised extensively for publication. I have not tried, of course, to write a political history of Scotland from the accession of George III to the French Revolution, though such a history is much needed. Rather, by focusing on Boswell's political career, I have hoped to add to our knowledge of the period as well as to contribute to a greater understanding of Boswell himself.

It is almost embarrassing to admit how much this work owes to others. The readers of my dissertation, Frederick W. Hilles, William P. Holden, and William K. Wimsatt, Jr. made many useful comments, as did A. S. Foord, who read part of the first draft. Besides Mr. Hilles and Mr. Wimsatt, my other colleagues in the Boswell Office at Yale have been most helpful; in particular, I should like to thank Harriet Chidester, Benjamin F. Houston, Herman W. Liebert, Robert F. Metzdorf, Marshall Waingrow, Robert Warnock, and Charles M. Weis. I have relied almost as heavily on my friends in the Walpole Office, especially George L. Lam, Robert A. Smith, and Warren H. Smith, who often claimed, with more justice than I cared to acknowledge, that this study would never be completed without their advice and assistance. Benjamin C. Nangle read the manuscript with his usual scrupulous attention.

To three individuals I owe a particular debt. Marion S. Pottle, whose bibliographical knowledge of the Boswell Papers is unrivaled, set me straight on several matters with the greatest courtesy. Sir James Fergusson of Kilkerran, Bt., Keeper of the Records of Scotland, has guided me everywhere in this work, both through his published studies and through his generous answers to many questions. The late Charles H. Bennett kindly encouraged me in every way almost from the moment I arrived, full of assurance and ignorance, at the Yale Graduate School. To his extensive and accurate research, every student of Boswell must be indebted beyond possibility of acknowledgment.

Any account of how much I owe to Frederick A. Pottle could only sound fulsome. I will merely paraphrase what a colleague once said: "Working with Fred Pottle is the finest education in scholarship a man could possibly have." There are still giants in the earth.

I wish to thank the following for generous permission to quote from manuscript and published material: Yale University, and the Boswell Editorial Committee in particular, as well as the McGraw-Hill Book Company, Inc. for material in the Boswell Papers at Yale; the Earl Fitzwilliam and the Wentworth Estates Co. for material in the Burke Collection, Central Library, Sheffield; Sir James Fergusson for material in the Kilkerran MSS; Mr. and Mrs. Donald F. Hyde for material in their collection; the Henry E. Huntington Library for material in the Loudoun MSS; the William L. Clements Library for material in the Shelburne MSS; the Trustees of the British Museum for material there. A research grant from the Pennsylvania State University helped to pay for preparing this work for the press, and Barbara Chatfield typed the manuscript with her accustomed speed and expertise. Sir James Fergusson and F. A. Pottle were kind enough to read the proofs.

F. B.

University Park, Pennsylvania
September 1964

Contents

Abbreviations and Cue Titles

Abbreviations, cue titles, and reference forms in this work have been styled, with certain modifications, to accord with the forthcoming research volumes in the Yale Editions of the Private Papers of James Boswell, to be published by McGraw-Hill and William Heinemann. Place of publication has been supplied only where the possibility of confusion exists. The following abbreviations refer to the Boswell Papers at Yale (Yale MSS).

A	Accounts
C	Correspondence: Letters received by James Boswell and other manuscripts not written by him
Journ.	Journals of James Boswell
L	Letters written by James Boswell
Lg	Legal Papers
Life MS	MS of the *Life of Samuel Johnson, LL.D.*
M	Manuscripts by James Boswell, not Journals or Letters
Mem.	Memoranda or Journal Notes of James Boswell
P	Printed Matter and other Non-Manuscript Material
Reg. Let.	Register of Letters

Catalogue numbers from the forthcoming Catalogue of the Yale MSS have been supplied for all references, except in the cases of the Journals (J 1–121), Life MS (M 144–67), Memoranda (found in J 1–121), and Register of Letters (M 251–55), where items can be easily located because they appear in chronological sequence in the Catalogue. "From" and "to" references indicate that Boswell was the sender or recipient of a letter. Since the great majority of the Yale MSS will be printed in the research edition, no attempt has been made to show what material has already been published; to have done so would have enlarged the footnotes beyond all measure. Where a published work is cited, followed by a Yale Catalogue number, e.g. to Wilkes, 7 May 1765 (*Letters JB,* i.74; L 1284), or in the rare instances where two Yale Catalogue numbers are given, e.g. to Dundas, 17 Mar. (*L 478.1; L 478), the first reference is to the original document and the second to a draft or copy.

The following non-Yale MSS cue titles have been used:

Adam	*View of the Political State of Scotland in the Last Century,* ed. Sir Charles Adam, 1887
Arniston Memoirs	*Arniston Memoirs . . . 1571–1838,* ed. G. W. T. Omond, 1887
Ayrshire	*Ayrshire at the Time of Burns,* Collections of the Ayrshire Archaeological and Natural History Society, vol. 5, 1959
Boswelliana	*Boswelliana,* ed. Charles Rogers, 1874
Boswelliana MS	MS from which the preceding item was derived in abridged form. In the Hyde Collection, Somerville, New Jersey
BP	*Private Papers of James Boswell,* ed. Geoffrey Scott and F. A. Pottle, 1928–34
Bute MSS	Loudoun Papers, now in the possession of the Marquess of Bute
Cald. Papers	*Selections from the Family Papers Preserved at Caldwell,* ed. William Mure, 1854

Carlyle MSS	MSS in the possession of the Misses Carlyle of Waterbeck, Dumfriesshire
Correspondence of George III	*Correspondence of King George the Third,* ed. Sir John Fortescue, 1927–28
Corsica	James Boswell, *An Account of Corsica,* 3d ed., 1769
Cumberland and Westmorland M.P.'s	R. S. Ferguson, *Cumberland and Westmorland M.P.'s,* 1871
EA	*Edinburgh Advertiser*
Fergusson, "'Making Interest'"	James Fergusson, "'Making Interest' in Scottish County Elections," *Scottish Historical Review,* xxvi, 1947
Fergusson, "Sir Adam and Sir John"	James Fergusson, "Sir Adam and Sir John: Sidelights on an Eighteenth Century Election," *Scots Magazine,* new series, xix, 1933
Fett. MSS	Boswell's letters to Sir William Forbes in C. C. Abbott, *A Catalogue of Papers Relating to Boswell, Johnson & Sir William Forbes Found at Fettercairn House,* 1936
Fitzwilliam MSS	Burke correspondence in the possession of the Earl Fitzwilliam on deposit with the Sheffield City Libraries. T. W. Copeland and M. S. Smith, *A Checklist of the Correspondence of Edmund Burke,* 1955, indicates what letters had been published by that date
Furber	Holden Furber, *Henry Dundas,* 1931
GM	*Gentleman's Magazine*
Hist. MSS Comm.	*Reports of the Historical Manuscripts Commission,* 1870 et seq.

Hypochondriack	James Boswell, *The Hypochondriack,* ed. Margery Bailey, 1928
Intimate Society Letters	*Intimate Society Letters of the 18th Century,* ed. [John, 9th] Duke of Argyll [?1910]
JHC	*Journals of the House of Commons*
Kilkerran MSS	Manuscripts in the possession of Sir James Fergusson of Kilkerran, Bt.
LC	*London Chronicle*
Letters JB	*Letters of James Boswell,* ed. C. B. Tinker, 1924. Texts of these letters have sometimes been corrected from originals or photostats
Letters of George Dempster	*Letters of George Dempster to Sir Adam Fergusson,* ed. James Fergusson, 1934
Life	James Boswell, *Life of Samuel Johnson,* ed. G. B. Hill, rev. L. F. Powell, 1934–50
Lit. Car.	F. A. Pottle, *The Literary Career of James Boswell, Esq.,* 1929
Loudoun MSS	Manuscripts relating to the Earls of Loudoun in the Henry E. Huntington Library, San Marino, California
Lowland Lairds	James Fergusson, *Lowland Lairds,* 1949
LPS 85	James Boswell, *A Letter to the People of Scotland,* 1785
Matheson	Cyril Matheson, *Life of Henry Dundas,* 1933
Mathieson	William Mathieson, *The Awakening of Scotland . . . 1747 to 1797,* 1910
Namier, *England*	Sir Lewis Namier, *England in the Age of the American Revolution,* 2d ed., 1961

Namier, *Structure*	Sir Lewis Namier, *The Structure of Politics at the Accession of George III,* 2d ed., 1957
Newhailes MSS	Manuscripts in the possession of Sir Mark Dalrymple of Newhailes, Bt.
Ramsay	John Ramsay, *Scotland and Scotsmen,* ed. Alexander Allardyce, 1888
Robinson	*Parliamentary Papers of John Robinson,* ed. W. T. Laprade, 1922
Shelburne MSS	Manuscripts relating to William, 2d Earl of Shelburne, in the William L. Clements Library, Ann Arbor, Michigan
SM	*Scots Magazine*
Tour	*Boswell's Journal of a Tour to the Hebrides,* ed. F. A. Pottle and C. H. Bennett, new ed. 1961. The work Boswell himself published is cited as *Life,* v.
Wight	Alexander Wight, *An Inquiry into the Rise and Progress of Parliament, chiefly in Scotland,* 1784

My practice has been to follow the spelling of manuscripts and printed works, apart from the expansion of certain conventional abbreviations, but punctuation has been occasionally supplied or altered, as has capitalization in a very few instances. Those of Boswell's journals and memoranda that appear in the *Private Papers of James Boswell* (*BP*) and *Boswell's Journal of a Tour to the Hebrides* (*Tour*) are printed as published in those works.

"It was generally supposed, that Mr. Boswell would have had a seat in Parliament; and indeed his not being amongst the Representatives of the Commons is one of those strange things which occasionally happen in the complex operations of our mixed Government."

Boswell on himself, 1791.
(*Lit. Car.*, p. xlii)

1

Introduction

A man's life seems largely shaped by the relationship between what he is and what he wants to be, between what his nature and environment inexorably make him and what his will demands he perform. If the "I am" expands naturally into the "I will be," the result is that enviable pattern, an harmonious life. More often, some discrepancies appear: a man strains for the wrong goal, and the disproportion between desire and attainment seems ironic or pathetic, tragic or grotesque.

The political career of James Boswell assumes all of these aspects at one point or another, but essentially it seems either like a nightmare or a bad joke. Boswell was a swan who insisted much of the time that he was a duck: a genius who aimed at a goal both beneath him and yet almost impossible to attain. The central and most persistent ambition of the greatest English biographer was to represent the County of Ayrshire in the House of Commons. Yet it is true that many Englishmen have combined careers in literature and politics: the involvement of the writer in the political life of his times was taken for granted by men like Milton, Marvell, Addison, and Swift; and in Boswell's own age, Burke superbly united his talents as statesman and writer.

There is a real difference, however, between Boswell and these men, a difference that transcends the contrast between his failure and their relative success: they tended to engage in politics only to the extent that it coincided with a natural gift. The prose of Milton's *Areopagitica* and Burke's *Reflections* retains its magnificence; Marvell was an able member of Parliament, and Addison rose higher in the state than perhaps nature had equipped him to. Swift's pamphlets were powerful, but who other than a specialist would care to read Boswell's second *Letter to the People of Scotland?* The contrast between Boswell and another political failure, Gibbon, is instructive. Gibbon sat in the Commons only so long as it was fairly easy and profitable to do so; he retired with little protest, since he knew that his real work lay elsewhere. But Boswell chased his mirage to the end.

One mark of Boswell's inability to estimate his own nature properly was that, except when indulging in absolute fantasy, his view of his own political role was so limited. He made no pretense to political theory, or even to a large view of affairs, like Burke. As a practical politician, he was at best middling: occasionally, his tactics were sound, but anything like a general strategy hardly entered his head. All he wanted was to be one of the 558 members of the House of Commons, not because he particularly hoped to do something for his country, like Savile or Wilberforce, or even to be conspicuous there; but simply because being an M.P. was a respectable position, which would enhance the reputation of the Boswells of Auchinleck, and ensure that he spend part of each year in London. There is nothing discreditable in Boswell's motives, which were on a level with those of the average M.P.; it is their ordinariness that shows, in Boswell's case, a misdirection of energy.

Only once in his political career, in his involvement with Corsica, did Boswell rise above mediocrity to achieve a reputation that hovered, typically enough, between success and notoriety. As well as wide public recognition, Corsica gave him a large and genuine cause, which he overplayed in characteristic fashion. At the same time, the publishing of the *Account of Corsica* was the crucial event of Boswell's early life, and in terms of his future it had all the aspects of the gods' double-edged gift. Boswell was already a practicing advocate, but unless his attention was caught by an unusual case, the law was no more than a day-to-day job; he rightly assumed that he could do reasonably well at the bar, but it is significant that among his fantasies he only occasionally dreamed of becoming Lord Chancellor. *Corsica,* however, opened up two major possibilities: he could actively pursue a career in literature or politics. Boswell had always liked to write, and *Corsica* proved to him that he could write and what kind of work he could write. Yet, at this time, he seems not to have understood his potential as a writer, or to have seriously considered writing as a career. On the other hand, the Corsican cause had given him a taste of what it was like, even in a minor way, to figure in public life; and he loved it. How much this experience channeled Boswell's ambition would be difficult to estimate, since a seat in Parliament had always been one of his goals; at the least, it must have considerably reinforced ambition.

Boswell's connection with Corsica might be called the paradox of the unfortunate success, since it encouraged him to pursue overlapping careers as writer and politician. Late in life his friend, W. J. Temple, pointed the moral when he told Boswell that he "aimed at uniting two characters that were incompatible. Had Dundas been ambitious of being a wit and an author, he never would have been Secretary of State."[1]

In short, Boswell's political career is the story of a man who mistook his own nature and fortune. From our perspective it is a blind alley, but it must be investigated if Boswell's conception of himself and his life is to be fully understood.

What Boswell could accomplish in politics was primarily governed, of course, by the political situation and electoral system of Scotland. The studies of Sir Lewis Namier and others

1. From Temple, [21 Apr. 1794] (C 2965).

have so clearly illuminated the structure of eighteenth-century English politics that it need not be summarized here, but it may be helpful to explain briefly the bases of Scottish politics, which was something of a special case. The small number of voters and the poverty of the Scots made the country particularly susceptible to governmental control and to the domination of a political manager who could deliver a large bloc of votes in return for past or promised favors. "The Scottish upper class looked to a parliamentary career chiefly as a means of earning the spoils of office; and, having a sufficient equivalent at command, they seldom failed to obtain their reward," according to William Mathieson.[2] He perhaps oversimplified the situation; the desire to participate responsibly in their country's government did motivate some men, but it was certainly true in Scotland as in England that "for the elector the vote, for the borough its representation, for the Member his seat in Parliament, were valuable assets from which advantages were expected."[3]

Scotland elected sixteen Representative Peers to sit in the House of Lords from an eligible group of seventy to ninety. In the first sixty years after the Union, the Government circulated a list of peers, which was generally adopted over some opposition. Resistance to this procedure became effective in the 1770s, and though Government interest remained strong for the rest of the century, it was never as decisive again.[4] The

2. *The Awakening of Scotland . . . 1747 to 1797* (1910), p. 22.

3. Sir Lewis Namier, *The Structure of Politics at the Accession of George III* (2d ed. 1957), p. 161. Especially in the absence of genuine political or religious issues, "power was used primarily to satisfy local or even personal needs" (ibid., pp. 133–34). Sir James Fergusson, however, remarks on the "high standard of ability, integrity, and public spirit" displayed by Scottish M.P.'s of the pre-Reform Bill period (*Lowland Lairds,* 1949, p. 20).

4. Alexander Wight, *An Inquiry into the Rise and Progress of Parliament, chiefly in Scotland* (1784), p. 128; Sir James Fergusson, *The Sixteen Peers of Scotland* (1960), pp. 75–95.

peers, however, as in England, exerted their influence most powerfully by the election of members to the Commons.

Of Scotland's 45 members in the lower House, 30 represented counties and 15 burghs. Since Scotland has 33 counties, 6 were paired off and elected members alternately: Bute, for example, elected a member in 1784, and Caithness in 1790. The county franchise was a tangled relic of feudalism. It was limited to those who held 40-shilling freehold lands "of old extent," a valuation of land supposedly dating from the reign of Alexander III (1249–86), who could produce a retour[5] of this land prior to 16 September 1681. It also extended to those who possessed land worth £400 Scots in valued rent (about £33 sterling), an assessment permanently fixed in 1667 which in the course of time became distinct from the real value of the lands. In either case land had to be held directly of the King, and not of a vassal.[6] This last qualification established what was known as a superiority.

This cumbersome system invited contention and abuse. Since the number of legal votes was extremely small, the creation of "nominal and fictitious" votes was a profitable business. A large landowner could divide his property into £400 parcels, for example, and by a complicated procedure invest the holders of these parcels with superiorities while retaining the property. A trust oath was required of all voters attesting that they were the real owners of the land by which they claimed the right to vote, but many voters did not hesitate to perjure themselves. The Court of Session, the highest civil court in Scotland, ruled several times against nominal votes in the 1760s and 1770s, but was either reversed by the House of Lords or circumvented by new subterfuges. It was not until 1790 that a decision of

5. "A Retour was the return, or answer, of a jury, by which on the death of the possessor of a landed estate, the successor was served, or declared, heir to his ancestor" (*View of the Political State of Scotland in the Last Century,* ed. Sir Charles Adam, 1887, p. xix n.1).

6. There were a few exceptions to this rule (ibid., pp. xvi n.3, xxvii–xxviii).

the House of Lords put a real check to these practices and even this check was not permanent.[7] In that year it was estimated that 1,235 of the 2,639 county votes were fictitious; parchment barons, as nominal voters were called, were especially numerous in Ayrshire, Boswell's home county.[8]

The regulations governing elections were equally complicated. Only those whose names were on the roll of freeholders could vote; those who wished their names added had to submit a claim to the Sheriff-clerk two months before the annual Michaelmas county meeting.[9] It was necessary for a prospective voter to have held his superiority for a full year at the time of an election to be eligible for enrollment and to vote. The Sheriff (i.e. the Sheriff-depute) fixed the date of election, so in some cases he was able to decide an election by choosing a day before or after new superiorities matured. Also, the order of business at a Michaelmas or election meeting was important.

7. Ibid., p. xxvi n.1. This decision was foreshadowed by a speech of Lord Chancellor Thurlow in 1787 (John Craigie, John Shaw Stewart, and Thomas S. Paton, *Reports of Cases Decided in the House of Lords,* 1849–56, iii.77–92, 169–88). See Journ. 26, 30 Apr. 1787; to [Robert Boswell], 14 Mar. (*L 211), from John Boswell, "Young Knockroon," 20 June 1787 (C 396), to Malone, 12 July 1788 (L 938); G. W. T. Omond, *The Lord Advocates of Scotland* (1883), ii.159–62. According to someone who signed himself C. D., writing in 1775, nominal and fictitious votes were a novelty in 1753, but had since been made in large numbers, especially during the elections of 1768 and 1774 (*A Letter to the Real Freeholders of Scotland upon the Bill for Regulating Qualifications,* 1775, pp. 8–9).

8. *Scots Magazine,* 52 (1790), 354 n.*, cited in Mathieson, pp. 19–20 (I have corrected Mathieson's addition). Holden Furber estimates from Adam's very similar figures that about 220 noblemen and large proprietors made and controlled these fictitious votes (*Henry Dundas,* 1931, p. 183). Many votes were obtained through straight purchase. Alexander Fergusson of Craigdarroch, for example, was said to have bought a half-dozen superiorities in Ayrshire in 1771 for about £2,300 (James Fergusson, " 'Making Interest' in Scottish County Elections," *Scottish Historical Review, 26,* 1947, 120 n.2).

9. The Michaelmas head-court was held for the purpose of revising the freeholders' roll. Curiously enough, it was unnecessary to submit a claim in advance to be enrolled at an election meeting (Wight, pp. 131, 151–52, 189–91).

The first matter taken up was the election of a preses (chairman) and clerk, with the last representative of the county in Parliament taking the roll, and casting an additional vote in case of a tie. The preses then took the chair, and adjustments to the roll were made in regard to claimants and objections to those already enrolled, such matters being decided by a majority vote of the freeholders present. The preses was influential since he held an additional vote in case of a tie, and could also alter the order of business by taking up claims in the sequence that best suited his purposes.[1] The final action of an election meeting, which could last a whole day, was the vote for member for the county.

The right to vote in the burghs was invested in the municipal councils, self-perpetuating bodies. Only Edinburgh among the royal burghs had a seat to itself, the other burghs being organized in groups of four or five. The procedure was as complex as in the counties, with this addition: each council elected a delegate, and the delegates in turn elected the parliamentary member, the delegate from the presiding burgh (the burghs presided in rotation) having the casting vote in case of a tie. The number of town council members in 1790 was 1,301,[2] so that out of a population of 1,500,000, there were about 4,000 voters in all Scotland![3]

When George III came to the throne, Archibald, Duke of Argyll had for many years been the manager of the ministerial

1. The procedure outlined above was, as Wight says, "surely the most regular mode of procedure," but he admits it was not established by statute, and was sometimes ignored (p. 151 n.*). Furber cites an interesting example of manipulating the Dunbartonshire election date in 1780 to prevent superiorities from "maturing" (p. 194), and Rosalind Mitchison provides a detailed account of the most elaborate maneuvers at the Caithness Michaelmas meeting of 1789 (*Agricultural Sir John*, 1962, pp. 68–81).

2. Furber, p. 184.

3. This sketch of the Scottish franchise is based on the works of Adam and Wight cited above; Edward and A. G. Porritt, *The Unreformed House of Commons* (1903), chs. 38–39; and Robert Bell, *A Dictionary of the Law of Scotland* (1807), s.v. Election Laws. Lord Auchinleck made some

interest in Scotland, or, as the Duke of Newcastle said, "the absolute Governor of one of His Majesty's Kingdoms."[4] On Argyll's death in 1761, his power fell to his nephew, the Earl of Bute, who managed Scotland through his brother, James Stuart Mackenzie.[5] Some opposition, connected to the "outs" in England, existed during this period, but the government which distributed places and pensions could always count on a solid bloc of Scottish votes, which in several cases it found indispensable for a majority. On the formation of the first Rockingham ministry in 1765, Newcastle offered Robert Dundas, Lord President of the Court of Session, the management of Scotland. Dundas thought it incompatible with his juridical duties, but his unofficial influence remained important.[6] From 1765 to 1775 no one figure dominated Scottish

---

interesting comments on the subject in his *Observations on the Election Law of Scotland* (1825), which Boswell took down from his dictation in 1771.

4. Brit. Mus. Add. MSS 32,922, f. 5, cited in Sir Lewis Namier, *England in the Age of the American Revolution* (2d ed. 1961), p. 173; Mathieson, pp. 28–30. Apparently Lord Milton managed affairs on the spot, under Argyll's direction (Alexander Carlyle, *Autobiography,* ed. J. H. Burton, 1861, pp. 211–12).

5. Mackenzie was made Keeper of the Privy Seal for Scotland in 1763 and, supported by the King, disposed of Scottish offices under the Grenville ministry (*Letters from George III to Lord Bute,* ed. Romney Sedgwick, 1939, pp. 210, 238). Grenville was not able to dismiss him from office until the spring of 1765 (Richard Pares, *King George III and the Politicians,* 1953, pp. 105 n.3, 107 n.4, 178); he was reinstated under Chatham as Privy Seal for life, but without control of Scottish patronage (*Selections from the Family Papers Preserved at Caldwell,* ed. William Mure, 1854, II.i.134 n.1*, II.ii.34–35, 42, 85–86, 89, 90). Alexander Carlyle asserted that Baron Mure, "a man of business and of sound sense," actually managed Scotland during Lord Bute's period in power, since Mackenzie "neither had talents nor inclination" for the job (*Autobiography,* pp. 336, 372–73). It is obvious from their correspondence, however, that Mackenzie retained control of Scottish patronage, while constantly consulting Mure about it (*Cald. Papers,* II.i–ii passim).

6. *Arniston Memoirs . . . 1571–1838,* ed. G. W. T. Omond (1887), pp. 177–79.

politics,[7] though Boswell in his *Letter to the People of Scotland* (1785) accused Sir Alexander Gilmour, former member for Midlothian, of once having managed affairs, undoubtedly sometime during these years.[8] Though it seems to have been meant seriously, the accusation was ironic: Gilmour was dependent on Robert Dundas's support, and Henry Dundas, the Lord President's younger half-brother, took Gilmour's seat away from him easily in 1774.[9]

7. Mathieson, pp. 54–55. John Ramsay says that the King consulted the Duke of Queensberry about Scotland during part, at least, of this interregnum (*Scotland and Scotsmen,* ed. Alexander Allardyce, 1888, i.346; see also, from T. D. Boswell, 30 May 1766, C 476). Grafton seems to have entrusted Mackenzie with some of his old functions in 1768–69 (*Cald. Papers,* II.i.134 n.1*). Probably the Secretary of State for the Northern Department handled routine patronage (Cyril Matheson, *Life of Henry Dundas,* 1933, p. 43; *Cald. Papers,* II.ii.35). Andrew Stuart told the Duchess of Hamilton in 1773 that a letter to the Secretary, Lord Suffolk, might "be attended with very usefull consequences," since "in the course of a contested Election there is frequently occasion to apply for favours in that quarter." Taking this advice, the Duchess provided Suffolk with an extended history of Lanarkshire politics and asked his support. Stuart explained Suffolk's friendly but noncommittal reply by saying, "Administration for the most part does not choose to take an active and decided part in the contentions between Great familys in Countys" (*Intimate Society Letters of the 18th Century,* ed. [John, 9th] Duke of Argyll [?1910], i.157–69).

8. P. 9. Gilmour started by supporting Newcastle against Bute (Namier, *England,* p. 404 n.2), and was one of the four Scottish M.P.'s to divide with the minority on the Preliminaries of Peace in 1762 (Mathieson, pp. 58–59). Later he supported, and may have had some influence under, the Rockingham ministry (*Correspondence of Edmund Burke,* ed. Thomas W. Copeland, 1958 et seq., i.235, n.3; *Cald. Papers,* II.ii.86), and, according to Alexander Carlyle, was a friend of the Duke of Grafton (*Autobiography,* p. 417). Gilmour may also have been a friend of Lord North, since North tried unsuccessfully in 1776 to have him brought into Parliament for Horsham through Lord Irwin (*Last Journals of Horace Walpole,* ed. A. Francis Steuart, 1910, i.572).

9. Matheson, pp. 23–31. Newcastle wrote to Robert Dundas (5 June 1763) to ask his "powerful support" in Midlothian for Newcastle's "good friend," Gilmour (*Arniston Memoirs,* p. 174). The next year John Dalrymple solicited Stuart Mackenzie's aid unsuccessfully against Gilmour,

Dundas was to become the greatest of Scottish political managers, and his rise is extremely important to the study of Boswell's political aspirations. The Dundases of Arniston were a famous law family: Robert Dundas was Lord President from 1760 to 1787, and Robert and Henry's father had held the same office from 1748 to 1753. Born in 1742, Henry Dundas was sent to Dalkeith Grammar School, and attended classes at Edinburgh University, where he, Boswell, and Temple took logic together. He was admitted to the Faculty of Advocates in Edinburgh in 1763, and three years later became Solicitor General. This promotion impelled Boswell to remark to Temple: "Do you remember what you and I used to think of Dundas? He has been making £700 a year as an Advocate, has married a very genteel Girl with £10.000 fortune, and is now appointed His Majesty's Sollicitor General for Scotland." Contempt mingled with envy, supplemented at times by admiration, was Boswell's usual reaction to Dundas throughout their lives.[1]

---

who was opposing the Grenville administration. In an estimate of Gilmour's electoral strength, Dalrymple credits the Lord President with controlling half of Gilmour's 22 supporters (*Cald. Papers,* II.i.283–90; see II.ii.86). Gilmour stood unsuccessfully for the Haddington burghs in 1774 as well as for Midlothian (Wight, p. 297; Sylvester Douglas, *History of the Cases of Controverted Elections,* 1775–77, ii.421–74), a course which Henry Dundas forced on him (*Arniston Memoirs,* pp. 183–84). See also *Parliamentary Papers of John Robinson, 1774–1784,* ed. W. T. Laprade (1922), pp. 17–18. Dundas's treatment of Gilmour was violently attacked by Eugene (Hugo Arnot) in his *Letter to the Lord Advocate of Scotland* [1777].

1. To Temple, 17 May 1766 (L 1235). Temple agreed: "we used to think little of" Dundas (8 Aug., C 2678; see 20 Nov. 1766, C 2679). Matheson says that the fortune of Dundas's wife, Elizabeth Rannie, was supposed to have amounted to £100,000 (p. 23), a very substantial sum indeed; Boswell's figure seems more likely. As late as 1786, Boswell spoke of Dundas's "coarse bellowing" in the House of Commons, and added: "It provoked me that he was so high, as I knew him all along to be my inferiour in learning and talents, and as he was a downright Swiss of every Ministry" (Journ. 17 Feb.).

Dundas's quick rise was due not only to his powerful connections, but to his undoubted legal ability. Always interested in politics, he had made up his mind to enter Parliament by 1771, when he wrote to Lord North to announce this decision and to indicate his sympathy with the Ministry. In 1775, he became Lord Advocate for Scotland, a promotion which testifies to his ability as well as to North's need for the support of the Arniston family and its influential friends. He soon made himself known in the Commons. From the first, he refused to restrict himself to Scottish affairs as most of his countrymen in Parliament did, or to the views of the North ministry, which he was nominally supporting. He favored stronger measures against the American colonies than North wished to take, supported relief for Catholic disqualifications in Scotland, and at the start of his career opposed fictitious votes in the Scottish counties. Secure in his seat, Dundas's independence was strengthened by his ever-increasing influence in Scotland; North also needed his help in the Commons debates, and Dundas was able to claim a reward for his services. In 1777 he was appointed joint Keeper of the Signet in Scotland, and was disturbed because the appointment was not given for life but only during the King's pleasure. His extended connection with India began in 1781 when he was made head of a board to investigate Indian affairs.

By this time North's days were obviously numbered, though Dundas fought hard to save his ministry.[2] After Rockingham's death in July 1782, Shelburne persuaded the King to appoint Dundas sole Keeper of the Signet for life in order to acquire his support; Shelburne also made him Treasurer of the Navy, and gave him the official management of all places falling vacant in Scotland. When the Fox–North coalition came in, however, Dundas resigned his Treasurership, and in August 1783 Fox dismissed him as Lord Advocate. But the rejoicing of

2. Ian R. Christie, *The End of North's Ministry, 1780–1782* (1958), pp. 283–98, 363.

his Scottish opponents did not last long, for Dundas returned to power with the young William Pitt.

From 1784 on, Dundas was Pitt's right-hand man and secure in office. He was made a member of the Board of Control for India, later becoming its President and the dominating figure in its management until 1800. After Hastings's return from India and impeachment, Lord Cornwallis became Governor-General of India, and he and Dundas worked harmoniously together; the patronage of a subcontinent rewarded Dundas's adherents. Dundas was also reappointed Treasurer of the Navy, and in 1791 he became Home Secretary, a post which included management of Irish and colonial affairs, as well as supervision of military operations. During his tenure of this office, he was chiefly concerned with suppressing reform movements in Great Britain inspired by the French Revolution. But military affairs claimed an increasing amount of his time, and in 1794 he gave up the Home Office for the newly created position of Secretary of State for War. The rest of his career falls outside the scope of this discussion but can be briefly summarized: he retired from office in 1801 except for a year as First Lord of the Admiralty (1804–05), was created Viscount Melville in 1802, was impeached on grounds of having misused funds as Treasurer of the Navy and acquitted in 1806, and died five years later.

Dundas's political attitude was summarized rather indignantly by George Dempster as " 'the Court has use for me and I for the Court'—such stuff!"[3] Yet this system of reciprocal benefits was the basis of most party politics of the time, and Dundas applied it with great success. His family influence gave him a start which he improved by the friendships he made; the Duke of Buccleuch was an early patron of his, the Duke of Gordon became his follower. Open, generous, and remarkably good-natured, he courted the good will of anyone who would

3. *Letters of George Dempster to Sir Adam Fergusson,* ed. James Fergusson (1934), p. 221. Dempster's letter is dated 3 July 1792.

be useful, though he was never servile and seldom hypocritical. His shrewd political tact enabled him time and again to reconcile opposing parties in counties or burghs, and leave both groups with a feeling of gratitude. As he wrote to Pitt, he was willing to fight on the "common public bottom" if he must, but preferred a comfortable give-and-take among gentlemen.[4] Once in control of Scotland, he was careful to assist everyone he could, except those actively in opposition.

The combination of Scottish support and political power is reflected in Dundas's domination of Scottish members of Parliament. Furber estimates that 10 counties and 2 burghs were controlled by his interest or by those friendly to him in 1774, 8 counties and 5 burghs in 1780, 15 counties and 7 burghs in 1784, 22 counties and 10 burghs in 1790, and at the peak of his power in 1796, 24 counties and 12 burghs.[5] Dundas's official duties became so heavy that he was forced to spend less and less time on Scottish affairs, and especially after 1790 he deputed many of them to his nephew and son-in-law, Robert Dundas. At all times, however, his interest was the best assurance of political advancement for a Scot.[6]

4. In a letter dated 11 Aug. 1788, cited in K. G. Feiling, *The Second Tory Party, 1714–1832* (1938), p. 167.

5. Furber, App. A.

6. This sketch of Dundas is based chiefly on the detailed studies of Furber and Matheson cited above.

2

Opinions and Directions: 1760–1773

Boswell recorded two remarks about himself which are significant guides to his approach to politics: "Ersk[ine] said I was a Tory with Whig Princip[le]s";[1] Burke said, "You have the art of reconciling contradictions beyond any man [I know]."[2] These comments apply only in part to Boswell's shifts in adherence from one group to another. Even his attempt to secure a place through Burke under the second Rockingham ministry, although he disagreed with its views, was not unusual in a time when friendship often counted more heavily than party or fac-

1. Journ. 9 Apr. 1778. See also Journ. 13 Oct. 1780. The Erskine referred to is Capt. James Francis Erskine, second son of James Erskine of Mar.

2. Journ. 23 Jan. 1790. Boswell ends a letter to Burke, 20 Nov. 1783, "believe me to be with old Tory steadiness, though you tell me I have a Whig constitution" (L 321). See also, to Dundas, 2 Jan. 1784 (L 450). According to an essay signed H., "Boswell's political principles seem to have been a medley of toryism and whiggism not very harmoniously intermingled" ("Memoir of James Boswell, Esq.," *Monthly Magazine, 15,* 1803, 550). Robert Warnock puts the matter more accurately when he speaks of "the peculiar turn of Boswell's mind at whatever age. . . . The same liberal point of view coupled with conservative principles" ("Boswell on the Grand Tour," *Studies in Philology, 39,* 1942, 661). Lack of clear party distinctions at the time is illustrated by Burke's remark, "I take the true Genius of this constitution to be, Tory Language and Whigg measure; Lingua Toscana in Bocca Romana" (from Burke, 1 Sept. 1782, C 687).

tional alignments.[3] But Boswell's convictions must have seemed more paradoxical. How could someone who almost worshiped the King support Wilkes's right to sit for Middlesex, or warmly defend the American rebels? What could be said for anyone who declaimed that he stood for the independent interest in Ayrshire against the influence of the aristocracy, while he was well known to be a creature of Lord Lonsdale, the most notorious boroughmonger of the time? In the case of Boswell's relations with Lonsdale, paradox became contradiction: temptation, in the form of a seat in Parliament, was too strong for Boswell, though he knew that he was falling below his own standards. In almost every other case, Boswell's motives and behavior were sincere; hypocrisy was never one of his failings.

The seeming lack of consistency in Boswell's political attitudes reflects certain aspects of his background and character. The Boswell family had been established at Auchinleck since 1504; pride of family was a tradition, and in Boswell himself the most deeply fixed of his emotions:

> I must own that Veneration and regard for my Ancestors, with a desire to continue their race, is A Principle, or a feeling, call it which you will, that I posess in a very strong degree, and which I retain at all times, whatever variation of sentiment I may have about other matters. . . . It is rooted in my heart; it is a part of myself.[4]

This statement, variously modulated, sounds like a *basso ostinato* throughout Boswell's writings; it is put most simply perhaps in the *Journal of a Tour to the Hebrides,* where Boswell describes himself as "a gentleman of ancient blood, the

3. Writing to Boswell at this time, Thomas Barnard, Bishop of Killaloe, expressed hopes for Boswell's political advancement through his personal friends now in power, though Barnard deplored their policies (2 Mar. 1783, C 81).

4. Journ. 24 Oct. 1762.

pride of which was his predominant passion."[5] Such deep regard for family was sometimes a source of disagreement between him and his wife, and after one conversation on the subject, Boswell blamed her in his journal for

> endeavouring to counteract the principle of *Family* which has prevailed in the Family of Auchinleck from generation to generation. She said, and perhaps with some truth, that our pride and high estimation of ourselves as if German Princes (my phrase) was ridiculous in the eyes of other people, who looked upon us not only as no better than any other Gentleman's family, but as a stiff and inhospitable family. But as I have great enjoyment in our fancied dignity, and cannot be persuaded but that we do appear of more consequence in the country than others, from a certain reserve which has allways been maintained, and am also of opinion that this pride makes us act in a nobler manner, I wish to encourage it.[6]

The gap between the ideal and reality is hard for most men to bridge, but Boswell found it almost impossible to reconcile family feeling and his particular situation. Lord Auchinleck, his father, was an honest, upright judge, with vigorous and rigid views, who found himself fatally handicapped in dealing with his eldest son by a complete lack of imaginative understanding. Everything that Boswell did, aside from becoming an advocate, struck him as a useless and dangerous waste of time, and while imbuing Boswell with his sense of tradition, he was unable to transmit his stern and limited outlook. Boswell respected and dreaded his father, and in consequence was torn between feeling that what his father wished him to do was what

5. *Boswell's Journal of a Tour to the Hebrides,* ed. F. A. Pottle and C. H. Bennett (new ed. 1961), p. 32.

6. Journ. 6 Jan. 1780. Boswell taught his eldest son, Sandie, in catechism form that after his duty to God his first duty was to "the Family of Auchinleck" (ibid.). See Journ. 24 Apr. 1778.

he should do, and knowing that he wanted a quite different career, though unsure of what sort. Boswell found relief from this irresolvable conflict by attaching himself to a number of older men who could offer him advice and approval. Johnson, the most famous of these, fitted this role perfectly, since he combined eminence of position and encouragement with the criticism that Boswell also found necessary to complete an acceptable father substitute. Deep analysis is not needed to see that Boswell's vocal dislike for Scotland and the law, for Scots dialect and custom, must have found much of its origin in his largely repressed hatred for his father, with whom they were closely identified.

In his relations with his father Boswell swung between dependence and independence, between an almost abject submission and a defiance reckless of consequences. Especially in Boswell's early years, Lord Auchinleck poured forth warnings, admonitions, and threats. He believed his motives were unimpeachable, as the end to one of his letters shows: "ffarewell My Dear Son believe all my advices intended for your good and not to claim Dependance."[7] But Boswell was treated like a child till he was past forty,[8] without being given the emotional support necessary to a child, and the pattern of his conflict with his father repeated itself continually in every phase of his thought and behavior, not least in politics. The cry of "Monarchy and liberty," of which he was so fond, was not only a Tory answer to "Wilkes and liberty," it was a response that

7. From Lord Auchinleck, [18 July 1763] (C 218).

8. "I knew a father who was a violent whig, and used to attack his son for being a tory, upbraiding him with being deficient in 'noble sentiments of liberty,' while at the same time he made this son live under his roof in such bondage, that he was not only afraid to stir from home without leave like a child, but durst scarcely open his mouth in his father's presence" (James Boswell, *The Hypochondriack,* ed. Margery Bailey, 1928, no. 45, June 1781). See F. A. Pottle's comment on Boswell's relationship with his father (*Private Papers of James Boswell,* ed. Geoffrey Scott and F. A. Pottle, 1928–34, xv.i–iv).

reflected Boswell's need to combine a sense of unshakable stability with freedom. A seat in Parliament was Boswell's fondest hope, because it would have allowed him to live in London—the negation of his father and Scotland—while directly maintaining the dignity and value of a Scots laird.

Politics was one of the many sources of disagreement between Lord Auchinleck and his son. We catch only glimpses of the political past of "the greatest Whig in Britain":[9] he supported his first cousin, Charles Cochrane, in the Ayrshire election of 1734 against the successful incumbent, Sir James Campbell; in 1740, he was on a list of promising young Whigs recommended to the Duke of Newcastle, who was responsible for his being made Sheriff-depute of Wigtownshire in 1748.[1] With the further help of Newcastle and Argyll he became a Lord of Session in 1754, and a Lord of Justiciary the following year.[2] Lord Auchinleck campaigned actively for the Earl of Loudoun's candidate in Ayrshire in the 1754 election, a county conflict which involved little more than a struggle for power

9. As William McQuhae, Boswell's tutor and friend, called him (from McQuhae, 26 Apr. 1763, C 1883).

1. He first refused the appointment, and then on the advice of Lord Arniston, Lord President and father of Robert and Henry Dundas, accepted it (Lord Milton to Alexander Boswell, 23 Mar., C 2028, Alexander, 6th Earl of Galloway to Alexander Boswell, 25 Mar., C 1330.2, John Stewart to Alexander Boswell, 9 Apr., C 2570.6, Andrew Mitchell to Alexander Boswell, 2 July 1748, C 2036.7; Lord Auchinleck, *Observations,* p. 22 n.*; Ramsay, i.162–63; *Albemarle Papers,* ed. C. S. Terry, 1902, ii.530, 536, 541).

2. Robert Dundas claimed that his late father's recommendation of Lord Auchinleck to Newcastle and Lord Chancellor Hardwicke had been highly influential in his appointment to the Justiciary bench (Robert Dundas to Lord Auchinleck, [?9 July 1755], C 1154.8), but Argyll had also recommended him (Argyll to Lord Auchinleck, 25 June 1755, C 39.4). See George Lewis Scott to Lord Auchinleck, 28 June (C 2434), 1 July (C 2435), Loudoun to Lord Auchinleck, 3 July 1755 (C 1784.7); *Boswelliana,* ed. Charles Rogers (1874), p. 5 n.*; *Hist. MSS Comm.,* 4th Report (1874), p. 531; George Brunton and David Haig, *An Historical Account of the Senators of the College of Justice* (1832), p. 518.

among the Ayrshire peers.[3] After that contest he seems to have had few direct dealings in politics until the election of 1774.[4] Through his connections with Newcastle and Argyll, he was a member of the Whig oligarchy which governed Scotland for many years; after they passed from the scene, he remained attached through friendship and political conviction to the group controlled by the Dundases of Arniston. His most famous remark on politics is characteristic if unoriginal; he is supposed to have told Dr. Johnson, when asked what Cromwell had done for England, that he "gart kings ken that they had a *lith* in their neck."[5]

Boswell wanted desperately to avoid the advocate's career which his father pressed on him. In his own words, "to get away from home where I lived as a Boy, was my great Object. It was irksom beyond measure to be a young Laird in the house of a father much different from me, of a mind perfectly sound, and who thought that if I was not a Man of business I was good

3. Fergusson, "'Making Interest.'" Lord Auchinleck's promotion to the Bench was closely connected to his electioneering activities. His appointment was pressed by Loudoun's friends and allies, Lord Cathcart and Lord Hyndford (Fergusson, pp. 122, 127 n.5; Brit. Mus. Add. MSS 32,995 f. 24v.—reference supplied by G. L. Lam). Lord Marchmont, supporting a candidate of his own, thought Boswell no more than a second-rater (*Hist. MSS Comm.*, Polwarth MSS, v, 1961, 282–83). Later Loudoun obtained a commission in his own regiment for Lord Auchinleck's second son, John, and was constantly concerned in his abortive military career (Bute MSS: Lord Auchinleck to Loudoun, 16 Mar., 6 June 1760, 28 Mar., 29 Apr. 1765, 7 Dec. 1770, 4 Feb., 13 Mar. 1771, John Boswell to Loudoun, 1 Mar. 1771).

4. He had been made a voter in Fife in 1734 for the superiority of Nether Glassmount (Freeholders' Minutes, Sheriff Court Records, Fife, in the Register House, Edinburgh. Information from Sir James Fergusson), and presided at a Fife election in 1763 (from Lord Auchinleck, 13 Jan. 1763, C 213).

5. See James Boswell, *Life of Samuel Johnson*, ed. G. B. Hill, rev. L. F. Powell (1934–50), v.382 n.2, where this apparently proverbial saying is discussed. In his French themes (M 87), Boswell attributes the same remark to his great-uncle, Thomas, 8th Earl of Dundonald (see *Tour*, pp. 442–43).

for nothing."[6] The alternative proposed by the young Boswell was a career in the Army, though he was unwilling to serve in any branch but the Guards stationed in London. The story of his unsuccessful attempt to obtain a commission is told in his London journal of 1762–63, and need only be summarized here. Boswell's father was dead set against the proposal; he agreed with the Duke of Argyll, who said that there was no reason why Boswell should be shot at for three and sixpence a day.[7] The friends on whose aid he counted, the Duke of Queensberry, the Earl of Eglinton,[8] and the Countess of Northumberland, were unable to do anything for him. A commission in the Guards would have been difficult to procure at any time; admission was highly selective, and the Guards "naturally comprised the greatest number of young men of Parliamentary rank";[9] Boswell was sufficiently handicapped by the fact that it was a period of demobilization and Scottish unpopularity, but, as well, he lacked the money to buy a commission.[1] Eglinton obtained a commission in a marching regiment for him, but Boswell wanted the Guards and London or nothing. By the end of spring 1763, he was forced to admit that a lawyer's career was best for him, and agreed with his father that a year in a Dutch university was desirable, on condition that he be allowed to make the Grand Tour afterwards. Lord Auchinleck sweetened the pill by writing, "In the plan I propose you have for your objects being respected, being usefull with your advice, getting in to Parl[iament] and having the power of conferring places in stead of going about begging one."[2]

6. Journ. 11 Dec. 1762.

7. *Boswelliana*, p. 229.

8. Eglinton, according to Alexander Carlyle, was "the second man in the kingdom while Bute remained in power" (*Autobiography*, p. 331).

9. Namier, *England*, p. 257.

1. *Boswell's London Journal, 1762–1763*, ed. F. A. Pottle (New York, 1950), pp. 20–21. Even the Earl of Buchan was unable to get a commission in the Guards for his son about this time (Lt.-Col. Alexander Fergusson, *The Honourable Henry Erskine*, 1882, p. 83).

2. From Lord Auchinleck, 30 May 1763 (C 214).

Whatever mistakes Lord Auchinleck made about his son's character, he hit exactly the right note this time. A seat in Parliament was a hope Boswell was never to abandon. The idea had already occurred to him; he had written to Andrew Erskine a year previously, that after a projected tour of the Continent, "I am thinking of returning to England, of getting into the house of commons, of speaking still better than Mr. Pitt, and of being made principal secretary of state."[3] A boyish dream, but Boswell took dreams seriously, and he had the example of his friend, George Dempster, before him. Dempster, whose social position was similar to Boswell's, had been elected in 1761 for the Perth group of burghs, and Boswell, impressed, had told him, "You talk with prodigious Modesty of your Metropolitan Connections. But by all accounts, you have made a bold push in the Senate; have attacked the great Pit, and raged against Continental Measures. This is flying at high Game indeed."[4] Dempster's example should also have been a warning; the election is said to have cost him as much as £10,000,[5] and Boswell would have had great difficulty in raising a comparable sum at any time.

During his stay in London in 1763, the prospect of Parliament teased Boswell's ambition. He indulged "noble reveries of having a Regiment, of getting into parliament, making a figure, and becoming a man of consequence in the state."[6] Grand plans for the future led to present caution; Boswell reminded himself that he should not become too much obliged to Eglinton, so that he could keep himself independent in Ayrshire: "Elections are very nice things. Nobody can tell what accidents

3. *Letters between the Honourable Andrew Erskine and James Boswell, Esq.* (1763), p. 105.

4. To Dempster, 19 Nov. 1761 (L 415).

5. *Letters of George Dempster,* p. 56. The Perth burghs were "very open, venal, and expensive" (Robinson, p. 7).

6. Journ. 20 Jan. 1763. See also Journ. 7 Feb. 1763; to Temple, 14 July 1763 (*Letters of James Boswell,* ed. C. B. Tinker, 1924, i.21).

may happen. I have a good family interest. I may indulge the idea of representing the County."[7] With his father's letter in his hands, his parliamentary ambitions received new impetus. He wrote to his friend, John Johnston of Grange ("worthy Grange," as Boswell often called him), with touching condescension that Lord Auchinleck "is truly a worthy Man. I assure you he is. All his little mistakes are owing to a confined and narrow Education. . . . He promises to give me all encouragement and mentions my getting into Parliament, as a noble Incitement."[8]

Then came Holland and political hopes lay dormant, while Boswell struggled with the terrible task of getting through each day.[9] His spirits revived on the Grand Tour, and he discussed possible careers with Andrew Mitchell, the British Minister at Berlin, and with the Earl Marischal. For a while, Boswell toyed with the idea of joining the eighteenth-century equivalent of the Foreign Service, or more accurately, he was attracted by the idea of becoming an envoy.[1] He was to regard himself half-seriously as Rousseau's personal ambassador to Corsica.[2] He asked Rousseau's advice on a political career, as he asked everyone else's, and Rousseau told him, "If you be-

7. Journ. 25 Jan. 1763.

8. To John Johnston, 16 June 1763 (L 707). See *Life,* i.427.

9. Boswell mentions his hopes of Parliament in letters to Temple, 25 Sept. (L 1215) and 9 Nov. 1763 (L 1216), and cites Parliament as an objective in his "Inviolable Plan" (M 88).

1. Journ. 9 June, 27 July, 6 Sept., 10 Oct. 1764; Mem. 24 Apr. 1765; to Wilkes, 7 May 1765 (*Letters JB,* i.74; L 1284), to Sir Alexander Dick [?9 Dec. 1766] (*Letters JB,* i.96). James Boswell, *An Account of Corsica* (3d ed. 1769), pp. 369–70. John Wilkes wrote to Boswell that he thought this career was the one which would make him most happy (22 June 1765, C 3089).

2. Journ. 15 Dec. 1764. Boswell encouraged the notion that his visit to Corsica was not purely personal through various letters and paragraphs contributed to the *London Chronicle.* (Almost all of these mysterious and intriguing items are printed in *Boswell on the Grand Tour: Italy, Corsica, and France,* ed. Frank Brady and F. A. Pottle, New York, 1955, pp. 322–

come a Member of Parliament, you must resemble the Abbé de St. Pierre. You must stick to your principles." Boswell replied, "A Member of Parliament who behaves as a strictly honest man is regarded as a crazy fool," to which Rousseau answered, "Well then, you must be a crazy fool of a Member; and believe me, such a man will be respected—that is, if he holds consistently by his principles."[3]

Despite his agreement with his father, Boswell still looked desperately for any escape from the drudgery of a lawyer's life. Parliamentary member, foreign minister, some sort of sinecure —any of these would do. From Berlin he had written to Temple, "Tell me that I shall pass many agreable days at my ancient Seat of Auchinleck, that I need not be a slave to the law, but may get into Parliament or be made a Baron of Exchequer, and have realy *Otium cum dignitate*."[4] The vision of either an active career in politics or a dignified sinecural idleness became inflamed when he met Lord Mountstuart, Bute's eldest son, in Italy. Boswell saw immediately that Mountstuart might be the lever that would raise him to power; his problem was how to handle the young nobleman. Mountstuart was amiable, intelligent, indolent, and spoiled, a man who, like his father, thought much of his family and dignity. Almost at once the two took to each other, and Mountstuart soon suggested that Boswell join him and his entourage, which consisted of Colonel Edmondstone, his governor, and Paul Henri Mallet, his tutor.

27, and discussed, pp. 244–46.) Lord Marischal told Boswell he had seen newspaper reports that he was an English emissary, and also that he represented the Young Pretender. Marischal added: "I believed neither, but supposed you intended to make a present of that Iland to the Infanta" (30 Apr. [1766], C 1953). Boswell remarks on his being taken for an official representative in *Corsica* (pp. 318, 340, 393).

3. Journ. 4 Dec. 1764 (trans. Geoffrey Scott).

4. 23 July 1764 (L 1224). See, to John Johnston, 11 May 1765 (L 753). The Court of Exchequer tried cases relating to the Crown revenue.

At first, all went well.[5] Boswell, four years older than Mountstuart, attempted to impress him with his superior knowledge and attainments, while preserving the intimacy engendered by personal confidences. But his eyes dazzled, and soon he had to remind himself to be prudent, *retenu,* and dignified. Boswell's rough notes and memoranda tell the story: "Supt My Lord's [Mountstuart's]. Saw you fawn'd a little. 'Tis realy better [to be] independent; by merit rise. His interest now and then. Be prudent."[6] A few days later they made a jaunt to Tivoli, and Boswell was able to report, "Lord MountStuart is ever your freind. Be [like Lord] Marischal, and with retenue preserve tranquillitatem animi."[7] This state of affairs did not last; Mallet, a clever, bitter man, could not endure Boswell, and Mountstuart found him odd at times and irritatingly stubborn. He resented Boswell's treatment of him as a youngster, and probably disliked Boswell's attempt to use him to gain access to Lord Bute, as well as his request that Mountstuart should help Temple's brother acquire a lieutenancy.

Before the tour started, Mountstuart had written to Baron Mure (5 June 1765): "Boswell is an excellent lad, full of spirit and noble sentiments; and (as the world goes,) it ought to be reckoned a fortunate thing for him going with me, and indeed fortunate for myself, as he goes on in the same studies as I do, and, if possible, rouses me up whether I will or no."[8] Less than two weeks later a sharp dispute arose because Mountstuart in-

5. Boswell's relationship with Mountstuart is discussed in detail in Robert Warnock's unpublished dissertation, "Boswell in Italy" (Yale, 1933), pp. 48–88.

6. Mem. 15 May 1765. That Mountstuart at least thought he had influence with his father appears from a letter he wrote to William Hamilton, British Envoy to the Court of Naples, 7 May 1764 (in error for 1765), offering his services as a favorite son "to the inaccessible Lord Bute" (from a photostat of the original, formerly in the possession of Capt. F. L. Pleadwell, M.D.).

7. Mem. 24 May 1765.

8. *Cald. Papers,* II.ii.39.

sisted on calling Boswell, "Jamie," an insult to one whose dignity had led him to assume the title of Baron while traveling in Germany and Italy.[9] A reconciliation followed, then more quarrels, until Boswell knew he should go his separate way, but he was incapable of renouncing his grand opportunity. He sadly reviewed the situation in an unsent letter to Rousseau:

> I found myself in my Lord's suite, and when I heard him hold forth on the pleasures of grandeur I began to wish for employment at Court. I thought of his great interest. Insensibly I tried to please him and was afraid of offending him. He soon noticed it, and could not keep from profiting a little from it. I realized it too. . . . I recollected myself. I made my Lord realize that I was as proud as ever. I did it too emphatically. We began to dispute about our characters, and each stated bluntly all the other's defects and all his own merits. . . . Finally our spirits subsided, and we were sometimes on a basis of puerile familiarity, and sometimes in the vilest humour possible, even to the point of not speaking to each other.

At Venice, Mountstuart was suddenly recalled to England. Boswell wrote further to Rousseau:

> On this last tour, my Lord and I got on better together. We admitted each other's virtues. My Lord said to me, "I have great esteem for you. I shall always be your friend in London. But you have a terrible disposition." . . . I felt an enthusiastic attachment for his ancient family.[1]

9. Mem. 17 June 1765. In Boswell's defense it should be remembered that a Scottish baron is not a peer; he is a landowner holding of the Crown with a baronial jurisdiction. See Journ. 10 Oct. 1764; "Ten Lines a Day," 30 Oct. 1764 (M 281).

1. To Rousseau, 3 Oct. 1765 (L 1115), trans. by F. A. Pottle and me. It hardly seems worthwhile to reproduce Boswell's French, which usually sounds like a simple, literal translation from English.

Once away from Mountstuart, Boswell's imagination had free rein; he minimized their disputes, and defended him from charges of indolence.[2] The relationship meant much less to Mountstuart, of course, and he was slower to forget their differences, especially when Boswell upbraided him for not sending some letters of recommendation he wanted.[3] By May 1766, peace had been restored once more, and Mountstuart wrote to him:

> You seem so desirous to keep up an acquaintance with me that I begin to think that you like me as well as you say, yet I think, the strange incoherency of your temper makes it dangerous to render that acquaintance intimate, you have fine old noble ideas, as I us'd to tell you, but the least thing alters you, the last man you see, of whom you have an opinion, carries away yours, add to that, I think you a little dangerous to trust. . . . Be assur'd that inspite of your oddities I take you to be a most excellent good hearted man and as such, will do every thing in my power (without shew and affectation) to oblige you.[4]

The situation had been clearly stated, but Boswell pressed on regardless. He dedicated his judicial thesis to Mountstuart, and wrote confidently to him, "I have no doubt of your Lordship's kind intentions to befriend me in whatever I shall undertake, and therefore I shall upon every occasion of consequence most freely apply to you."[5] Boswell seems to have felt that it was possible to maintain a dignified independence, while demanding

2. For example, Mem. 9 Aug. 1765.

3. Journ. 15 Feb. 1766; from Sir John Pringle, 28 Jan. 1766 (C 2294). In this letter, Pringle says that he had advised Mountstuart not to send Boswell the letters of recommendation he wished, so that Boswell would return to Scotland more quickly. See, from Mountstuart, 27 Dec. 1765 (C 716).

4. 29 May 1766 (C 717).

5. 6 Aug. 1766 (L 344). Johnson wrote to Boswell, 21 Aug. 1766, "Why did you dedicate it to a Man Whom I know you do not much love?"

political favors for which he could make little return except friendship.[6] He had adopted Mountstuart as his Maecenas, and thought of him fondly as a devoted and disinterested patron who would further his interests at every opportunity. This was not the case; Mountstuart had a sincere, if intermittent, regard for Boswell but, like many others, found it difficult to take him seriously. In any case, his chances of helping Boswell had been much diminished by the break between George III and Bute. Yet for many years he remained Boswell's chief hope for obtaining a sinecure.

"You have fine old noble ideas," Mountstuart had said, and indeed the enthusiastic inflexibility with which Boswell clung to his ideas impressed all who met him. His basic convictions about government and politics seemed to have been formed very early. One of the few surviving anecdotes about his childhood dates from the '45: as a boy of five, Boswell wore a white cockade and prayed for King James, until his uncle gave him a shilling to pray for King George.[7] The story illustrates his early attitude almost too neatly: romantic sentiment made him partial to the Stuarts, while prudence and interest attached him to the Hanoverians. Of monarchy as a form of government, he had no doubts. "Surely," he once commented, "a regular limited Royal Government is the best and the most conducive to the happiness of Mankind. A Republic is in my opinion a most confused, vulgar system whereas a Monarchy inspires us with gay and spirited ideas."[8]

His stay in Utrecht confirmed this opinion. At the time of

(Life MS). In the *Life,* Boswell deleted everything after "Why did you" (ii.20).

6. Boswell might well have applied to himself what he wrote of Rousseau: "He has ideas of independence that are completely visionary, and which are unsuitable for a man in his position" (to Alexandre Deleyre, 15 Oct. 1766, L 413, trans. F. A. Pottle and me).

7. *Life,* i.431 n.1.

8. Journ. 25 Mar. 1763.

Wilkes's difficulties over *North Briton,* no. 45, and the *Essay on Woman,* he wrote:

> Beleive me Temple that an english Republican is either a weak or a wicked Politician. I thank God we have got a monarchy, limited as much as a true Patriot and true lover of order could wish. I rejoyce to find that the King begins to show real firmness. I hope he will make it be remembered that *The Crown* is the head of our Constitution.

Then in a characteristic burst, he added: "Poor Wilkes! Sad dog as he is! who will not be sorry for him! I long to hear his history."[9]

Temple disagreed sharply with what Boswell proudly called his "old-fashioned ideas":

> Your notions of government surprise me. They are slavish and unworthy of an Englishman. . . . The English government is not a Monarchy; it is a mixed Republic, where the supreme power is equally divided amongst the three Estates. . . . You say Locke has made you a Christian; read his immortal treatise on Government and be no longer a slave.[1]

Boswell did experience somewhat of a revulsion from monarchy in its despotic form on his visit to Prussia. "I have seen my Royalty in full force," he wrote to Temple from Leipzig, "and I have seen it's sad effects on mankind. I am now the warmest Briton that ever adored Liberty."[2] This temporary reaction was nullified by the pleasant reception which "Baron" Boswell met with at some of the petty German courts, notably that of the Margrave of Baden-Durlach, and he wrote to Temple from Ferney:

9. 6 Dec. 1763 (L 1217).
1. From Temple, 7 Jan. (in error for Feb.) 1764 (C 2669).
2. 14 Oct. 1764 (L 1225).

> Why am I not in power? I may be so perhaps yet before I die. Temple I am again as loyal as ever. I abhorr a despotic Tyrant. But I revere a limited Monarch. Shall I be a British Courtier? Am I worthy of the Confidence of my King? May George the Third chuse that the most honest and most amiable of his Subjects should stand continually in his Royal Presence? I will if he says, "You shall be independent."[3]

Geneva cured him completely; in the crudity of its citizens, he beheld "a nauseous example of the manners of Republicans."[4]

Jacobitism was dead by 1760; Pitt had won over its last stronghold, the Highlands, by recruiting regiments there during the Seven Years' War, but Boswell never quite lost his feeling for the Stuarts. He warmly maintained in 1763 that the Stuarts, though unfortunate, did nothing to warrant being expelled from the country, and that the changes introduced by Cromwell and the Revolution of 1688 had confused the minds of the people and loosened ties of loyalty.[5] Boswell knew that the only Jacobites left were diehards, and that conceivably he could hurt his prospects by voicing such opinions too loudly, but his enthusiasm for the old cause often flared up. At Utrecht he was forced to remind himself that he might be a Tory and still be loyal to King George; it was easy to slip into Jacobitism.[6] He met Andrew Lumisden, secretary to the

3. 28 Dec. 1764 (L 1226). Ironically enough, "no king was ever less fond of plebian society than George III. He liked to be surrounded by lords at court" (Pares, *King George III and the Politicians,* p. 57).

4. Journ. 30 Dec. 1764.

5. Journ. 17 Jan. 1763.

6. Journ. 31 Jan. 1764. See French themes (M 87) and *Tour,* pp. 162–63. Boswell fully stated his attitude toward the Stuarts in a conversation with that sturdy but disillusioned Jacobite, the Earl Marischal: "He and I talked of Jacobitism, as how there was something pathetic and generous in it, as it was espousing the cause of a distrest and ancient Royal House. My Lord however owned that they deserved to lose the throne of Britain. I own so too. I am sorry for them. I wish to forget them; and I love from my Soul 'Great George our King'" (Journ. 23 July 1764).

Old Pretender, in Rome, and spent a good deal of time with him, but for once took care not to indulge in any open anti-Hanoverian sentiments.

The fascination of the Stuarts for Boswell lay in their connection with the past of tradition, custom, and ceremonial; they were adherents of Anglicanism and Catholicism; they were dramatic in their recklessness, and gallant in their daring rebellions. Like himself, they had been confined and thwarted by strict, gloomy Presbyterians. Boswell saw the prototypes of Tory and Whig in Charles I and William III. He kept the feast day of the Blessed Charles King and Martyr whenever he could and, as late as 1793, he wrote to the Marchioness of Salisbury that his loyal Tory soul had been delighted when she said, "I do love Charles the First."[7] William III, a stolid brute of a Dutchman, was a usurper, and the Revolution of 1688 was "a desperate doze of mercury."[8]

In his legal work, Boswell was a persistent advocate of lost causes, but in politics he recognized that the Stuarts were irrevocably gone, and he must accept the Hanoverians. His acceptance of the situation was eased by his strong, initial attachment to the young King. On hearing the Speech from the Throne which opened Parliament in 1762, Boswell wrote: "His Majesty spoke better than any man I ever heard: with dignity, delicacy, and ease. I admired him. I wished much to be acquainted with him." A later appraisal was more restrained: George III "is born a Briton," he wrote in one of his French themes; "he is a perfectly amiable man; perhaps his virtues are more amiable than great."[9] One sign of amiability was the return of some Tories to Court favor, or so Boswell thought.[1]

7. 16 May 1793 (L 1125).

8. Journ. 15 Apr. 1773; "Ten Lines a Day," 9, 10 Dec. 1763 (M 276); "Parliament a Poem" (M 279).

9. Journ. 25 Nov. 1762; French themes (M 87), c. 14 Nov. 1763, trans. F. A. Pottle.

1. Boswell wrote in the same French theme: "The Court undoubtedly does well to show favour to so respectable a party [as the Tory], who are

But when Wilkes assured him, two years later, that he thought George III every bit a Stuart, Boswell replied, "Then I fall down and worship the Image that he has set up. I reason not. 'Tis my taste."[2] Even allowing for the tone of banter in which Boswell and Wilkes often discussed politics, there was a seriousness in Boswell's attitude which time only deepened.

Affection for the King did not necessarily indicate respect or regard for the members of his family. Boswell had met the King's brother, the Duke of York, on his first trip to London and, elated by the Duke's notice of him, Boswell dedicated his ode, *The Cub at Newmarket,* to him without permission, and to his displeasure. Boswell was hurt by this; he told Grange, "as to the Dedication, I think I did the D[uke] of Y[ork] a favour, and am angry that he did not take it properly."[3] He wrote austerely at Utrecht: "The Duke of York was not a man of dignity nor of extraordinary genius. He was sunk in debauchery and sometimes made himself the companion of the vilest of the human species. I knew him only very little and he never did me the least service,"[4] a statement translucent with injured pride.

Boswell considered the Union of 1707 as he did the fall of the Stuarts, an unfortunate but perhaps necessary event. Its makers roused him, on occasion, to unimpressive rhetoric: "O Infamous

---

in truth the firmest friends of the Constitution." Boswell must have meant Bute and his friends; George III told Pitt in 1765: "You can name no Whig familys that shall not have my countenance; but where Torys come to me on Whig principles let us take them." Few came (Pares, p. 72 and n.2).

2. Mem. 18 Feb. 1765.

3. To John Johnston, 21 Dec. 1762 (L 687).

4. French themes (M 87), c. 9 Nov. 1763, trans. F. A. Pottle. Boswell made a bitter comment when he heard of the death of the King's uncle, the Duke of Cumberland (Journ. 22 Dec. 1765), but inserted something in his defense in the *Life* (ii.375 n.1). He called the Duke of Gloucester "a man above common" (to Sir Alexander Dick [1779], *Letters JB,* ii.289).

Rascals, who sold the honour of your country to a Nation against which our Ancestors supported themselves with so much glory. But I say no more, only Alas, poor Scotland!"[5] Boswell harped on the same note throughout his Continental tour, lamenting the decline of real Scots patriotism, and congratulating himself on his own value as "a rare Scot."[6] Always jealous of Scottish rights, he contributed a series of letters in 1771 to the *London Chronicle* applauding a movement among the Representative Peers to break away from the usual ministerial influence.[7] It is hard to believe, however, that Boswell in his cooler moments would ever have favored repealing the Union.[8]

Throughout his life, Boswell's approach to politics was conservative, idealistic, and emotional. As a conservative and idealist he believed in "the grand scheme of subordination," that tidy feudal theory in which each kept his place and performed the duties it required. His own place was assured; at worst, he was a Scots laird, a high rank, or so Johnson told him.[9] From this, it might be possible for him to rise, but below it he was determined not to fall. Such a situation in life carried both power and responsibility, but as a young man Boswell may be pardoned for being more conscious of his eventual power. He reported with some self-irony at one point: "I raged in the cause of pride, and said my greatest satisfaction was to have

5. Journ. 6 Oct. 1764, and see *Tour,* pp. 23–24. When Johnson outlined the benefits of the Union, Boswell thought his account exaggerated (*Tour,* p. 95). The false tone of the eloquence quoted above perhaps indicates that Boswell did not find the subject vital. He attacked the Union, however, in a correspondence with the Bishop of Derry, published in 1785 (*LC,* 10 Sept.), and as late as 1790 said it had destroyed Scotland as a nation (Journ. 15 Feb.).

6. Journ. 6 Sept., 3 Dec. 1764, 26 Dec. 1765.

7. F. A. Pottle, *The Literary Career of James Boswell, Esq.* (1929), p. 247.

8. For general Scottish sentiment on this question, see Sir Henry Craik, *A Century of Scottish History* (1901), i.448–51.

9. *Life,* i.409.

power over others, to have which I would suffer many evils, and I thanked heaven for having given me noble sentiments and the rule over Lands."[1] Since his own security was bound to that of the social order, he supported monarchy without reserve as "the Image of divine rule,"[2] of which his own status was an even more microcosmic version.

The Revolution of 1688, however, had put an end to any pretensions of absolute rule, and Parliament was essential in a limited monarchy as a defender of the people's liberties. In his more censorious moments, Boswell felt that it had degenerated from its ancient model, the Roman Senate. He said, in a French theme, that Walpole had introduced a regular system of corruption; and further,

> There are many persons with places and pensions who are members of the House of Commons. And if you also include the number of those who expect to receive such favors, you have a pretty Parliament. How can the people entrust their liberty and their property to those gentlemen who want to obtain property for themselves, or rather who want to find some method of escaping their creditors; and as for liberty, if one wishes to tell the truth, they never think of it apart from its value, for they count on selling it.

Two days later, Boswell admitted that he had been too harsh in speaking of the Commons: "I never intended to condemn that respectable body *in toto.* I spoke only of 'interested' persons, who are ready in consequence to give their support to

1. Journ. 10 Sept. 1764. He told Rousseau: "I have leanings towards despotism. . . . On our estates, I am like an ancient laird, and I insist on respect from the tenants" (Journ. 15 Dec. 1764, trans. Geoffrey Scott and F. A. Pottle). Though Boswell disliked living at Auchinleck, he always believed that "there is a feeling of dignity and consequence in being master of land above any thing else" (*Hypochondriack,* no. 36, Sept. 1780).

2. "Parliament. An Epistle" (M 278).

everything that will please the Court." It is almost possible to see a finger raised in dramatic warning as Boswell continues:

> for if Parliament is corrupted, farewell to the [Constitutional] balance of which we boast so much. We have only a king and two or three ministers to make laws and reduce the people to slavery itself. Thank God, however, the English people are inspired by noble sentiments of liberty, though sometimes ill-directed by artful men. But so long as they hold to such ideas, the Court cannot encroach far on the rights of the people without their being well aware of it.[3]

These innocent maxims also inspired Boswell in verse:

> Why still affirm ye rash satyric tribe
> That no Elector can refuse a Bribe
> Why still exclaim in melancholy rote
> Alas! alas! how venal is a vote!
> In every Borough what corruption reigns
> None now a seat except by cash obtains,

and so on for many more couplets of equal merit. He warns Dempster, to whom these lines are addressed, to beware pride and "the high horse of Independence," i.e. adherence to the Rockingham Whigs, or he may find that he has sold his country for a place. For his own part, says Boswell, "Should I be entrusted with the office of a British Lawgiver, I shall act to the best of my judgment with calm Integrity. . . . Should I not get into Parliament, I shall bound my views to the courts of Caledonia, place myself on the Exchequer Board by Baron Maule, cultivate my lands, and live hospitably with my neighbours at Auchinleck." But

> To serve my country half my land I'd give
> Not to be member, freinds, is not to live.

3. French themes, c. 30 Nov., c. 2 Dec. 1763 (M 87), my translation.

Who at his seat contentedly would stay
Who would not be in great preferment's way?
Who'd grudge the money at elections spent?
A *Place* is not too dear at *cent per cent.*[4]

This whole long epistle is a *jeu-d'esprit* which gives full play to the contradictory elements in Boswell's convictions. He could leap from the defense of royal rule here to the vision of tyranny by king and minister in his French themes, and hold both positions simultaneously. It might be maintained that Boswell was taking the middle way, like Gibbon's tremulous ball of orthodoxy vibrating within almost indistinguishable limits, but moderation was not in Boswell's character: he preferred to jump from one extreme to the other. Men of Boswell's nature were dangerous in practical politics; they were independent and unreliable; it was impossible to tell when they might suddenly feel compelled to ignore the advice of their patrons.

Boswell as yet lacked any practical experience in politics, but his personal relations showed how indiscreet he could be. As a Tory and a Scot, he thought a great deal of Bute, whom he praised highly in his French themes, blaming his downfall on too rapid advancement, and on the fact that a minister of state "unhappily must answer to a furious and irrational multitude." He was aware that Bute "had a natural pride and disdained to pay court or even act graciously towards the most important peers" of England, but he was "a man of genius and good principles," fortified by the knowledge of his own integrity.[5] After meeting Mountstuart, Boswell wrote to Wilkes:

4. "Parliament. An Epistle" (M 278). In the last couplets, the MS has "grand" above "great" (l.4), and "of" above "at" (l.6).

5. French themes, c. 22–24, c. 29 Nov., c. 10 Dec. 1763 (M 87), my translation. Earlier, in an unpublished letter to *The North Briton* signed "Risor," Boswell had compared, in a detached and supposedly humorous way, the changes of ministry to the Scottish game of *"Hop-romp"* (Brit. Mus. Add. MSS 30,876, ff. 20–21). See Journ. 13 Feb., 18 July 1763.

> My intimacy with him has brought me acquainted with the character of Lord Bute whom I shall ever admire. His letters to his son prove him to be a man of the most generous soul and most tender heart. . . . As a Statesman, I am sure his intentions were grand and honourable. What his Administration has been upon my honour I have not yet knowledge nor abilities enough to judge. He writes with an eloquence which would charm you.[6]

Unfortunately, Boswell was equally charmed by Wilkes himself. His attitude toward the author of *The North Briton* was fixed even before he met him; as he told Grange, "I differ much from Mr. Wilkes . . . yet I love his cleverness."[7] After meeting Wilkes in London in 1763, he encountered Wilkes again during his Italian exile and was fascinated by his wit and cosmopolitanism. True, Boswell insisted on the divergence of their political views, but he thought it a proof of his tolerance to write to Wilkes:

> You may think as you please, but I have no small pride in being able to write to you with this gay goodhumour; for, I do in my conscience beleive you to be an ennemy to the true old British Constitution, and to the order and happiness of Society. That is to say, I beleive you to be a very Whig and a very Libertine. . . . I am Dear Sir as much yours as a Scots Royalist can be.[8]

Though he knew Wilkes was loathed by most respectable Englishmen and all Scotsmen, Boswell broadcast their friendship all over Europe.[9] He had the excuse that Wilkes was

6. 13 July 1765 (*Letters JB,* i.83; L 1286).

7. To John Johnston, 22 Feb. 1763 (L 697). See Journ. 9 Feb. 1763, and the verses, "O Wilkes, He is a rare dog" (M 272).

8. 22 Apr. 1765 (*Letters JB,* i.72, 74; L 1283). See Journ. 9 Jan. 1765; to Wilkes, 7 May (*Letters JB,* i.75; L 1284), 15 June 1765 (*Letters JB,* i.81; L 1285).

9. To Deleyre, 3 Apr. (L 411), to John Johnston, 11 May (L 753), to the Margrave of Baden-Durlach, 11 May (L 23), to Sir Alexander Dick,

genuinely kind to him, as he was to be throughout their lives, but there was certainly no need for Boswell to thrust this unpleasant intimacy in Mountstuart's face, when he knew that Wilkes and Bute were bitter opponents. But Boswell could not resist this experiment any more than he could resist bringing Johnson and Wilkes together in those brilliant scenes recorded in the *Life*. When Mountstuart told him that Wilkes was a rascal, Boswell showed him a letter he had written to Wilkes and asked him if Bute would be angry if he knew; the natural reply was that Bute would not like it much.[1] A month later when Mountstuart told Boswell, during a quarrel, that all the English disliked him, he was repeating a variant of what Nathaniel Dance had told Boswell earlier, that the English said he despised his countrymen and spent his time only with Wilkes.[2]

Important as his relationships with Mountstuart and Wilkes were to be in Boswell's life, they hardly compare in significance with his jaunt to Corsica. Curiosity and Rousseau led him to that island, but the experience had far-reaching consequences that could hardly have been anticipated. Boswell was filled with an intense admiration for Pascal Paoli and the Corsican people whom he led in their struggle against the Genoese and

---

22 May (*Letters JB,* i.80), to Rousseau, 3 Oct. 1765 (L 1115). The letter to Rousseau was never sent.

1. Mem. 19 May 1765. Possibly it was a letter from rather than to Wilkes, since the memorandum is not clear. The Register of Letters lists a letter to Wilkes on 8 May 1765, probably the one sent dated 7 May. Much later Boswell persuaded Mountstuart and Wilkes that the three of them should dine together (to Wilkes, 14 May [1776], *Letters JB,* i.253, 27 Feb. 1779, L 1293). See, to Wilkes, 20 Apr. [1776]; (*Letters JB,* i.248–49; L 1292).

2. Mem. 29 Mar., 29 June 1765. Wilkes's attitude toward Mountstuart was quite different. He wrote to Boswell, "I was very glad to hear you had form'd a great intimacy with Lord Mountstuart. He is by all accounts a most amiable young nobleman. . . . I congratulate you on that connection, which I hope will be advantageous to you" (22 June 1765, C 3089).

later against the French, and his enthusiasm crystallized in his *Account of Corsica* (1768). Here, Boswell sounded his theme of "monarchy and liberty" fully for the first time.[3]

The *Account of Corsica* opens with an apostrophe to liberty:

> Liberty is so natural, and so dear to mankind, whether as individuals, or as members of society, that it is indispensibly necessary to our happiness. . . .
>
> There is no doubt, but by entering into society, mankind voluntarily give up a part of their natural rights, and bind themselves to the obedience of laws, calculated for the general good. . . . Keeping the original intention of government ever in view, we should take care that no more restraint be laid upon natural liberty, than what the necessities of society require.[4]

This was the keynote of Boswell's presentation of the Corsicans. Corsica, he maintained, was "a compleat and well ordered democracy," exhibiting "a gradual progression of power, flowing from the people, which they can resume, and dispose of at their pleasure, at the end of every year."[5] The executive power of Corsica rested in a nine-man Council, and a General, President of the Council, whose position resembled that of the Stadholder in Holland. The power of the General was limited, but the power of Paoli as a person seemed to have no bounds; it was a species of despotism founded on love.[6]

3. A typical statement of this theme occurs in Boswell's Ayrshire Election Address of 1784: "My political principles I have avowed, in the most direct and public manner, to be those of a steady Royalist, who reveres monarchy, but is at the same time animated with genuine feelings of liberty; principles which, when well understood, are not in any degree inconsistent, but are happily united in the true British constitution" (*Ayrshire at the Time of Burns,* Collections of the Ayrshire Archaeological and Natural History Society, *5,* 1959, 84).

4. *Corsica,* pp. 33, 35.

5. Ibid., p. 182.

6. Ibid., pp. 179–80, 190.

Boswell saw Corsica in classical terms: Paoli was a hero from Plutarch, and the Corsican government resembled Sparta in its form and spirit. Paoli satisfied Boswell's need to see a ruler in a hierarchical system, while the Corsican fight for independence stirred all his vigorous sympathy for the underdog.[7] The cry of liberty enchanted Boswell, though it is sometimes difficult to tell what he meant by it. He had no sympathy with republicans like Mrs. Macaulay who "whined about liberty as an old Puritan would whine about Grace," or with the Genoese, whom he contemptuously described as a nation of republican oppressors;[8] since he lacked a mind which dealt readily in abstractions, Boswell's statements about liberty tend to be resounding clichés. On one hand he could fully agree with Johnson that "in this country the people are the superintendants of the conduct and measures of those by whom government is administered";[9] on the other, he declared that Johnson, his model in theoretical matters, "was at all times indignant against that false patriotism, that pretended love of freedom, that unruly restlessness, which is inconsistent with the stable authority of any good government."[1]

Such vague views gave Boswell a good amount of intellectual leeway. He showed his interest in liberty by responding emo-

7. Boswell emphasized the model of Plutarch in the closing paragraph of *Corsica* in which he quotes Chatham as saying of Paoli: "He is one of those men who are no longer to be found but in the lives of Plutarch." See, to Rousseau, 4 Jan. (*L 1191.1; L 1119), to Sir Alexander Dick, 23 Oct. 1766 (*Letters JB,* i.92), and Joseph Foladare's unpublished dissertation, "James Boswell in Corsica" (Yale, 1936), i.115–16, 146.

8. Journ. 30 Mar.–20 Apr. 1768; *Corsica,* p. 104.

9. *Life,* i.311. Boswell here seems to distinguish the "people," the upper and middle classes, from the "rabble." The "people" were "the whole body of enfranchised or qualified citizens, considered as the source of power" (OED, s.v. people, 5). Goldsmith similarly differentiates the people, the "middle order of mankind," from the rabble (*Vicar of Wakefield,* ch. 19).

1. *Life,* i.424. The statement immediately follows the passage in which Johnson is quoted as justifying revolution against "a corrupt political system."

tionally to concrete situations like the struggles of the Corsicans and Americans for freedom. In Great Britain, liberty consisted in maintaining the constitutional balance of powers, and he was particularly voluble against the encroachments of Parliament, either on the prerogative of the Crown as in the case of Fox's East India Bill, or on the rights of the people as in the Middlesex election.

Corsica was written with a more specific purpose than merely to expound the virtues of Paoli, liberty, and the Corsicans; it was intended to rouse the British and the Government to do something about the situation. As Boswell was writing his book in 1767, Corsican affairs were becoming rapidly worse. The French, who were garrisoning certain towns under arrangement with the Genoese, began to increase their demands upon both Paoli and Genoa. Boswell had started his campaign for aid to Corsica as soon as he returned to the Continent. He flooded the London papers for the next three years with accounts of himself, with mysterious rumors about a Corsican envoy, and with inventions about the aid other European countries intended to offer Paoli. *Corsica* was written to appeal to all interests; Boswell pointed out the excellence of the island's harbors, its value to England as a check on France, and the ethical appeal of the Corsican cause: "When we thus view the Corsicans gloriously striving for the best rights of humanity, and under the guidance of an illustrious commander and able statesman, establishing freedom, and forming a virtuous and happy nation, can we be indifferent as to their success?"[2]

Many Britons evidently thought not; the public response to Boswell's book was enthusiastic. William Guthrie said in the *Critical Review* (March 1768): "Our author has, in the person of Paoli, realized all the ideas which the most vigorous imagination could form of a chief, a patriot, and a legislator,

2. *Corsica,* p. 250. Boswell's immediate aim was repeal of the British Proclamation of 1763, which cut off aid to, and trade with, the Corsican rebels (Foladare, pp. 15–16, 25–26).

embellished with the ornaments of an understanding cultivated by polite literature,"[3] and the *Monthly Review* and *Gentleman's Magazine* were equally complimentary. By May 1768, when the French announced their intention of invading Corsica, the English government, incited by public reaction, made firm representations. Rochford, the English ambassador to France, informed Choiseul that the Corsican expedition was regarded as a violation of the treaty of Aix-la-Chapelle "by far the greatest Part of the Nation." Choiseul replied that "He knew It; that Boswell's Account of Corsica had made a great Noise."[4]

Upon his return from the Continent in 1766, Boswell had tried to interest Chatham in Corsican affairs, but had been unable to rouse him to take any definite steps.[5] Chatham was living in retirement by 1768, and Grafton, despite some initial moves, was dissuaded from making the Corsican situation a major crisis by difficulties with the Bedford group.[6] As soon as Choiseul learned of Grafton's hesitancy, he went ahead with his plans and openly attacked the Corsicans, while the British supplied only limited secret aid.[7]

3. *Critical Review,* 25 (1768), 181, cited in Foladare, i.124. For other reactions, see Foladare, i.119–51.

4. Shelburne MSS, vol. 40, pt. ii, no. 69, cited in Foladare, i.158.

5. Journ. 22 Feb. 1766; to Chatham, 15 Feb. (*Boswell on the Grand Tour: Italy, Corsica, and France,* pp. 289–90; L 364), from Chatham, 16 Feb. (C 785), to Chatham, 19 Feb. (*Letters JB,* i.87–88; L 365), 18 Sept. 1766 (L 366), 3 Jan. (L 367), from Chatham, 4 Feb. (C 786), to Chatham, 8 Apr. 1767 (*Boswell in Search of a Wife,* ed. Frank Brady and F. A. Pottle, 1956, pp. 52–54; L 368). Boswell had always admired Chatham, though with some reservations: French themes, c. 16–21 Nov. 1763 (M 87); "Parliament. An Epistle" (M 278); the verses, "A Ludicrous Hodge-Podge" (M 273), and in "Ten Lines a Day" the poem called "The Whoremonger," c. Apr. 1767 (M 292).

6. Though David Hume told Boswell that the Duke of Bedford liked his book (to Temple, 14 May 1768, *Letters JB,* i.160).

7. In the Cabinet, only Shelburne, Secretary of State for the Southern Department, seems to have wished to oppose France vigorously (see Foladare's excellent summary of the whole affair, i.152–65).

Boswell continued to do everything in his power to encourage support of the Corsicans. He founded a Corsican Club, transmitted genuine items from the *Gazetta di Corsica* to the London newspapers under the heading of the "Corsican Gazette," approached influential people,[8] and edited a volume called *British Essays in Favour of the Brave Corsicans,* which appeared in December 1768. He also solicited subscriptions to send money and buy arms for the Corsicans. Apparently between £10,000 and £20,000 were collected,[9] and ordnance eventually costing £740 was shipped from Scotland under a separate subscription.

The ordnance shipment involved Boswell in a quarrel with Sir Adam Fergusson, later M.P. for Ayrshire. Boswell maintained that Fergusson had promised £100 in the summer of 1768 for the Corsican cause. On the strength of this and some other money he had raised, Boswell ordered the military supplies to be sent with one third the money actually in hand to pay for them. Fergusson then refused to pay, saying that he had never promised the money for arms, and Boswell and a fellow advocate, Andrew Crosbie, who had assumed responsibility for the purchase, were forced to pay an additional £129 apiece over their original subscriptions of £50.[1] Boswell asked Henry Dundas, as Dean of the Faculty and Fergusson's friend, to adjudicate the dispute but he declined, and Boswell sued Fergusson in a case which dragged on until finally decided in

8. This tactic backfired at least once. Lord Lyttelton told Boswell that he should be careful not to present himself at people's doors as an envoy from Corsica; rather he should get himself introduced and "speak as hinting, not as pointing out" (Mem. 3 May 1768).

9. Foladare, i.177–80, 189–94. Most of my account of Boswell's exertions on behalf of the Corsicans is based on Foladare's work. See also *Letters and Journals of Lady Mary Coke,* ed. J. A. Home (1889–96), ii.419.

1. To Temple, 24 Aug. (*Letters JB,* i.164), to Sir Alexander Dick, 24 Sept. 1768 (*Letters JB,* i.165–66), from Charles Gascoigne, 24 Jan. 1769 (C 1353), 3 Jan. (C 1354), to Gascoigne, 11 Jan. 1771 (L 572), to Fergusson, 30 Aug. (L 536), 11 Nov. 1780 (L 537); Corsican ordnance (A 22).

Boswell's favor in 1790.[2] Though no open breach occurred between them for a long time, this quarrel was to become the starting point of Boswell's bitter dislike for Fergusson, a dislike intensified by their disagreement in politics.[3]

Grafton's weakness in dealing with the French was one of a number of reasons which led Shelburne to resign in October 1768, and Chatham relinquished the Privy Seal, his nominal position, almost simultaneously. As soon as Parliament convened in November, Burke and Grenville led a movement to give active aid to the Corsicans, but they chose a poor way to force the Ministry's hand. The Opposition's motion demanded that the Ministry turn over to the Commons all negotiations relating to Corsica; in other words, it infringed the Cabinet's right to direct foreign policy, and was defeated, 230 to 84.[4] With this decision, all hope of official British action vanished, and private subscriptions were unable to offset French troops. When Paoli was forced to board an English ship in June 1769, the revolt was over.

Corsica was Boswell's introduction to the active scene; as he said in his often quoted remark to Paoli, "I had got upon a rock in Corsica and jumped into the middle of life."[5] His efforts had brought him new friends like Lord Lyttelton and General Oglethorpe, and impressed his old ones. His fame in his own day was secure; indissolubly connected with Paoli and liberty, he

2. At least there is a draft of a letter from Boswell to Dundas, 4 Dec. 1780 (L 447), submitting the matter to his consideration. Dundas, however, in a letter to Boswell, 12 May 1782 (C 1133), says, "It was only lately, as you know, that I knew any thing of the little pecuniary Quarrel betwixt Sir Adam Fergusson and you." In any case, Fergusson declined to submit the question to Dundas's arbitration (to Dundas, 20 Apr. 1782, *Letters JB,* ii.523–24; L 448). See also Journ. 30–31 Aug. 1780, and post, p. 168.

3. In a deleted section of the MS of *LPS 85* (now in the Hyde Collection) Boswell stated that his "objection" to Fergusson was based primarily on his refusal to pay the Corsican subscription (Paper Apart, marked 3).

4. Sir Henry Cavendish, *Debates,* ed. J. Wright (1841–43), i.52–61.

5. *Boswelliana,* p. 328, dated 27 May 1783.

was called "Corsican" Boswell by the Dowager Countess of Eglinton in 1768, and he was still "Corsican Boswell" to Lord Fife over twenty years later.[6] Success increased Boswell's self-confidence. He was aware that his sober Scottish friends were doubtful of his stability,[7] and his brother, David, warned him that his self-publicity was giving him a bad name. David had seen a long paragraph in the Edinburgh papers, taken from the *London Chronicle,* which, as he wrote to Boswell, provided "a pompous Account of your Expedition to Corsica. . . . What gives me and your Friends here greatest pain, is that indifferent people generally imagine the Intelligence comes from yourself, and are Zealous in condemning you for it, as the Effects of Vanity and Self Conceit."[8] But Boswell was able to assure himself, "it is amazing how much and how universally I have made myself admired. This is an absolute fact. I am certain of it; and with an honest pride I will rejoice in it."[9]

By no means all of Boswell's energy was absorbed by Corsican affairs during 1767–69. He took an active part in the

6. From Susanna, Countess of Eglinton, 31 Oct. 1768 (C 1185). *Lord Fife and his Factor,* ed. Alistair and Henrietta Tayler (1925), p. 222. Foladare gathers several such references (i.197–99).

7. For example, William Rouet to Baron Mure, 10 Jan. 1766, "You see what a figure your friend Boswell cutts in Corsica! I fear he is mad" (*Cald. Papers,* II.ii.58). David Hume described Boswell to the Comtesse de Boufflers (12 Jan. 1766) as "very good-humoured, very agreeable, and very mad" (*Letters of David Hume,* ed. J. Y. T. Greig, 1932, ii.11).

8. From T. D. Boswell, 3 Feb. 1766 (C 469). David followed this admonition with another, disapproving of a letter of Boswell's printed in the *London Chonicle:* "The people of Edinburgh in general are now beginning to look upon you as a man like Lord Kames, who does the most extravagant things without thought or reflexion" (28 Apr. 1767, C 492; see also, from T. D. Boswell, 19 May 1767, C 494).

9. Journ. 31 Aug. 1769. His efforts on behalf of the Corsicans made Boswell popular with contemporary liberals, and he belonged to a club which Benjamin Franklin, also a member, called "The Honest Whigs" (Journ. 14 May 1768, 21 Sept. 1769, 26 Mar. 1772. See R. A. Leigh, "Boswell and Rousseau," *Modern Language Review,* 47, 1952, 309 n.3; Carl Van Doren, *Benjamin Franklin,* 1941, pp. 420–22).

Douglas Cause with various pamphlets and poems: *Dorando, The Essence of the Douglas Cause,* and two odes, *The Douglas Cause* and *The Hamilton Cause.* He also edited (if that is the proper word) the *Letters of Lady Jane Douglas,* snippets taken from official documents in the case; this effort had great influence on popular opinion.[10] After the House of Lords, reversing the Court of Session, had upheld Douglas, Boswell exuberantly played a prominent part in the Edinburgh mob which attacked the houses of the Lord President and Lord Hailes, and broke Lord Auchinleck's windows because he refused to illuminate in honor of the victory.[1]

Boswell's exertions gained him the friendship of the Douglas family; he became a visitor at Bothwell Castle, and considered accepting Douglas's offer to travel with him on the Continent. For a moment it even looked as if his contributions would receive a tangible reward. Alexander Maconochie, one of Douglas's lawyers, wrote to Boswell in February 1768 suggesting he might become Sheriff-depute for Stirlingshire, if George Cockburn Haldane, present holder of the office, ran for Parliament that year as expected. Maconochie further advised Boswell to apply to Haldane and to the Duke of Queensberry, who was not only a friend of Boswell's but an ardent supporter of Douglas. Haldane, however, must have declined to run; he retained his Sheriffship for at least another two years, and the project came to nothing.[2]

10. The Duke of Queensberry testified to the effect of *The Essence of the Douglas Cause* (from Queensberry, 5 Jan. 1768, C 2335).

1. From Lord Hailes, 4 Mar. (C 1439), from Dempster [c. 12 Mar.] (C 940), from Lord Marischal, 26 Aug. 1769 (C 1965). Ramsay, i.172–73; *Anecdotes and Egotisms of Henry Mackenzie,* ed. H. W. Thompson (1927), pp. 105–06.

2. From Maconochie, 3 Feb. 1768 (C 1868). *Edinburgh Almanack for . . . 1768,* p. 89; *Edinburgh Almanack for . . . 1770,* p. 118. Haldane is not mentioned as a Parliamentary contestant in the *Gentleman's Magazine's* list (*38,* 1768, 280) or the *Scots Magazine's* list (*30,* 1768, 424–25), but apparently he later had Parliamentary ambitions (General Sir J. A. L. Haldane, *The Haldanes of Gleneagles,* 1929, p. 299).

"I fear this great D[ouglas] Cause has been something of a political one," Boswell told Lord Mansfield,[3] and its results were not altogether favorable for Boswell's future. The friendship of Douglas was emotionally satisfying rather than politically beneficial, and the case made Boswell enemies. The Dowager Duchess of Hamilton, who was Duchess of Argyll, treated Boswell very coldly when he and Dr. Johnson appeared at Inveraray during their tour of the Hebrides.[4] The publication of *Dorando* was a tactless move, since it appeared while the Court of Session was still arguing the case, and the Lord President, infuriated, had certain newspaper publishers arrested for printing extracts from it.[5] Lord Hailes, one of Boswell's best friends, suspected him of leading the mob against his house, and though this incident was forgotten or overlooked, Boswell's later attack upon Hailes's brother, the Lord Provost of Edinburgh, led to a coolness never entirely overcome.[6] These incidents, which illustrate Boswell's lack of restraint, were to have a powerful indirect influence on his career.

Boswell proceeded in his course of alienating the powerful by supporting Wilkes's rights in the Middlesex election dispute.[7] "So fascinating is success," Boswell wrote, "that I began

3. Journ. 20 May 1768. Feeling ran very high on both sides: see Boswell's remarks about Andrew Stuart, one of the Hamilton lawyers (Journ. 16 June 1769), and the comments of Stuart and others in the *Caldwell Papers* (II.ii.148–56). See also *Arniston Memoirs,* p. 180.

4. *Tour,* pp. 351–56, and see Journ. 23 Sept. 1777.

5. *BP,* vii.135–36; *Lit. Car.,* p. 32; Ramsay, i.172–73.

6. From Hailes, 4 Mar. 1769 (C 1439), [early Dec. 1771] (Newhailes MSS). Earlier, Hailes had asked Boswell whether he had spread a false rumor that Hailes had changed his opinion in the Douglas Cause (15 Aug. 1768, C 1438). Boswell condemned the Lord Provost in the *London Chronicle,* 24 Oct. and 28 Nov. 1771, for failing to confer the freedom of the city on Paoli (*Lit. Car.,* p. 247; C. M. Weis's unpublished dissertation, "The Correspondence of James Boswell and Sir David Dalrymple," Yale, 1952, pp. 102–03, 109–10, and Appendix II).

7. *Life,* ii.111–12, iii.221. In the latter passage, Boswell says he had differed with Johnson on only two political matters: the Middlesex election and the taxation of the American colonies.

to quit the determinations of my own reason, and to imagine him really a Patriot and like a Roman." Though "a little reflection" soon cured him of this, he was "ÉTOURDI" enough to talk of Wilkes to Lord Mansfield, who "did NOT relish" it.[8] Mountstuart told Boswell that Mansfield had relished it so little indeed that he had declared he would never let Boswell into his house again. Boswell responded typically by calling on Mansfield, whom he found courteous, though describing him on later meetings as cold and artificial; and many years later he wrote to Mansfield that he realized he had offended him by speaking well of Wilkes.[9]

Boswell did not admire what Wilkes stood for politically but, like more important people such as Grenville, he thought Wilkes unfairly deprived of his seat in the Commons. In the *Political Register,* Wilkes had sniped at Boswell as "that primitive Christian, that admirer of every thing opposite and contradictory,"[1] and Boswell remarked in 1769 that "the Petitioners [for Wilkes] to his Majesty at this season of opposition, when they tried to appear sensible amidst their madness, were like a drunken man trying to seem very grave and rational."[2] He had already asserted in a letter to the *London Chronicle* that Wilkes had once offered his services to Bute, and therefore his conduct had been motivated by malice and self-interest, and in the same newspaper Boswell returned to the old charge that Wilkes and Churchill had shamefully abused Scotland.[3]

8. Journ. 29 Mar., 22 May 1768.

9. Journ. 29 Mar. 1772, 11 Apr. 1773, 17 Mar. 1776; to Mansfield, 14 Feb. 1783 (L 948).

1. March 1768, reprinted in John Almon, *Correspondence of the late John Wilkes* (1805), iii.252. Wilkes's remark was apropos of Boswell's assertion in *Corsica,* "better occasional murders than frequent adulteries." Wilkes offered to supply Almon with a critique of *Corsica,* but it was never written (ibid., iii.238). See, from Temple, 27 May 1768 (C 2702).

2. Journ. 12 Sept.

3. *LC,* 14, 24 May 1768, 26 May 1770, and see *Caledonian Mercury,* 25 Mar. 1769 (P 12.8). Boswell had first heard the story of Wilkes's offer

When the two met at the Lord Mayor's dinner in 1772 for the first time in six years, Boswell told Wilkes that he was glad to meet him, but had not come to visit him in jail because "I am a Scotch Laird and a Scotch Lawyer, and a Scotch married man. It would not be decent."[4] Wilkes seems to have passed off this remark with his usual geniality and the two resumed friendly relations.

Boswell had indeed settled down in Scotland, settled in the law because he had to. Dempster had reviewed his prospects in 1766 with cruel logic:

> With regard to Your getting into Parliament . . . it is a noble Object of Ambition, but the roads to it are so various and thorny and so precarious that you cannot be too circumspect. Indeed I dont see how you can point at it while Your Father Lives. A Seat in Par[liamen]t is stormd like a Breach, by people drunk and desperate, Nay Boswell I aver a little degree of Madness is a necessary ingredient. Had I talkd of Parliament in the hearing of my Father or Grandfather they would have thought of Bedlam, cast their Eye towards my Younger Brother or tied up my Estate beyond human reach. I am sure You will be amongst us; but the means are not Yet clear to me.[5]

The means were not forthcoming, and three years later Dempster continued: "Were You never so much bent upon getting into Parliament you should only apply so much the harder to the practise and Study of Law. It is the best school for acquiring

---

from John Home, the author of *Douglas* and Bute's private secretary (French themes, c. 11 Dec. 1763, M 87). Bute later denied that the accusation was true (Journ. 15 May 1781).

4. Journ. 20 Apr. 1772. As late as 1785, Boswell asked his countrymen to forgive his friendship with Wilkes, because Wilkes was such a pleasant companion (*A Letter to the People of Scotland,* 1785, p. 70).

5. From Dempster, 10 Jan. [1766] (C 937).

eloquence, and the best Education for a Legislator is that of a Lawyer." He proceeded to sharpen Boswell's desires by adding:

> To a man who has money enough or few desires or uses for what he has I am clearly of Opinion Parliament is the most desireable Line. Take it as a business, take it as an Amusement, take it as the means of Learning wisdom, acquiring knowledge of men, forming Connections among the greatest and consequently the best people in the State, where is there its fellow? I cannot therefore wonder at your desire to be in it, nor approve too much of Your endeavouring to get there.[6]

The upshot of Boswell's consultations with his friend, the Member for the Perth burghs, was that "We agreed that I might be happy with a seven years' seat in Parliament, if it could be had easily, But, in the mean time, I was very well with the law in Scotland."[7]

Notable as Dempster was for his integrity, he was far more easygoing in his attitude toward the workings of Parliament than Temple, who was sheltered from the temptations of office. Thinking of the House of Commons in pre-Cromwellian days, Temple wrote to Boswell that he once valued it highly:

> I mean when it was composed of men of honour and independent fortune. . . . [But now] of what is the lower house composed? Above one half of them are the retainers of the Nobility, absolutely brought into Parliament by them and obliged to vote as they direct. Among the rest there are a few men of merit and fortune, several gamblers of desperate circumstances, and not a few merchants who procure a seat to avoid a bankruptcy. Such a motley tribe is the once independent House of Commons! Such is our

6. From Dempster, 13 Apr. 1769 (C 941). Other friends of Boswell gave him the same advice: from Sir John Pringle, 10 June 1766 (C 2295), from Andrew Lumisden, 15 Dec. 1770 (C 1801).

7. Journ. 21 Sept. 1769. See, to Dempster, 1 Jan. 1767 (L 419).

> grand bulwark against a kingly or oligarchycal tyranny. In short the present house of Commons are no better than the lackies of the Lords.[8]

Boswell was aware that some of these strictures were just, and he asked Johnson during the Hebridean tour whether the peers should have so great an influence in the choice of the Commons. Johnson replied with that most orthodox of eighteenth-century premises: "Influence must ever be in proportion to property, and it is right it should." The dialogue continued:

> BOSWELL. "But is there not reason to fear that the common people may be oppressed?"
> JOHNSON. "No, sir. Our great fear is from want of power in government. Such a storm of vulgar force has broke in."
> BOSWELL. "It has only roared."
> JOHNSON. "Sir, it has roared till the judges in Westminster Hall have been afraid to pronounce sentence in opposition to the popular cry. You are frightened by what is no longer dangerous, like Presbyterians by Popery."[9]

Such arguments left Boswell impressed but not always convinced.

Though he could not make his way immediately into Parliament, Boswell hoped mightily to obtain some sinecure through his influential friends. In the spring of 1772, he listed among his purposes for going to London visits to Queensberry, Mountstuart, and Douglas, to see what they could do for him or his friends; he also wanted to find out whether he could practice profitably at the English bar, and escape Scotland in that way.[1] The trip was not very encouraging. Though Mountstuart prom-

8. 25 Oct. 1769 (C 2712).

9. *Tour,* p. 37, and see p. 73.

1. Journ. 20 Mar. 1772. Temple was one of the friends Boswell wished to help (from Temple, 27 Dec. 1771, C 2728, 26 Mar. 1772, C 2729). The idea of practicing at the English bar was an old dream (Journ. 13, 17

ised to obtain a seat in the Court of Session for him, Boswell must have realized the uncertainty of this prospect.[2] His other friends received him cordially, but were unwilling or unable to do anything for him at the moment. He thought of applying for the Sheriff-deputeship of Ayrshire, which involved giving the incumbent, William Duff, its salary for life, so as to have it after his death. This might be a step toward the Bench, as it had been for his father, but Johnson advised him against it and Boswell finally decided it would be irksome and unprofitable.[3]

All around him was talk of Parliament. Sir Alexander Macdonald was thinking of standing for Inverness-shire, and Dempster told Boswell that "he would not give up the enjoyment of the two sessions which he had sat in Parliament for any consideration."[4] Boswell even felt a moment of hope himself. Major Craufurd of Craufurdland made, Boswell wrote, "a very genteel offer. He said if I would stand candidate for the shire of Ayr at next election, he would pass a charter and give me his vote." Unfortunately, Craufurd seems to have been able to promise only his own vote.[5]

Dec. 1762, 22 May 1768, 8 July 1769; to Thomas Sheridan, 27 Sept., L 1156, from Sheridan, 21 Nov. 1761, C 2484, to Garrick, 18 Sept. 1771, *Letters JB,* i.184; L 558).

2. Journ. 25 Mar. 1772.

3. Journ. 18 Apr. 1772, 16 Nov. 1774. The sheriff-depute was in effect sheriff during this period, and the position, which was not a sinecure, became increasingly important during the latter half of the century (Thomas Hamilton, "Local Administration in Ayrshire, 1750–1800," *Ayrshire,* p. 177). It paid £200 a year in Ayrshire (*Edinburgh Almanack for . . . 1770,* p. 118).

4. Journ. 20, 22 Mar. 1772.

5. Journ. 28 Mar. 1772. To "pass a charter" refers to a method of qualifying as a voter. Little relevant is known about Major (later Lt.-Col.) Craufurd. He dabbled in Renfrewshire politics (*Cald. Papers,* II.ii.133–34 [238]), but did not qualify as a voter in Ayrshire until 1781, when he supported Montgomerie (Kilkerran MSS). He was actively interested in later Ayrshire campaigns (to Eglinton, 8 Mar. 1781, L 493; E. H. Coleridge, *Life of Thomas Coutts,* 1920, i.178–79, 275, 277, 303).

Boswell kept his opinions before the public with *Reflections on the late Alarming Bankruptcies in Scotland,* a pamphlet published anonymously in November 1772. Its occasion was the failure of Douglas, Heron & Company (the Ayr Bank). This firm, set up in 1769 with an impressive capital of £150,000, was organized and managed by a group of wealthy amateurs, including the Dukes of Queensberry and Buccleuch, and Douglas of Douglas. With the praiseworthy aim of aiding the expansion of Scottish trade, industry, and agriculture, they lent money recklessly, much of which is said to have been spent on the purchase and cultivation of land in the West Indies and the erection of expensive houses in Edinburgh. The closing of a prominent London banking house in June 1772 brought about the failure of this company, which was now much overextended, and the downfall of many small banks. A meeting of peers and gentlemen in Ayr on 1 July passed a resolution giving thanks to the Company and expressing continued confidence in it, but no resolution could alter the fact that it had already stopped payment on its notes. Though it opened again in September, the partners decided to suspend operations in August 1773, and the stockholders' final loss was over £660,000.[6] Many Scottish landowners, especially in the west, were ruined by its failure.[7]

This calamity was Boswell's pretext for the *Reflections,* a "little Essay intended to serve not only for immediate admonition but as a sketch of the present manners in Scotland so much altered to the worse from what his Lordship remembers."[8]

6. The best account of this disaster appears in Henry Hamilton, "The Failure of the Ayr Bank, 1772," *Economic History Review, 8* (1956), 405–17. See also Sir William Forbes, *Memoirs of a Banking-House* (1860), pp. 39–43; C. W. Boase, *A Century of Banking in Dundee* (1867), pp. 88–89; A. W. Kerr, *History of Banking in Scotland* (1926), pp. 83–94; R. S. Rait, *The History of the Union Bank of Scotland* (1930), pp. 164–67.

7. *Lowland Lairds,* p. 22.

8. Boswell's draft of his inscription for Lord Kames's presentation copy (M 249) of the *Reflections.*

Boswell discerns three general causes of bankruptcy among the upper classes: extravagance, negligence of household accounts, and "the desire of being precipitantly rich." He argues that the Union increased the riches and barbarity of the Scots, and condemns their indiscriminate entertaining, heavy drinking, and inattention to dress. But much of the *Reflections* is a hymn to hierarchy, and an attack on the "abominable spirit of levelling all those distinctions which ages of civilized society have, through all the gradations of politeness introduced amongst mankind." He incorporates with approval an unnamed French writer's division of society into two classes, the nobles and the plebeians: "the functions of the former are to defend it; those of the latter to feed and to enrich it, without ever aspiring to useless honours, which are not made for them."[9] Boswell concludes with the hope that the bankruptcies, "however distressing to individuals, deserving and undeserving, may be of general utility, if they have the effect which we may suppose they will have on every rational and well-disposed person, by restoring just notions of subordination, frugality, and every other principle by which the good order of society is maintained."[1]

As the tone of the *Reflections* sufficiently demonstrates, Boswell had no personal reason for writing it, since he had not suffered himself from the Company's failure. Rather it shows his general discontent with the state of Scottish society, and mirrors the dislike of the conservative, highly stratified landowning class for the merchants and nouveaux-riches who were moving into positions of power. Like his later pamphlets, the work is not notable for its discretion in regard to his friends. Though it makes no specific references, neither Queensberry nor Douglas, if they knew of it, could have been pleased with its condemnation of "unprincipled men" who cheated the public. We do not know whether Boswell carefully concealed his

9. *Reflections*, pp. 7–10.
1. Ibid., p. 23.

authorship but, considering the presentation copy to Lord Kames, it seems likely that several of his friends knew he had written it.[2]

Boswell's closest contact with active politics at this time came through his legal practice: during the court sessions of 1772–74, he was engaged in cases which concerned "Earl Fife's Politicks." Fife was fighting with the Duke of Gordon for political control of the counties of Banff and Elgin, and both men were going through the usual routine of making as many votes as they could, while contesting the other's additions to the freeholders' roll. Boswell was only one of Fife's lawyers, but he threw himself into the cause with his usual enthusiasm. It is coincidental, but prophetic, that Dundas was enrolled on Gordon's side, and that Gordon won most of the cases.[3]

The year 1773, however, ended in a burst of glory, the tour of the Hebrides which brought Mahomet to the mountain, or Dr. Johnson to the Highlands. The *Journal of a Tour to the Hebrides* reveals Boswell at a high pitch of romantic Toryism. Johnson's common sense tempered Boswell's enthusiasm for the "old cause," though Boswell shed tears at an account of the Battle of Culloden, and both felt "a kind of *liking* for Jacobitism, something that it is not easy to define."[4] The Highlands moved Boswell to lament that he was not the head of a clan,

2. Ibid., pp. 4–5. The bank crisis also inspired Boswell to write a poetic squib on Sir Adam Fergusson (*LC,* 3 Sept. 1772), who is described as suffering from want of *"Air,"* and to remark further on Fergusson's speaking at great length at a meeting of the Ayr Bank stockholders (*LC,* 28 Dec. 1773). Fergusson was one of the larger shareholders in Douglas, Heron & Co., and its failure cost him about £4,400 (information from Sir James Fergusson).

3. Mem. 10, 28 Dec. 1772, 23 Feb., 2 Mar., 7 June, 20 Dec. 1773, 24 Jan., 22 Feb. 1774; Journ. 15, 20, 27 June 1774, etc. These and other political law cases in which Boswell was employed during 1772–74 are discussed by John Murray in an unpublished dissertation, "James Boswell in Edinburgh" (Yale, 1939), ii.146–74.

4. *Tour,* pp. 106–07, 163. When Boswell published this work, he omitted or radically revised the references to the Stuarts.

and that hereditary jurisdictions had been abolished; he rejoiced at seeing a feudal chief in action. When he maintained, however, that mankind was happier "in the ancient feudal state of subordination than when in the modern state of independency," Johnson replied realistically that the chief was, but that the rest having once escaped from this state were never willing to return.[5]

There was also talk of parties and elections. Boswell regretted that family position counted less than the wealth of a Nabob in securing a Parliamentary seat, and Johnson responded warmly that "there is a *scoundrelism* about a low man"; neither had much respect for a man who made money in trade.[6] Johnson attacked Burke's policy of adhering to one set of men politically, though he could admit in theory loyalty to a party guided by principles, and Boswell when he prepared the *Tour* for publication added a long note agreeing wholeheartedly with his friend.[7] Between Whig and Tory, there was no option: "every bad man is a Whig; every man who has loose notions," Johnson declared, while Boswell explained that "we are both *Tories;* both convinced of the utility of monarchical power, and both lovers of that reverence and affection for a sovereign which constitute loyalty, a principle which I take to be absolutely extinguished in Britain, which is one of the worst consequences of the Revolution."[8]

5. *Tour,* pp. 77, 103, 151–52, 212–13. Later, Boswell once admitted that "the *old barons* lived in savage tyranny, and their vassals in servile dependence" (*Hypochondriack,* no. 52, Jan. 1782).

6. *Tour,* pp. 76–77, 319–20.

7. *Tour,* pp. 20–21; *Life,* v.36 n.3. Johnson was evidently distinguishing between a faction, like the Rockingham, and a party, like the Whig.

8. *Tour,* pp. 162–63, 236. Boswell omitted the latter statement quoted above in the published work, and replaced it with a long justification of Hanoverian rule on the grounds of expediency and possession sanctioned by time (*Life,* v.202–05). An extended defense of a limited monarchy and of the necessity for subordination in government occurs in *Hypochondriack,* no. 19 (Apr. 1779).

3

Ayrshire and Practical Politics: 1774–1782

The county of Ayrshire lies like a triangle on the southwestern coast of Scotland, with its long side on the sea and its eastern frontiers bordered by hills. About 60 miles by 28 at its greatest extent, it is divided historically and topographically into three parts: the plain of Cunningham in the north, which extends into the central district of Kyle, and the hills of Carrick in the south divided from Kyle by the river Doon.

Throughout most of the eighteenth century, political power in Ayrshire rested in large part in its peers, with their large estates and extensive family connections. The Earls of Eglinton and the Montgomeries, the Earls of Loudoun and the Campbells, the Earls of Cassillis and the Kennedys were naturally prominent forces in county politics, as to a lesser extent were the Earls of Glencairn and Dumfries. Also, the Dukes of Argyll and the Earls of Bute from outside the county exerted influence in the Ayr group of burghs. But Ayrshire was never controlled by its peers as Argyll was long dominated by the Duke of Argyll, or Elginshire was disputed by the Duke of Gordon and Earl Fife. A number of long-established, independent families, the Craufurds of Auchenames, the Fergussons of Kilkerran, the Dunlops of Dunlop, the Fullartons of Fullarton, the Whitefoords of Ballochmyle, and the Boswells of Auchinleck, among others, felt entitled to their share of power. Because of these varied "interests," Ayrshire inevitably invited the possibility of highly complicated political maneuvering.

Local politics can hardly exist in a vacuum, but the relation of local to national politics in eighteenth-century Scotland depended so much on particular circumstances that it is impossible to generalize about it. While there was a good deal of interplay, especially in the more populous and less controlled counties, it was not very often that a change of government in London was the most important factor in a local contest. Yet it did play a major role in the 1741 Ayrshire election. At that time, the seat was held by Sir James Campbell, brother to the third Earl of Loudoun and a supporter of Walpole. He was defeated by Patrick Craufurd of Auchenames, representative of an old Ayrshire family, who was backed by the anti-Walpole group.[1] Craufurd was reelected in 1747, but was turned out in 1754 by James Mure Campbell, son of the former member. In this election, Campbell's campaign was managed by his cousin, the fourth Earl of Loudoun, who had the ministerial support of Newcastle, but the struggle had little relation to national politics apart from some slight residue of feeling left from Walpole's time. Craufurd obtained the aid of Alexander, Earl of Eglinton, in return for a promise to support Eglinton's candidate at the next election. Loudoun, however, conducted such a vigorous campaign that his candidate won easily.[2]

The accession of George III had important repercussions in the political world of Scotland. The Earl of Bute was now in a position to displace his uncle, the Duke of Argyll, as political manager, but for the moment it was not clear which one was in charge of affairs. Not much is known directly about the Ayrshire election of 1761, but something may be learned by look-

1. W. L. Burn, "The General Election of 1761 at Ayr," *English Historical Review,* 52 (1937), 105 n.1.

2. Fergusson, " 'Making Interest,' " pp. 125–28. This article discusses the elections of 1754 and 1774 in detail. A sketch of Patrick Craufurd and his son, John, appears in *Lowland Lairds,* pp. 68–74, and of John alone in Norman Pearson, " 'Fish' Craufurd," *Nineteenth Century and After,* 75 (1914), 389–401.

ing at the situation in the Ayr group of burghs. Of these, Campbeltown and Inveraray in Argyll were firmly controlled by the Duke, as was Rothesay in Bute by the Earl; Loudoun and Eglinton supposedly had some interest in the two Ayrshire burghs, Ayr and Irvine.[3] Loudoun was closely attached to Argyll while Eglinton was a personal friend of Bute, whose brother, James Stuart Mackenzie, was the sitting member. To avoid a contest, a compromise seems to have been reached in 1761 by which Archibald Montgomerie, Eglinton's brother, was to be brought in for the county, while Lord Frederick Campbell, Argyll's nephew, was to be chosen for the burghs.

Burgh elections, however, tended to be expensive and uncertain affairs. In this instance, the Town Council of Ayr, irritated by this arbitrary arrangement made without reference to it, chose Sir Adam Fergusson of Kilkerran as its candidate. Fergusson seems originally to have had some encouragement from Argyll, who wished to contest Bute's control of the burghs, but once the two peers had come to an agreement he was only an embarrassment.[4] Fergusson was willing to retire at Argyll's desire,[5] but he felt committed to the Town Council, and he was also supported by Patrick Craufurd's former adherents in the county, led by Sir Thomas Wallace of Craigie; irritated because their interest was minimized by the Bute–Argyll alliance, they were doing their best to create trouble. Delicate negotiations were required before the Ayr electors would con-

3. Robinson, p. 8; Mathieson, p. 104. The account of the Ayr burghs elections is based on Burn's article.

4. Before the death of George II, Argyll accused Bute of having "set up the Prince of Wales's standard in Scotland against the King" in two burghs, and also declared that Eglinton, Bute's friend, would never become Governor of Dumbarton Castle if he could prevent it (Namier, *England,* pp. 117–18). They were reconciled, however, toward the end of 1760 (Burn, p. 107), and collaborated unsuccessfully in the Edinburgh election of 1761. Argyll's death on 15 April 1761, five days before the Ayr burghs election, left Bute undisputed management of Scottish affairs (Namier, *England,* pp. 162 n.1, 173).

5. *Letters of George Dempster,* p. 50.

sent to release Fergusson from his candidacy and clear the way for Campbell.[6]

Archibald Montgomerie was elected without a contest for the county and expected to be returned again in 1768, but David Kennedy, brother to the Earl of Cassillis, suddenly emerged as a candidate and was chosen, after having obtained Loudoun's votes by promising to support whatever man Loudoun named at the next election.[7]

The election of 1774 was the first in which Boswell took an active part. It is a fine example of the most complicated intrigue, and a detailed survey of the background must be undertaken if any sense is to be made of it. Colonel William Fullarton of Fullarton estimated in 1793 that the upper class of proprietors in Ayrshire, those with estates worth from £100 to £10,000 per annum, numbered about 180, of whom 114 were voters. In addition, there were the five or six peers who owned considerable property.[8] The number of real proprietors could not have changed greatly in twenty years, but the number of voters fluctuated sharply. There were 128 voters on the freeholders' roll in 1774, before nominal votes were created in large numbers; 206 in 1780, 235 in 1781, 230 in 1784, 218 in 1788, and 221 in 1790.[9] The sharp drop thereafter was the

6. Campbell chose to sit for the Glasgow burghs, for which he had also been returned, and the Ayr seat was given to Alexander Wedderburn (later Lord Loughborough). Bute retained his hold on the Ayr burghs for many years. Craufurd was returned for Renfrewshire with Bute's help (Namier, *England,* p. 162).

7. Fergusson, " 'Making Interest,' " pp. 125, 128; *Cald. Papers,* II.ii.125–29. Boswell was neutral in this election, but when pressed by Eglinton felt he should have supported Montgomerie (Journ. 16 Jan. 1768).

8. *General View of the Agriculture of the Country of Ayr* (1793), p. 91.

9. *Ayrshire,* p. 102, the figure for 1774 being corrected from the detailed tabulation on pp. 107–13. There are slight differences between these figures and those given in Adam, p. 42; in [T. H. B. Oldfield], *An Entire and Complete History of Boroughs* (1792), iii.[p. 8 in section on Scotland]; and in the *View of the Political State of Scotland* (1790), attributed to Alexander Mackenzie, pp. 41–60. These differences result from the tabulations having been made at various times during election years, or

obvious result of the House of Lords' decision on nominal and fictitious votes in 1790.[1]

The elections so far considered were mainly factional struggles among the nobility, primarily between the houses of Loudoun and Eglinton. A relatively new situation arose in 1774. Many of the independent gentlemen of the county combined with two of the peers, the Earls of Glencairn and Dumfries, to support Sir Adam Fergusson, and faced with this challenge the dominant peers, Loudoun, Eglinton, and Cassillis, joined forces.

The most powerful member of this aristocratic coalition was Archibald, eleventh Earl of Eglinton, who had succeeded to the title on the death of his brother in 1769. Eglinton was colonel of various regiments and eventually a full general and Governor of Edinburgh Castle; for him as for the other peers, politics and his career were closely tied together. In private life he was a hard drinker and unfortunate in his marriages: his first wife died young, and he divorced his second in 1788 for adultery with the Duke of Hamilton.[2] Eglinton was a passionate Scotsman; he lacked the urbane gaiety of his elder brother, Boswell's early friend, and according to his factor, Alexander Fairlie of Fairlie, he was touchy about granting favors.[3] Boswell, who was his counsel in several lawsuits and dutifully loyal to him for many years as his political chief in Ayrshire, was sometimes unhappy in Eglinton's company, feeling that they had little in common and that Eglinton had no high opinion of him.[4]

---

from the figures referring either to the number of voters at the Michaelmas head-court or at the General Election.

1. Ante, pp. 5–6; post, p. 152.

2. In 1778, Boswell referred to Eglinton Castle as a "den of drunkeness" (Journ. 10 Nov.). (Only direct quotations, or facts taken from other than well-known sources like the DNB, *Complete Peerage,* etc. are footnoted in these descriptive sketches.)

3. From Fairlie, 20 Nov. 1786 (C 1227).

4. Journ. 9 Nov. 1778, 12 Jan. 1780. Earlier, however, Boswell had referred proudly to Eglinton as his "very good friend" (to Henry, 10th

John, fourth Earl of Loudoun, was at one time Commander-in-Chief of the British forces in North America and held several other high military posts, but he was more successful as a politician than as a soldier. After Argyll's death, Loudoun quickly transferred his allegiance to Bute,[5] and he had an aptitude for being on the winning side in local elections. Boswell described him after his death as one "who did more service to the county of Ayr in general, as well as to individuals in it, than any man we have ever had." Praising Loudoun's honesty, benevolence, and good humor, Boswell particularly emphasized that Loudoun did not raise false political expectations in others.[6]

The Earls of Cassillis of the period were undistinguished. Thomas, the ninth Earl, was an army officer; he was succeeded in 1775 by his brother, David, an advocate. Calling on the then M.P. for Ayrshire in 1773, Boswell thought him "the same joker as formerly," and added: "It struck me a little to think that the Gentlemen of Ayrshire should be represented in Parliament by a good, honest, merry fellow indeed, but one so totally incapable of the business of Legislation, and so devoid of the talents which distinguish a man in publick life."[7]

On Fergusson's side, Patrick, sixth Earl of Dumfries, was also an army officer, like so many of the Scottish nobility. A close neighbor of the Boswells at Auchinleck, he quarreled with Lord Auchinleck about a road that he wanted to construct through the Boswell property; by 1777 they were no longer

---

Earl of Pembroke, 20 Oct. 1777, L 1036. See, to Pembroke, 12 Jan. 1778, L 1037, to Jean, Countess of Crawford, 28 May 1779, L 393).

5. Burn, pp. 108–09. See Loudoun MSS 9,446, 9,450, 9,453, 12,660. Loudoun subsequently supported Grafton (Loudoun MSS 8,913, 8,914).

6. *Life,* v.372. This last comment may have been intended to reflect on Dundas.

7. Journ. 5 Apr. Quoting a song Kennedy was fond of, Boswell said "the only delights of the bed" that Kennedy cared for "were the delights of a bed of Oysters which he could eat with social laugh over a bottle of Claret or a bowl of punch" (Boswelliana MS).

on visiting terms, and Boswell agreed with Lady Auchinleck when she said that Dumfries "was the most dangerous creature that could be: *a cunning fool*."[8] William, twelfth Earl of Glencairn, is a dim figure. A major general, he died in 1775 and was succeeded by his son, James, the patron of Burns.[9]

Sir Adam Fergusson himself was a classic example of the Scottish country gentleman. Admitted advocate in 1755 at the age of 22, he was an outstanding "improver" of his estate and also a good scholar: he could read Greek, Latin, French, and Italian with facility, knew enough Hebrew to look up a Biblical reference, and was something of a paleographer as well. His virtues were solid and useful, perhaps a little austere, as Burns's characterization of him as "aith-detesting, chaste Kilkerran" implies. The one adjective that his contemporaries instinctively applied to him was "respectable."[1] His father, who sat on the Bench as Lord Kilkerran, had been a strong supporter of Loudoun, and this connection, through Loudoun's relationship with Argyll, seems to have given Fergusson his abortive start in politics in 1761. Thereafter he was politically on his own.[2]

Preparations for the election began early. Fergusson had

8. Journ. 23 Mar. 1777. See Journ. 14, 27 Oct. 1782; Margaret, Countess of Dumfries to Margaret Boswell, 22 Aug. 1778 (C 1116). Contemporary opinion of Dumfries seems not to have been very high. Around 1787 Katherine Mure wrote that if elected a Representative Peer he would never understand the business of the House of Lords: "it is his wife is the reall candidate: if she could be the peer, it would do very well" (Fergusson, *The Honourable Henry Erskine,* p. 200). For Dumfries's extensive road construction, see Sir John Sinclair, *Statistical Account of Scotland,* 1791–99, vi.415.

9. Sir James Fergusson describes Earl William as "a stout and touchy old man" in connection with the 1761 election ("'Making Interest,'" p. 123). His son later supported the Prince of Wales (*Letters of Robert Burns,* ed. J. De L. Ferguson, 1931, ii.59).

1. This sketch of Sir Adam is based on Sir James Fergusson's descriptions of him in "Sir Adam and Sir John: Sidelights on an Eighteenth Century Election," *SM, 19* (1933), 221; in *Letters of George Dempster,* pp. xxi–xxiv; in *Lowland Lairds,* pp. 93–105; and in letters to me.

2. Burn, p. 106; Fergusson, "'Making Interest,'" pp. 128–29.

made Dempster a nominal voter in his interest by 1770, and he also created superiorities for his own brothers. The Duchess of Argyll, remembering his services as counsel in the Douglas Cause, told Andrew Stuart and Baron Mure, trustees for her son, the Duke of Hamilton, that she intended to give Fergusson the three Hamilton votes in Ayrshire, and they concurred.[3]

As Boswell once declared, "the politicks of one county are often warped in with those of another,"[4] and this was certainly true for Fergusson and the Duchess. She was primarily interested in the campaigns in Renfrewshire and Lanarkshire, where the Hamilton and Argyll families had great interest. Andrew Stuart was their candidate in Lanarkshire, and John "Fish" Craufurd, son of Patrick Craufurd of Auchenames, in Renfrewshire. "Fish" Craufurd, who momentarily lost his head, made overtures to an opposition group headed by Daniel Campbell of Shawfield, which had successfully opposed Stuart at the last Lanarkshire election and which was connected with Douglas, the archenemy. This proposal horrified Stuart, who suggested instead an alliance with the Lord President and his friends, urging his personal intimacy with the President and his brother and the fact that they had not joined the coalition against him at the last election.[5]

Baron Mure carried on the negotiations between the Duchess and the Dundases. He reported to her on 21 October 1773 that while matters had not been brought to any conclusion, the delay proceeded from no disinclination on the other side and

3. *Letters of George Dempster*, pp. 69, 205; Fergusson, "'Making Interest,'" p. 129; *Intimate Society Letters*, i.145–46.

4. Reg. Let. 26 June 1784.

5. Apparently the bitter hostility between Stuart and Lord Mansfield, who was a great friend of the Dundases (*Arniston Memoirs*, p. 185; Furber, pp. 5–6; Matheson, pp. 16, 29, 37, 43), offered no impediment to this alliance. In Craufurd's defense, it should be added that the Duchess of Argyll had also suggested a compromise, though a much more advantageous one, with Shawfield (Horace Bleackley, *The Beautiful Duchess*, 1927, p. 189).

would soon be removed.[6] Our sources fade out at this point but it is quite likely that the two groups reached an agreement that guaranteed Stuart's election.[7]

Stuart, Dundas, and Fergusson were all friends,[8] and the probable intervention of the Dundases in Lanarkshire seems parallel to the help they gave Fergusson in Ayrshire. Friendship was interwoven with political expediency: Fergusson represented a rising political group which needed backing, and this the Dundases could supply. The Lord President persuaded his good friend, Lord Auchinleck, to exert himself in county politics for the first time in twenty years, and Auchinleck, who had previously given Boswell permission to support "the ancient

6. *Intimate Society Letters,* i.178–89.

7. Christie claims that the Dundases' "political connections in Lanark were placed at his [Stuart's] disposal in alliance with the Hamilton interest" (*The End of North's Ministry,* p. 294), but the sources he cites do not support so definite an assertion. Dundas, however, served as Stuart's "nominee" (i.e., representative) on the Select Committee when his election for Lanarkshire was unsuccessfully challenged by Shawfield in 1775 (Douglas, *History of . . . Controverted Elections,* ii.366). They worked closely together in the Fife election of 1776 (Furber, pp. 192–93), and were appointed joint Keepers of the Signet in Scotland in 1777. Dundas refused to accept appointment as sole Keeper of the Signet in 1779 until provision had been made for Stuart (Matheson, pp. 56–57; see also post, p. 81 n.9), who became a Commissioner of Trade and Plantations. For examples of their continuing relationship, see *Hist. MSS Comm.,* 10th Report, App. VI (1887), pp. 42, 242–43; *Correspondence of King George the Third,* ed. Sir John Fortescue (1927–28), vi.56–57.

According to C. D., 89 of the 91 votes in the Lanarkshire election were fictitious (*A Letter to the Real Freeholders,* p. 31).

8. Stuart and Fergusson had been closely associated in the Douglas Cause. Letters from Stuart to Fergusson, as well as a presentation copy of Stuart's *Letters to Lord Mansfield,* survive at Kilkerran (information from Sir James Fergusson). In 1774, Fergusson was trying to help Col. James Stuart, Andrew's brother, in his difficulties with the East India Company (*Letters of George Dempster,* pp. 79–80), and Andrew held an Ayrshire vote in Fergusson's interest (Adam, p. 25).

Fergusson and Dundas were two of the five Extraordinary Directors appointed for the Ayr Bank in November 1772 (*SM, 34,* 1772, 636), and Dundas later reminded Boswell that Fergusson had long been a friend of his (from Dundas, 12 May 1782, C 1133).

and respectable Interest of Ayrshire,"[9] now made a number of fictitious votes in favor of Fergusson.[1] Boswell resented this step bitterly, claiming that it both frustrated his "general wishes for old Interest in Elections," and made him insignificant in his own county. He never quite forgave the Dundases for their interference.[2]

It was while negotiations were going on between the Duchess of Argyll and the Dundases that Boswell and Johnson visited Inveraray Castle. Boswell mentioned to Johnson at this time the approaching "violent contest" in Ayrshire,

> where one of the candidates, in order to undermine the old and established interest, had artfully held himself

9. Such, at least, was Boswell's recollection in 1782 (to Dundas, 20 Apr. 1782, *Letters JB,* ii.523–24, L 448), but Temple wrote to him at the time, "Was ever anything so imprudent, so disrespectful, as to engage your interest without your father's approbation" (15 Feb. 1774, C 2752). An account of how the situation probably developed appears in *Boswell for the Defence,* ed. W. K. Wimsatt and F. A. Pottle (1959), pp. 201–03.

1. On 24 March 1774, Lord Auchinleck disponed most or all of his estate, including Dalblair, to ten liferenters for the obvious purpose of making votes, though the votes did not "mature" in time for the election of that year (H. M. Register House, General Register of Sasines, vol. 314, ff. 271–86; Particular Register of Sasines, Ayr, vol. 23, ff. 294–313. Information from Sir James Fergusson). Some of these voters had scruples about taking the trust oath (Journ. 27 Jan. 1775). It is probably these votes that Boswell was afraid Dundas was going to obtain from Lord Auchinleck at the time of the 1780 election (Journ. 18, 22 Oct. 1780). Boswell purchased Dalblair on 16 April 1767 (Journ.), but his father had held the superiority since 6 November 1752 (Register of Deeds, Dur., 20 June 1763); he may have felt further justified in disposing of it as he pleased since he was a surety to Boswell's creditors for £1,200 of the purchase price, and finally paid over £1,000 when the debt was settled (Journ. 17 Nov. 1775, 1 Jan., 18 Oct. 1776).

Boswell thought his father's conduct particularly reprehensible since Lord Auchinleck had previously condemned fictitious votes, as is implied in his *Observations on the Election Law of Scotland;* see also Journ. 6 Aug. 1774, 21 Nov. 1776; Ramsay, i.176–77, 341 n.1.

2. Journ. 11 Nov. 1774, 23 Dec. 1775, 16 Jan. 1776, 16 Mar., 28 Nov. 1777, Nov.–Dec. 1779 (*BP,* xiv.4), 6 Apr., 12 Oct. 1780; to Dundas, 20 Apr. 1782 (*Letters JB,* ii.523–24; L 448); *LPS 85,* pp. 60–61.

> out as a champion for the independency of the county against aristocratick influence, and had persuaded several gentlemen into a resolution to oppose every candidate who was supported by peers.[3]

Boswell meant such gentlemen as Sir John Whitefoord, John Dunlop of Dunlop, and his son, "Sir" Thomas Wallace,[4] a group closely identifiable lineally and politically with Patrick Craufurd's one-time backers. These men shared the fear of an anonymous writer in the *Scots Magazine* that the noble families of large estates were overwhelming "the private gentlemen of property in each county";[5] their confederacy inspired George Dempster to tell Fergusson in January 1774:

> I had heard of the noble association against you in Ayrshire and consider'd it as fatal to your views. You revive my spirits much by what you say in your letter of the effect this association has had upon the independent part of the gentry of the county, and of your own resolution to persevere in the contest.[6]

David Kennedy, running for reelection as the candidate of the "noble association," was also having his troubles. His aunt, Susanna, Dowager Countess of Eglinton, wrote to her son-in-law in February 1774 that "elections in this place occasions great divisions. All thos was of my son's partie last time is now against his man. Captain Montgomerie,[7] Lord Cassillis, and

3. *Life,* v.354–55. Boswell heightened the original account (*Tour,* p. 353) for publication.

4. Maternal grandson to Sir Thomas Wallace of Craigie, whose name and title he assumed. The title was disallowed (G. E. C[okayne], *Complete Baronetage,* 1900–09, iv.277–78). Miss Harriet Chidester has pointed out to me that the younger Dunlop was the grandson of the 4th Baronet (mentioned ante, p. 58) and not of the 3d (who died in 1728), as asserted by G. E. C. See, to Pembroke, 22 Jan. 1779 (L 1041), and James Paterson, *History of the Counties of Ayr and Wigton* (1863–66), i.295–96.

5. *35* (1773), 13.

6. *Letters of George Dempster,* p. 80.

7. Hugh Montgomerie, later M.P. and 12th Earl of Eglinton.

Mr. Kennedy joyns him; but it's hard to know who will succeed, though Lord Loudon asists." A month later (10 March 1774) she reported to the same correspondent:

> There never was such a bustle about elections as now in this countie. Lord Eglintoune, Lord Casstels, and Lord Loudon, are joynd for Mr. Kennedy, and making manie new vottars. All the votars that joyn'd my son against Mr. Kennedy at the last is jainst, and against my son to a man. The evant is doubetfully talked off. I'm told great strugalls is thoroug all poor Scotland, and nothing prevaills but coruption.[8]

Alexander Montgomerie of Coilsfield, Eglinton's cousin and henchman, offered a more detailed and cheerful estimate of the situation to Baron Mure in June 1774. Montgomerie tabulated the probable votes on each side as follows:[9]

Lord Eglinton	48	Sir Adam Fergusson	16
Lord Cassilis	41	Sir John Whyteford	11
Lord Loudoun	27	Lord Dumfries	23
Sir John Cathcart	8	Sir T. Wallace	21
[John Hamilton of] Bargeny	3	[John McAdam of] Craigengillan	7
[John Craufurd of] Auchenames	2	Lord Auchenleck	8
Baron Mure	2	John Dunlop	3
[Hugh Ross of] Kerse	2	[William Fullarton of] Rosemount	3
J. Orr [of Barrowfield]	2	Duke Hamilton	3
[John Hamilton of] Sundrum	1	Alex. Fergusson [of Craigdarroch]	4
		Lord Glencairn	10
	136		109

8. William Fraser, *Memorials of the Montgomeries* (1859), i.373.

9. *Cald. Papers,* II.ii.234–35. "Great numbers of new votes are made on both sides, but it is thought Mr. Kennedy will in the end carry his election" (30 June 1774), according to Robinson (p. 18).

This list is a remarkable illustration of the crosscurrents of Scottish politics. Though, as noted, Baron Mure had concurred in the Duchess of Argyll's decision to give the Hamilton interest to Fergusson, he was also an old friend of Eglinton and his connections, and Montgomerie confidently assumed he would vote for their candidate.[1] John Craufurd, as the Hamilton nominee in Renfrewshire, was naturally reluctant to vote for Kennedy, but he and his father had pledged their votes to the Eglinton candidate, and Montgomerie refused to release them.[2] The Craufurd following, Wallace, Whitefoord, et al., suffered no such impediment; they disassociated themselves not only from their former leader, but also from Eglinton whom apparently they had supported in 1768.[3] Bargany and Sundrum were brothers-in-law of Montgomerie. Cathcart was a nephew of the Earl of Cassillis, who was in turn Eglinton's first cousin. Craigengillan was much obliged to Lord Auchinleck,[4] who possibly influenced him to vote for Fergusson. Craigdarroch was standing in Dumfriesshire against the nominee of the Duke of Queensberry,[5] a pillar of the Bute interest and an ardent friend of Douglas, so his support of Fergusson was logical.

The election itself, which took place on 13 October,[6] was tersely described by an anonymous correspondent in the *Scots Magazine.* Kennedy and his friends, having succeeded in the election of a preses and clerk, were confident of victory when

1. Mure probably voted for Kennedy (*Cald. Papers,* II.ii.241).

2. Ibid., II.ii.236, [237].

3. Almost nothing is known about this "independent" group, but it seems reasonable to infer that its members had no obligations to be loyal to the Craufurds. That this group supported Eglinton is inferred from Lady Eglinton's letters quoted above; possibly she refers to Dumfries and Glencairn.

4. Journ. 4 Oct. 1776.

5. Robinson, p. 18.

6. Wight, p. 156. The Michaelmas head-court, referred to below, was held on 4 October.

George Fergusson, Sir Adam's brother, proposed putting the trust oath. This did not alarm Kennedy since his side had made only one fourth the number of nominal votes that Fergusson and his friends were responsible for, and (according to this embittered account) "the *property-voters* in favour of Mr. Kennedy exceeded those in favour of Sir Adam by near twenty." However, five of Kennedy's voters, including Hugh Montgomerie, refused to take the oath, while all twenty of Fergusson's superiority holders, including a parson, swore without scruple.[7] Now possessing a majority, Sir Adam's friends "immediately fell to reviewing the procedure of the Michaelmas head-court; and having picked out the names of the claimants in the interest of Sir Adam, whose titles to be inrolled had been rejected by the judgement of the freeholders in their court, they ordered them to be added to the roll . . . and which being done, they returned Sir Adam by a majority of thirteen."[8]

The "noble association" was an ill-united group. Boswell, who had been zealous in its cause, was shocked to realize in November 1774 that Loudoun was ready to join Fergusson if it was to his advantage.[9] In the same month at an election of the Representative Peers, Cassillis, the ministerial choice, was opposed by Eglinton. Cassillis won handily, 32 to 20, with the backing of the Earls of Bute, Loudoun, March (Queensberry's heir), and the other candidates on the ministerial list; Eglinton

7. "Gentlemen of honour feel it a very unpalateable oath, witness what happened at Air and Kirckudbright" (C. D., *A Letter to the Real Freeholders,* p. 5).

8. *36* (1774), 674–75. The letter is dated Ayr, 14 October. The *Edinburgh Advertiser,* 18 October 1774, supplies one or two further details about the election. Its bitterness is also indicated by the formal protest of 13 October which Sir Adam drew up against William Duff of Crombie, the Sheriff-depute, for supposedly irregular proceedings during the election (Kilkerran MSS). The vote was 60 to 47 (*Letters of George Dempster,* p. 81).

9. Journ. 16 Nov.

was supported by the Duke of Buccleuch, Henry Dundas's friend, and the Earl of Dumfries.[1]

Boswell, who considered Fergusson a parvenu, expressed his attitude fully in an anecdote:

> Sir Adam Fergusson who by a strange coincidence of chances got in to be a Member of Parliament for Ayrshire in 1774, was the Great Grandson of a Messenger. I was talking at Rowallan on the 17 of March 1777 with great indignation that the old families of the County should be defeated by an Upstart. Major Dunlop urged the popular topick that the other candidate Mr. Kennedy was supported by noblemen who wanted to annihilate the influence of the Gentlemen, and he still harped on the coalition of three Peers. "Sir," said I, "let the ancient respectable families have the lead, rather than the Spawn of a Messenger. Better three Peers than three Oyeses."[2]

This misleading and not very funny story illustrates only one of Boswell's objections to Fergusson. Another was aroused by Fergusson's claim of representing the independent gentlemen against the peers; this claim Boswell later attacked in his *Letter to the People of Scotland* (1785): "Sir Adam Fergusson wrote a circular letter against peers interfering in our county election, and several very worthy gentlemen joined the standard of *independency,* as they imagined, which he erected. Carrying

1. *SM,* 36 (1774), 618–20. The account in *Hist. MSS Comm.,* 11th Report, App. V (1887), pp. 369–70, gives Cassillis's majority as thirteen, but the *Scots Magazine* lists the voters on both sides. See also *Calendar of Home Office Papers, 1773–75* (1899), pp. 255–59, and Loudoun MSS 9,045. Perhaps to satisfy those who resented governmental dictation, Eglinton was returned as a Representative Peer in 1776 (see Fergusson, *The Sixteen Peers of Scotland,* pp. 85–87).

2. *Boswelliana,* pp. 283–84 (corrected from photostats of the MS). No basis has been found for Boswell's sneer, presumably directed at Sir Adam's great-grandfather, Simon Fergusson of Auchinwin. The Fergussons, an ancient and respectable family, had been established in Ayrshire since the 14th century.

them along with him, and yet 'having his peers as well as we,' he contrived to possess, for two parliaments, the representation of Ayrshire, by means of *those superiority votes,* which that county has declared to be *nominal and fictitious,* while the REAL INTEREST was unrepresented."[3] This statement provoked a reply from "An Ayrshireman" in the *Public Advertiser* (14 July 1785) that the gentlemen of the county "were long most disgracefully led by a contending aristocracy, but at last they resolved to shake off the servile yoke, and choose a Member independent of the Peerage." Despite the coalition of the peers, "the excellent character of Sir Adam Fergusson had gained him the good-will and affection of all the independent Gentlemen of the county, who united cordially in electing him to be the Member," and "An Ayrshireman" reminded Boswell that this group had included Lord Auchinleck.[4] In reply, Boswell asserted that in 1780 Montgomerie "had a *considerable majority of real votes,*" that without the assistance of the Dumfries, Glencairn, and Hamilton votes Fergusson would never have been chosen, and that when Dumfries and Glencairn abandoned him in 1784, Fergusson had been forced to compromise with Eglinton.[5]

Undoubtedly Fergusson saw himself as the leader of the county gentlemen,[6] in Boswell's terms a "democratical coali-

3. P. 53.

4. "An Ayrshireman" obviously knew Boswell and his father quite well. After comparing Boswell to Lord George Gordon, he says, "from the regard I had for your worthy father, I wish that your petulant vanity, and violent versatility, did not mark you out so conspicuously an object of contempt and ridicule" (P 60.2).

5. *Public Advertiser,* 27 July 1785.

6. Fergusson wrote to Lord Hailes (25 Oct. 1774): "I know the sincerity of your Lordship's congratulations for my success in an attempt, which, in the opinion of many, and even in my own at the beginning, seemed almost desperate. It gives me in reality more satisfaction on account of the County than my own. How far it is for my advantage may be questioned. It is certainly for their honour; because, however much mistaken in their object, a great proportion of those who voted for me, did so from good and public motives" (Newhailes MSS).

tion,"[7] but it is equally certain that without the support of the peers mentioned by Boswell, Fergusson would never have been successful. No Ayrshire candidate at the time could win without the backing of at least several of the peers, since their power to make votes was so extensive.

Perhaps the deepest, if least tangible, source of conflict between Boswell and Fergusson arose from the question of party. The terms Whig and Tory may have retained little practical significance in the later eighteenth century, but they indicated a difference in attitude toward Church and Constitution and they still carried an emotive charge.[8] It was Fergusson's remark that "in the British constitution it is surely of importance to keep up a spirit in the people, so as to preserve a balance against the crown" which led Dr. Johnson to call him "a vile Whig."[9]

7. Journ. 15 Oct. 1774. The connotation Boswell gave to "democratical" may be gathered from his later remark about Johnson's political opponent, Dr. Joseph Towers: "I abhor his Whiggish democratical notions and propensities, (for I will not call them principles)" (*Life,* ii.316).

8. It is well known that modern historians disagree as to what meanings the terms Whig and Tory had during this period. I have mainly followed Richard Pares, who says that the terms were being revived early in George III's reign "to indicate differences of opinion between people hitherto called whigs, about the constitutional rights of the crown and their proper exercise. Whigs called other whigs by the name of tories, and 'pure' whiggism was increasingly identified with a kind of anti-monarchism" ("George III and the Politicians," *The Historian's Business,* 1961, p. 100). Other relevant discussions of "party" occur in Namier, *England,* pp. 179–215; Pares, *King George III and the Politicians,* pp. 55–60, 70–72; Sir Lewis Namier, "Monarchy and the Party System," *Personalities and Powers* (1955); Herbert Butterfield, *George III and the Historians* (1957), pp. 219–24; W. R. Fryer, "The Study of British Politics between the Revolution and the Reform Act," *Renaissance and Modern Studies, 1* (1957), 105–14; J. M. Price, "Party, Purpose and Pattern: Sir Lewis Namier and his Critics," *Journal of British Studies, 1* (1961), 71–93.

9. *Life,* ii.170. The journal on which the Life MS is based at this point continues: "He was disgusted by Sir Adam, and called him to me a narrow whig with just the commonplace arguments. I however told him afterwards that Sir Adam was a man who distinguished himself by his regard for

And Boswell, whom heredity, principles, and ambition made very sensitive to party distinctions, later wished to check Henry Dundas, "a branch of a whig family," through Mountstuart's "noble Tory interest."[1]

Much as Boswell resented Fergusson's victory, he resented the Dundases' intervention even more. Their intervention, while minor in scope, illustrated both the methods Henry Dundas was to use to acquire power and the conditions that permitted him to do so. Apart from the Secretary of State for the Northern Department, acting in his official capacity, North's ministry, like all ministries since Bute's, lacked both an agent for Scotland and a "party" organization there. Also, the direct influence of the government was limited. In John Robinson's notes covering 43 Scottish seats in the 1774 election, the words "money" or "government," indicating that direct pressure could be applied, occur in connection with only six burgh seats.[2] As a result the ministry was forced to deal separately with each figure of political importance. Each county and burgh acted autonomously. In some, one man or one family was entrenched, but in most, two or three factions struggled for power; on some occasions they could compromise on a candidate, on others they fought bitterly amongst themselves, as the Grants, Duffs, and Gordons did in the northern counties. Any ministry was forced to be careful when faced with such a situation, and its task was eased tremendously when one Scot could be found with both sufficient control and sufficient tact to keep these varied elements in line. Dundas was in a favor-

---

religion, though his politicks were bad. 'O Sir' said Mr. Johnson, 'Politicks go but a little way with me, in comparrison of religion. I forgive him his Politicks for his religion' " (31 Mar. 1772).

1. Journ. 17 Mar. 1776; to Temple, 22 May 1775 (*Letters JB,* i.225).

2. Robinson, pp. 5–9. This list was drawn up in December 1773. In a later résumé of contested counties, Robinson mentions Government interest in Kirkcudbright (pp. 17–20). In the earlier list he forecast the results of 27 elections correctly, was wrong in 6 cases, and left 10 doubtful.

able position to become this man from the start, and he made use of every opportunity.

In 1774 there was no combined force of any strength in Scotland except the remains of the Bute interest. Bute was unassailable in his own county, and he gained control of the Ayr burghs by agreement with the Dukes of Argyll.[3] Stuart Mackenzie, member for Ross, Sir William Augustus Cunynghame, member for Linlithgowshire, the Duke of Queensberry, with his immense influence in Dumfriesshire and elsewhere, and the noble coalition in Ayrshire were all closely connected to Bute.

Dundas's ambition became quickly apparent to such interested spectators as Boswell and Mountstuart. Boswell reported in April 1775 that he enjoyed hearing Mountstuart talk of the Bute interest, and that Mountstuart had only contempt for the Duke of Buccleuch's dream of being prime minister of Scotland with the help of Dundas. It soon became obvious that Dundas was going to be the chief of this group rather than the Duke, and the central figures of this "*Scotch ministry*" began to emerge: Dundas, Buccleuch, Fergusson, Andrew Stuart, and probably several others whose welfare depended on their good relations with the administration in office.[4]

The emergence of this inner circle might well have drawn Bute and his friends closer to the independent politicians in Scotland who disliked Dundas. Among them were Sir Lawrence

3. Ante, pp. 57–58, and see *Cald. Papers,* II.i.133–34.

4. Journ. 6 Apr. 1775, 26 Jan., 17–18 Mar. 1776. Furber says that Dundas "could probably count upon the friendship of about ten of the Scottish members" in the Parliament of 1774 (p. 191), but his estimate is not completely accurate. He lists among Dundas's friends John Lockhart-Ross as M.P. for Lanarkshire, where he had been replaced by Stuart, and Lord William Gordon, who did not come into Parliament until April 1779. On the other hand, John Craufurd in view of his Hamilton connections was unlikely to be hostile to Dundas, as Furber claims. Craufurd did not act with Fox before 1782 (Christie, *The End of North's Ministry,* p. 212; and see Pearson, "'Fish' Craufurd," pp. 394–96). For Dundas's connections in 1782, see Christie, pp. 294–95.

Dundas, who controlled the city of Edinburgh, his son, Thomas, who sat for Stirlingshire, and Sir Lawrence's brother, Thomas, who with his sons represented in succession the stewartry of Orkney and Shetland. The Wemyss family in Fife, the Elphinstones in Dunbartonshire, Lord Fife and his friends in the north, Dempster in the Perth burghs, Gilmour in Midlothian, Sir Gilbert Elliot in Roxburghshire, and Douglas of Douglas with his friends: all had reason to oppose any extension of Dundas's control of Scotland.

Here was the nucleus of a powerful opposition, but it failed to coalesce in the crucial years between 1774 and 1784. Three or four factors help to explain this failure. The basic difficulty, as Boswell pointed out in 1776, was that political interest in Scotland had become so divided among private families after the death in 1761 of Archibald, Duke of Argyll, that it would be hard for any one family to establish an extensive influence.[5] This difficulty did not discourage Dundas, but apparently none of his opponents could conceive of any larger goal than using the two or three seats they controlled as bargaining points with the ministry in power. The absence of a great political issue may have impeded cohesion; with the exception of Dempster and Lord Fife they seemed to have supported North's conduct of the American War until shortly before the end of his ministry.[6] Yet it is still somewhat surprising that they did not combine to counteract Dundas's growing power. Boswell mentions one dinner at Gilmour's that looks like a partial roll call of the disaffected: the guests included Mountstuart, his brother James Stuart, Capt. John Elphinstone (later eleventh Lord Elphin-

5. Journ. 17 Mar.

6. Sir Lawrence Dundas and his connections went into opposition in 1780, and the younger Sir Gilbert Elliot's speech against the Ministry in 1782 was a sign that the end was close for North (Christie, pp. 213–14, 337–39). Alexander Garden of Troup also supported North and Dundas, but opposed the American War (Christie, pp. 295, 332 n.5, 359–61). For Fife's independent position, see Robinson, p. 99, and Christie, p. 330 n.3.

stone), Douglas, and Campbell of Shawfield,[7] but not even a hint survives that at any time did they contemplate a coordinated opposition.

Perhaps the most important factor in their failure to unite was the lack of a leader. In the absence of modern party organizations, factions tended to cohere loosely around a man. The logical leader of this group was Mountstuart; he could probably have counted on a nucleus of four or five Scottish votes, as well as on two members for Bossiney and Cardiff, boroughs where his family had interest,[8] and his sponsoring the Scots Militia Bill of 1776 might well have rallied further support.[9] But there were certain severe drawbacks to Mountstuart's position and character. He suffered from his father's bad political reputation,[1] and his own pride, indolence, and indifference to others were even more damaging factors. Boswell thought him "quite a Prince," but Mountstuart's revealing preference for a

7. Journ. 12 Apr. 1775.

8. Robinson, pp. 84, 95, 99.

9. The elder Sir Gilbert Elliot, Dempster, and Fergusson spoke in favor of the Bill (*Parliamentary History of England, 1774–77* [ed. William Cobbett, 1806–20], xviii.1228–37).

1. William Combe, in his gossip sheet, *The R--l Register,* blamed Mountstuart's troubles on the unpopularity of his father (5, 1781, 46–49, 175–76). Lady Mountstuart (if she wrote the unsigned letter to Thomas Coutts, 16 Nov. 1782, ascribed to her) claimed that debt and regard for his father made Mountstuart's position delicate: "Joining any party is joining the enemys of his father!" (Coleridge, *Life of Thomas Coutts,* i.150), and Mountstuart thought himself out of favor with the North ministry (to Burke, 18 Mar. 1782, Fitzwilliam MSS).

Bute complained bitterly of being unable to do anything for his son, Charles, in 1773 (Henry Mackenzie, *Account . . . of John Home,* 1822, p. 151), and Charles's military career seems subsequently to have been impeded (*New Records of the American Revolution. The Letters . . . Sent by Lieut.-General Sir Charles Stuart, to his Father, the Earl of Bute, 1775–79,* 1927, pp. xxxi, 115). Bute successfully negotiated with North, however, in 1780 for a seat for his son, James, which cost £1,000 (Christie, pp. 97–98, 99, 178 n.3). Louis Dutens claimed that the Ministry neglected Bute because they were persuaded "he would never take a part in opposition" (*Memoirs of a Traveller,* 1806, iv.184).

seat in the House of Lords rather than one in the Commons and the arrogance he showed in refusing to consult other Scots about the Militia Bill were hardly conducive to political success.[2] The Bute family and their connections never learned the truth that Mountstuart's future father-in-law tried to impress upon them: "Act firmly together, and you must be of consequence, otherwise no side will look at you, and you will be ill-treated by all in turn."[3] Mountstuart finally settled for a brief diplomatic career as Envoy to Turin, and for an appointment as Ambassador to Madrid under Shelburne and the Coalition ministry, a post he never took up.[4]

Each of Dundas's original opponents hanged separately: either they fought only when attacked on home ground, or they were won over by patronage. Sir Lawrence Dundas and his relatives remained inveterate enemies of the Arniston branch of the family, but his death in 1781 delivered the town of Edinburgh into Henry Dundas's hands. George Keith Elphinstone, M.P. for Dunbartonshire, remained in opposition until he vacated his seat by agreement in 1790. However his elder brother, Lord Elphinstone, who controlled this county in con-

2. Journ. 29 Mar. 1775, 17 Mar. 1776. Mountstuart was made a British peer in May 1776 (see Mem. 11 May 1776). Boswell summarized Mountstuart's character with some objectivity in 1777: "I was hurt by Lord Mountstuart's neglect when I had been so confidential with him. But his style is peculiar in every respect, and I must take him as he is: with Nobleness of mind and generosity, and gleams of affection, but with Indolence in the extreme, which in effect not only prevents his virtues from acting, but, to those who do not know him perfectly, makes him be thought to have what may be called Vices: Inconstancy, Fallaciousness, and other such qualities" (Journ. 30 Mar.). Mountstuart was described by Dutens, his adviser in Turin, as proud, "fond of splendour," careless about money—with an income of 10,000 guineas a year—and obliging (*Memoirs,* iv.7, 14–15).

3. Thomas Coutts to Charles Stuart, 4 Mar. 1783. At this point, James Stuart was voting against the Shelburne ministry (*A Prime Minister and his Son,* ed. E. Stuart Wortley, 1925, p. 199).

4. *British Diplomatic Representatives, 1689–1789,* ed. D. B. Horn, 1932, p. 137; *A Prime Minister and his Son,* pp. 200–03.

junction with the Marquess of Graham, became Lt.-Governor of Edinburgh Castle in 1781, and in the same year was petitioning Dundas to help him obtain a vacant pension of £400 a year.[5] Douglas had become a supporter of Pitt by 1784 and was rewarded with a British peerage six years later.[6] Elliot was defeated in Roxburghshire in 1784 and, though he came over to Pitt and Dundas during the war years, Dundas in 1796 was unable to help him regain his county seat.[7] Dundas attached the Wemyss family with appointments. Lord Fife remained independent until he entered into a restless alliance with Dundas in 1787.[8] Dempster survived in cheerful isolation, while Gilmour sank into political oblivion.[9]

5. Adam, pp. 89–91; *Hist. MSS Comm.*, 10th Report, App. VI, p. 43. Mountstuart, whose first cousin was married to Elphinstone (their youngest son was named Mountstuart Elphinstone), also wrote to Dundas on Elphinstone's behalf (ibid.).

6. Robinson, pp. 101, 104. Douglas's earlier political position is obscure. He had close personal ties with the third Duke of Queensberry (who died in 1778), and was elected in 1782 for Forfar, where Dundas's violent enemies, Lord Panmure and his family, had a strong interest (Furber, pp. 192, 261–62); at the same time, Dundas was allied with the Hamiltons in Lanarkshire, where Douglas had interest (Adam, p. 212). These facts suggest that he was initially opposed to Dundas, but Dundas had been one of his counsel in the Cause and was still reaffirming his legitimacy as late as 1789 (*Mrs. Montagu*, ed. Reginald Blunt, n.d., ii.236). In any case, Douglas played a waiting game by not taking his seat during the crucial period of North's fall (Christie, p. 357). His marriage to the Duke of Buccleuch's sister in 1783 may have been a decisive factor in his later support of Pitt and Dundas.

7. Furber, pp. 259–60. See post, p. 177.

8. Furber, pp. 192–93, 220; *Lord Fife and his Factor*, pp. 2, 163, 185–87, 245–47, 249, 252–53; *Domestic Papers of the Rose Family*, ed. Alistair and Henrietta Tayler (1926), pp. 32–34. Furber's summary of the relationship between Fife and Dundas is a little misleading (pp. 206–15, 243, 258–59, 271–72).

9. Ante, p. 9 nn.8–9. In 1768, when they were rival suitors for Catherine Blair, Boswell described Gilmour as "a young man about thirty who has £1600 a year of estate, was formerly an officer in the guards and is now one of the Clerks of the board of green cloth £1000 a year in short a noble match, though a man of expence and obliged to lead a London life"

Boswell had been on good terms with the Dundases until their intervention with his father, in spite of the envy which Henry Dundas's appointment as Solicitor General had aroused; but after hearing what his father had been persuaded to do Boswell refused to dine with the President, and by February 1775 they were not on speaking terms.[1] This dislike was quickened by Henry Dundas's appointment as Lord Advocate. In announcing this event to Temple, Boswell admitted that "Harry" Dundas had "strong parts," but continued, "he is a coarse, unlettered, unfanciful dog. Why is he so lucky? Is not such an office degraded by his getting it."[2] He stood ready to oppose Dundas's election as Dean of the Faculty of Advocates in the summer of 1775, and had ideas of attacking him in the press, though he conceded honestly at one point that Dundas was "upon the whole a man of abilities and a man of Worth."[3]

The Fife by-election of 1776 nearly brought about a duel between the two. Boswell joined his cousin, Claud Boswell of Balmuto, and the Wemyss party in supporting James Oswald of Dunnikier against Sir John Henderson, who was backed by his uncle, Andrew Stuart, and Dundas. The election hinged on the validity of the vote of a Capt. Hew Dalrymple, one of

---

(to Temple, 8 Feb., *Letters JB,* i.143). Gilmour was in severe financial trouble by 1778, and appealed directly to George III for help in 1782 (*Correspondence of George III,* vi.118–19). He had lost his Clerkship in 1780 (*Royal Kalendar . . . for . . . 1780,* p. 80; *Royal Kalendar . . . for . . . 1781,* p. 80; see *Correspondence of George III,* iv.352). In 1781, Dundas remarked "no idea could be more wild" than Gilmour's "thinking of representing the Town of Edinburgh" (Furber, pp. 195–96). He retired to Boulogne where, involved in further financial difficulties, he died (*Letters of George Dempster,* p. 133; *GM,* 62, 1792, 1220).

1. Ante, p. 10. Journ. 6 Aug. 1774, 23 Feb. 1775.

2. To Temple, 22 May 1775 (*Letters JB,* i.225); see, from Temple, 16 June 1775 (C 2763).

3. Journ. Review of the Summer Session, 1775 (*BP,* x.229); to Temple, 16 Oct. 1775 (*Letters JB,* i.243). See Journ. 23 Dec. 1775; from Temple, 6 Oct. 1775 (C 2765); *Life,* iii.213.

Oswald's adherents, and when the case came before the Court of Session, Lord Auchinleck, who was presiding, affirmed the vote. Dundas, in an election petition submitted to the House of Commons, charged him with having spoken on one side of the question and having voted on the other. Though Lord Auchinleck did not resent this accusation, Boswell did, and he became uneasily convinced that it was his duty to call Dundas out for this slur on his father. His friends, however, unanimously declared that he had no reason to take offense in what was a public and not a personal difference, and Boswell allowed himself to be placated.[4]

This was not the only election in which Boswell was involved outside of Ayrshire; at the time of his own county election he had been employed by Lt.-Col. Archibald Campbell in his contest for the Stirling group of burghs against Lt.-Col. James Masterton, the nominee of Sir Lawrence Dundas. Campbell carried the day in a campaign marked by double-dealing, bribery, and a violent attack from the pulpit which led to a lawsuit, and he chose Boswell to be his formal delegate from the burgh of Culross at the election meeting. Boswell accepted, and then suddenly realized that he might be forced to swear to the Formula, an oath abjuring the Roman Catholic church and certain of its doctrines. This he was unwilling to do, since he was not sure that he really abhorred a belief in purgatory and the invocation of angels and saints, as the oath read; he knew, however, if he refused to swear that he would never be able to sit in Parliament or even vote in an election. Fortu-

4. Journ. 13 Dec. 1775, 16 Jan., 6–16 Mar. 1776; from John Johnston, 15 Mar. 1776 (C 1634); Furber, pp. 192–93. An account of the election and court judgment appears in the *Scots Magazine, 38* (1776), 160–61. Ramsay apparently invented a controversial exchange between Dundas and Boswell on the subject of Lord Auchinleck's vote, though Boswell's supposed remark, "You and your brother have made him a politician, and you have not improved him," sounds characteristic (i.177 n.1; see Journ. 6 Mar. 1776).

nately, no one proposed that the oath be administered, so Boswell was able to escape the choice between the strictures of his literal conscience and the unpleasant consequences of refusal.[5] He was also concerned as an advocate in the Clackmannan election of the same year, which involved an unsuccessful petition before the Commons on behalf of his friend, Capt. James Francis Erskine of Mar.[6]

These contacts with the world of politics sustained Boswell's ambition, and he prodded his London friends to help him to a place. Mountstuart, "*Carus Mæcænas,*" and "Tutelary Patron" of Scotland as well as personal patron of James Boswell, was his chief hope.[7] During Boswell's spring visit to London in 1775, Mountstuart's promises of help encouraged him to look about for an opening. He first thought of David Ross's position as a judge in the Commissary Court of Edinburgh,[8] but a week later a more lucrative idea occurred to him: perhaps Mountstuart, Queensberry, and Douglas could combine to persuade Baron Maule to resign his sinecure as Clerk to the Register of Sasines in the Court of Session; as late as October, Boswell was still pursuing this mirage.[9] The pressure on him to secure some office during his father's lifetime was strong, since it would

5. Journ. 11 Oct.–1 Nov. 1774, 4 Feb., 19 Dec. 1775; *Life,* iii.58–64; *SM,* 36 (1774), 556–58, 620–22, 675–76.

6. Journ. 1–3 Nov. 1774, 3–7 Apr. 1775. Douglas summarizes the case in *History . . . of Controverted Elections,* ii.343–64.

7. Journ. 21 June 1774, [23 Nov.] 1775. See Journ. 16 Mar. 1775; to Temple, 4 Apr. (*Letters JB,* i.218), from Temple, 9 Apr. (C 2760), to Temple, 3 June 1775 (*Letters JB,* i.229), 1 May 1776 (*Letters JB,* i.252).

8. A court concerned with such matters as divorce, execution of wills, petty claims, etc. The job paid £80 a year (to Mountstuart, 13 Nov. 1775, L 346).

9. Journ. 22, 29 Mar., 11 Apr. 1775; to [Margaret Stuart], 27 Oct. 1775 (L 1200). Maule's position, which was worth £200 a year (*Parliamentary Register, 1779–80* [ed. John Almon, 1775–80], xvi. extra page 2), was finally given to Andrew Stuart as part of the bargain by which Dundas became sole Keeper of the Signet (*GM, 51,* 1781, 396; see *Correspondence of George III,* iv.353; ante, p. 64 n.7).

make him less dependent on his father while at the same time proving him worthy of parental regard. Even more important, Boswell may have clearly suspected that his legal practice would fall off after his father's retirement, which it did. He still hoped to escape the Court of Session for the more congenial life of the English Bar, and in the spring of 1775 went so far as to start eating the obligatory meals in the Inner Temple, but he was not ready to make a bold move without some position to ease the way.

Suddenly an actual, though minor, vacancy appeared, and Boswell recapitulated his hopes in a letter to Mountstuart:

> When I was in London last spring I had the happiness of being assured by your Lordship of the continuance of your friendship for me, and that you would assist me with your interest when a proper opportunity should happen. There is now a vacancy of the office of one of the Commissaries of Edinbr. by the death of James Smollet Esq.; your Lordship will remember that we talked of a much better thing—Baron Maule's office of Clerk to the Register of Seasines; and that your Lordship kindly promised to concert measures with the Duke of Queensberry for trying to get it secured for me. I know not if any thing has been done towards it and your Lordship will excuse me for troubling you with this memorandum. . . .
>
> Now it would be of great consequence to me to shew my father, that I am effectually patronized by your Lordship; and for this reason I would beg that if there is no immediate view of bringing about a resignation of Baron Maules office which your Lordship suggested might perhaps be done by means of Lord Panmure and Baron Mure you would apply for the office of Commissary; and if it cannot be had for me, at this time, a promise may be obtained of it upon the promotion of David Ross which cannot be distant.

Boswell continued with some compliments on Mountstuart's speech in Parliament on the Scots Militia Bill: "Such an exertion as this places you above far above any puny pretender to the government of Scotland. You understand me."[1]

But Dundas, the "puny pretender," was either quicker or had greater interest than Mountstuart, and George Fergusson, Sir Adam's brother, was appointed Commissary, while Mountstuart soothed Boswell's feelings by promising that he and Queensberry would get something for him yet.[2] Sir John Pringle put the matter in a different light: "You place a confidence in the interest of a certain Lord and a certain Duke, for procuring you means for executing your Scheme. I do not doubt their liking you, but I doubt of their ability to obtain so much favour from a Minister, for one that has no parliamentary interest in himself." Boswell could not evade the truth of this remark, but in reply he told Pringle that he must make his usual jaunt to London so as not to "lose sight of such probable means" for advancing himself.[3]

The events of 1776 repeated those of the previous year: there were more conversations about a place but nothing achieved, and Queensberry, moreover, seemed reluctant to try to do anything about Baron Maule. Boswell helped Mountstuart with his Militia Bill, and they were as friendly as ever, but the only solid result of his London trip of this year was his employment as counsel for Douglas, who was fighting with the Hamiltons over his estate.[4] In 1777, the situation grew darker. Boswell received no invitation to come to London from Mountstuart in spite of strong hints, and when in June he spoke to Mountstuart in Edinburgh about a place, he received the cold answer

1. To Mountstuart, 13 Nov. 1775 (L 346). See Journ. 13 Nov. 1775. Commissary Smollett receives honorable mention in his cousin's *Humphry Clinker*.

2. Journ. 25 Nov., 1 Dec. 1775. Loudoun and Cassillis were also disturbed by the influence of Dundas and Fergusson (Loudoun MSS 9,047).

3. From Pringle, 6 Jan. (C 2315), to Pringle, 26 Feb. 1776 (L 1080).

4. Journ. 17, 30 Mar., 3 Apr. 1776; Mem. 21 Apr., 6, 14–15 May 1776.

that it would be a shame to waste one on him, since his father would soon die and he would not need it.[5]

Boswell's hopes died hard. By 1778, his father was urging him to stick close to Mountstuart, though previously he had been skeptical of Boswell's chances of profiting from his friendship; Mountstuart, however, had grown bored with Boswell's ever-present reminders, though he still showed him some of his old regard and gave him a £100 note which Boswell regarded as a loan.[6] Queensberry promised to write to George Clerk-Maxwell, a Customs Commissioner in Edinburgh, to ask him to resign his sinecure as Lord Treasurer's Remembrancer in the Court of Exchequer, which was worth £200 a year, but nothing materialized from this gesture either.[7] There was no real way of avoiding the fact that Boswell had nothing to offer in return for such a favor except personal regard, and though others sometimes obtained places on this basis, it was not a common occurrence. As Dr. Johnson said, there were "so many connections and dependencies to be studied"[8] in dispensing political posts that interest was essential, and this Boswell lacked. Even if he had been in a position to influence his father, as he was not, his father's county votes were useless to Queensberry or Mountstuart.[9] Yet Boswell refused to give up. He applied again to Mountstuart in August 1779 for the "survivancy

5. Journ. 30 Mar. 1777; Mem. 26 June 1777; Reg. Let. 1 Mar., 24, 28 Apr. 1777.

6. Journ. 27 Dec. 1775, 8, 13, 20 Mar., 9–10, 24–25 Apr., 18 May 1778; Mem. 5 Apr. 1779. Boswell had previously borrowed £100 from Mountstuart in 1776 (Journ. 1 Jan. 1777; "Note of debts without evidence," M 206). General Paoli also advised him to attach himself to Mountstuart (Journ. 22 Apr. 1778; Mem. 30 Mar. 1778).

7. Journ. 7 Apr. 1778; *Edinburgh Almanack for . . . 1778,* p. 128. Boswell's remark to Burke that he wished he could be a commissioner or one of the secretaries to the Commission on Conciliation with the Colonies (8 Mar. 1778, *Letters JB,* ii.274–75) reflected his pro-American views rather than representing a serious bid for a position.

8. *Life,* ii.157.

9. Boswell even lacked a vote of his own (Journ. 6 Oct. 1780).

of the office of Solicitor to the Stamp office," but Mountstuart had been appointed Envoy to Turin; bidding him a "cordial adieu" as he embarked in October, Boswell saw his prospect for advancement vanish with him over the horizon.[1]

Just as Boswell pestered the great for a place, so his relatives and friends begged him to exert his influence in the great chain of preferment. Boswell's efforts on behalf of people like Grange, John Boswell at Ayr ("Young Knockroon"), and his wife's nephews, Sir Walter Montgomerie-Cuninghame, David, Alexander, James, and Henry Cuninghame help to show his relations with the local magnates who were his usual recourse. The old Earl of Loudoun very obligingly forwarded the Cuninghames' military careers,[2] but Cassillis's attitude was less genial until Boswell finally began to press him. He reminded Cassillis of his efforts in the 1774 election, remarked that Cassillis never called on him though Eglinton always did, and complained that Cassillis had not employed him in a lawsuit which Sir Adam Fergusson had brought against him. Cassillis was not convinced that Boswell's strictures were just, but he did promise to do what he could to get Grange a small sinecure or pension, which had been Boswell's specific objective.[3]

Meanwhile, Boswell's relations with the Dundases remained strained. His father did not allow him to forget their importance and the friendship which had existed between the two

1. Reg. Let. 3 Aug. 1779; *Life,* iii.411.

2. To Loudoun, 18 Apr. [1771], 30 Oct. 1777, 19 Jan. 1778, 8 Feb. 1779 (all in *Letters JB,* ii.520–23), from Loudoun, 17 Feb. 1779 (C 1785). The Register of Letters records further correspondence between them on military appointments and promotions (4 Nov., 24, 30 Dec. 1777, 24 Jan., 9, 13, 16 Feb., 26 June 1778, 22 Feb., 20 Dec. 1779).

3. Journ. 24 Apr. 1779, Reg. Let. 24 Feb. 1777, 22 May 1779. Johnston then, as later, remained unbenefited. The lawsuit concerned a fire which broke out in some of Cassillis's coal workings, spread to the surface, and destroyed several acres of Fergusson's plantations. Fergusson unsuccessfully claimed damages (*Lowland Lairds,* pp. 97–99, and information from Sir James Fergusson).

families for several generations; for Lord Auchinleck's sake Boswell professed to be willing to put their relationship once more on a friendly footing, but occasionally his intense dislike of them burst forth openly. They had made "a cipher" of him, and he did not forget it.[4]

Most of his resentment was directed against the President, whose coarseness offended him though he admired Dundas's conduct of business. Boswell felt he could not visit the President without an acknowledgment that wrong had been done him,[5] and since this was not forthcoming no rapprochement was possible. He had remained on speaking terms with Henry Dundas, whom he considered overbearing and proud of his position, but they saw little of each other in the social interchange of dinners, suppers, and tavern meetings which constituted the staple of Edinburgh society.[6]

By the end of 1778, however, Boswell realized that he was suffering more than the Dundases by the breach between them. Henry Dundas was now a man of influence, and Mountstuart's failure to do anything for his self-appointed protégé was increasingly evident. Boswell, therefore, took the opportunity presented by Lord Auchinleck's illness to visit Dundas, and his reconciliation with the President was confirmed by a dinner at Arniston in the spring of 1780. When he was departing, Boswell reports,

> the President shook hands with me and said, "My dear James, Nobody wishes you better than I do." And Dr.

4. Besides the references listed in pp. 74 n.4 and 79 nn.1–3, Boswell's varying reactions to the Dundases appear in Journ. 18 Nov. 1775, 13 Mar. 1778, 8 Dec. 1780; *Boswelliana,* p. 275.

5. Journ. 21 Nov. 1776. See Eugene's strictures on the Lord President's conduct in court (*A Letter to the Lord Advocate,* p. 13). Ramsay called him "the most efficient and useful President . . . since the Revolution" (i.338).

6. Journ. 18 Mar. 1776, 20 Oct. 1778; Mem. 4 July 1777. Temple fed Boswell's jealousy with his similar contempt for Dundas (from Temple, 7 May 1776, C 2769, 15 June 1779, C 2798).

> Webster [the mediator] told me he said to him, "I'm very happy with this meeting." Thus was a reconciliation at length brought about between the President of the Court of Session, the hereditary freind of our family, and me. It was sincere on my part. For I had forgiven him for some time.

Lord Auchinleck was pleased with this meeting, and the future looked serene.[7]

The election of 1780 found Boswell still linked to the aristocratic interest, and actively engaged in rounding up votes for Major Hugh Montgomerie, who had been chosen this time to stand against Fergusson. The parties had not changed: Eglinton, Loudoun and Cassillis backed Montgomerie, while the Lord Advocate and Lord Auchinleck favored Fergusson.[8] Dundas, however, was now recognized as the ministerial leader in Scotland, and he probably persuaded North to throw his influence behind Fergusson, even though Montgomerie was as strong a supporter of the Government's policies; and North's offer of aid to the Earl of Glencairn, who wished to become a Representative Peer, assured Fergusson of the Earl's ten votes.[9] But twenty-five of Fergusson's votes were disqualified in the meetings of the freeholders, and Montgomerie was elected on 16 October 1780 by 65 votes to 55.[1] Boswell, who was "anxious to uneasiness" over the outcome, was even more

7. Journ. [14 Jan.], 12 Aug. 1779, 6, 24, 27 Apr. 1780; to Robert Dundas, 14 June 1779 (L 482).

8. Journ. 8 Sept., 6 Oct. 1780. See Loudoun MSS 9,217.

9. Journ. 12 Oct. 1780, 1 Apr. 1781; Loudoun MSS 11,031, 12,374; *SM*, 42 (1780), 555; *Correspondence of George III*, v.127–28, 130–31; M. A. Thomson, *The Secretaries of State, 1681–1782* (1932), p. 38.

1. Journ. 19 Oct. 1780; to Pembroke, 17 Feb. 1781 (L 1045); *SM*, 43 (1781), 336. *The Official Return of Members of Parliament* (1878, 1890–91) gives the date of the election as 18 October, but Wight says it took place on 16 October (pp. 189–90, 206), as does John Philipps (*Election Cases*, 1782, i.6). This date sounds probable from Boswell's journal (16–19 Oct.). The Michaelmas meeting was held on 3 October (Wight, p. 206).

elated than Eglinton, but Cassillis "did not much rejoice" in the success of the Eglinton family. Jealousy among the peers died hard.[2]

Refusing to accept defeat, Fergusson appealed to the Court of Session for a review of the freeholders' votes, and by 8 March 1781 it had ruled on a sufficient number of cases to give him a majority of two. A Select Committee of the House of Commons investigating these cases agreed with the decisions of the Court of Session, and Fergusson was declared duly elected on 2 April.[3]

One minor development during this protracted struggle indicates the fluidity of factional lines in this period. When it became obvious that the election would go to a Select Committee, Boswell, who was intensely involved in the legal proceedings as one of Montgomerie's counsel, suggested to Eglinton that he apply to Col. Barré, or through the Marquess of Rockingham to Burke, to serve as Montgomerie's "nominee" on the Committee, since Henry Dundas was to be Fergusson's "nominee." What Eglinton and Montgomerie thought of these suggestions is unknown; in any event, Thomas Dundas, Sir Lawrence's son, was chosen instead.[4] The Dundases were closely connected to Rockingham, but it seems likely that Eglinton turned to them mainly because of their dislike of the Arniston Dundases, and because Sir Lawrence "was a warm freind to

2. Journ. 18–19, 26 Oct. 1780. Both sides had been confident of victory. Fergusson had assured "Fish" Craufurd as late as 10 September that his election was "not now certain. It is only highly probable" (*Lowland Lairds,* p. 149). By 24 September, Boswell felt Montgomerie's victory was "morally certain" (Journ.).

3. Journ. 10 Mar. 1781; to Eglinton, 8 Mar. (L 493), to Montgomerie, 8 Mar. 1781 (L 499); *LPS 85,* pp. 48–50; *Life,* iv.73–74; *Journals of the House of Commons* (1780–82) xxxviii.62, 315–16, 327; *SM, 43* (1781), 185. See Loudoun MSS 8,281. Some of the cases are discussed in Wight, pp. 145–46, 189–91, 201–02, 206–07, 230–33, 236–37, 255, 282–83, 286–87, and some in Philipps, pp. 1–130.

4. Journ. 21 Mar., and 22 Feb.–1 Apr. 1781; to Eglinton, 8 Mar. (L 493), to Montgomerie, 8 Mar. 1781 (L 499); *JHC* (1780–82) xxxviii.316.

the Montgomery interest."[5] However, the choice does imply the political possibilities open to Eglinton: he could hope for Rockingham's return to power; he could continue to support North while opposing Dundas; or he could make a bargain with Dundas.

Eglinton chose the last of these alternatives. Fergusson was appointed a Commissioner of Trade and Plantations in July 1781, which necessitated a by-election. To obviate another struggle, North asked Eglinton as a favor to allow Fergusson to be reelected without opposition, and Eglinton found that he could hardly do otherwise: in the state of the freeholders' roll, Fergusson would win in any case. A *quid pro quo* was expected; Boswell asked Dundas to help Montgomerie obtain the command of a battalion to go to the East Indies, and Dundas seized on the idea. Montgomerie never went to the Indies, but he was promoted to Lt.-Colonel in March 1782.[6]

In this way matters were arranged fairly well for the major interests concerned, but not for Boswell.[7] He still wanted to be in Parliament himself; even as he was campaigning for Montgomerie, he spoke to Loudoun about standing at the next election and Loudoun seemed to approve.[8] Boswell could not in conscience, however, make the usual Scottish claim that he supported the group in office, since he was disgusted by the Ministry's conduct of the American War. For a long time he had been shrewd enough to see that force would not be decisive, and generous enough to believe that taxing the unrepresented

5. Journ. 12, 18, 22 Oct. 1780; Christie, pp. 213–14.

6. Journ. 23 July–6 Aug. 1781; Loudoun to Eglinton, 20 July, Fairlie, Boswell, and John Wauchope to Montgomerie, 24 July, to Montgomerie, 27 July 1781 (these three letters are in the Scottish Record Office, unsorted Eglinton Muniments); *SM, 44* (1782), 223.

7. Eglinton was made Governor of Edinburgh Castle in May 1782, which pleased him less, according to Pembroke, than either the Colonelcy of the 2nd Dragoons (Scots Greys) or of the 1st Foot (Royals) would have (from Pembroke, 18 May 1782, C 2212).

8. Journ. 12 Oct. 1780. See, to Temple, 3 Sept. 1780 (*Letters JB,* ii.307).

Americans was not a fair solution to English economic problems.[9] He wrote to Temple after the General Election of 1780:

> *The state of the Nation* is indeed wretched; nor do I see any prospect of our being better. It is shocking to think that a new Parliament is returned which will be as subservient to Ministry as the last. . . . I would not have been one of those who rejected the Petitions from America—no not for half the British Empire. Yet I am a tory still; for, I distinguish between our *limited Monarch,* and a *despotick Ministry.*[1]

Boswell's most important problem then was to find a local source of support. Even if he could claim Loudoun's interest he would still have to approach Eglinton and Cassillis among the peers, and Montgomerie had a prior claim. To seek the backing of Dundas was another possibility; they had been on good terms during the 1780 Ayrshire election, and Boswell had even teased him about his neglect of Lord Auchinleck's fictitious votes. The residue of distrust, however, which was always at the back of Boswell's mind when he thought of the Dundases, needed little fuel to make it flare up. When the President declared during the Court of Session's determination of the Ayrshire election cases in 1781 that there was not an independent vote in Ayrshire, Boswell had resented the remark deeply, had demanded a retraction and got it. He remarked when the election

9. Boswell had a great deal to say about the American Revolution which is not discussed here because it does not seem to have much affected his political career. Though in 1769 he spoke "with force and spirit on Britain's right to tax her colonies" (Journ. 27 June), he in general supported the Colonists later. For contrary instances, however, see, to Pembroke, 22 Jan. (L 1041), to Oglethorpe, 25 Feb. 1779 (L 1002); two "Rampager" essays in the *Public Advertiser,* 11 Mar., 14 Aug. 1775 (P 75.3). D. I. Fagerstrom discusses Boswell's views in "Scottish Opinion and the American Revolution," *William and Mary Quarterly, 11* (1954), 262–63.

1. To Temple, 3 Sept. 1780 (*Letters JB,* ii.309). See, to Oglethorpe, 23 Dec. 1779 (L 1003).

proceedings moved to London before the Select Committee that the Lord Advocate was the sworn enemy of the Montgomerie faction. Yet when Boswell and Henry Dundas dined together at Melville, Dundas's country place, in October 1781, they were once more on friendly terms. It could not be expected that they would ever be close friends; Dundas was too sure of his eminence, and Boswell too quick to resent any slight. At this dinner Dundas made a remark to Boswell which may have been meant as a warning: "It never does to go against old connections. It never succeeds," which evoked a spirited and tactless reply: "Why, My Lord . . . I will not say that. You have been very fortunate. But it never *should* succeed."[2] The give and take of such conversations had too much edge to it to foreshadow any lasting friendship.

The help of a patron still seemed to Boswell a reasonable method for making his way into Parliament, and since Mountstuart had disappeared from the scene he widened the scope of his efforts. He tried to get Paoli to hint to the King that Boswell wished to serve near him, and he even thought for a moment of attempting to interest Edward Eliot, the famous boroughmaster of Cornwall and the political benefactor of Edward Gibbon, in providing him with a seat in Parliament.[3] But his most singular attempt of this sort was a spectacular and forlorn assault on the "thane" of Bute in 1781. Boswell had never met Bute, but this did not deter him from writing to the now old and retired statesman, to ask for permission to wait on him. This was not a purely political maneuver, since Boswell had the same desire to meet Bute that he had had to meet Rousseau, Voltaire, Chatham, and other famous men; he was curious to

2. Journ. 18, 22 Oct. 1780, 6–10 Mar., 7 Apr., 22 Oct. 1781; to Robert Dundas, 7 Feb. (in error for March) 1781 (L 483).

3. Mem. 14 Apr. 1781; to Paoli, 27 July 1781 (L 1010). Later he remarked to Burke on "how pleasant would it be" if the King of his own volition were to "transplant" him from Edinburgh to London, but added that he did not wish "to indulge romantick visions" (to Burke, 18 Mar. 1782, Fitzwilliam MSS). See Journ. 10 Jan. 1784.

see how the minds of the great worked, and whether they would respond to his personality. Nevertheless, it is hard to believe that Boswell was being perfectly truthful when he told Bute that he had no intention of troubling him directly or indirectly with any demands either for himself or for any other person. Boswell was granted his interview, in fact two, and he was gratified with a gracious reception and a few tidbits of intimate political history, but Bute was too busy with his own concerns to pay much attention to this professional sightseer, so that the connection was without consequences.[4]

Boswell's final alternative was to attach himself to the Opposition, either through Burke in England or through one of the seven Scottish M.P.'s who voted for Dunning's resolution: Dempster, Sir Lawrence Dundas, Thomas Dundas, Sir Gilbert Elliot, Lord Fife, and two minor figures.[5] Among this group, only Fife and Sir Lawrence controlled more than his own seat. Having been one of Fife's lawyers, Boswell wished to keep up their acquaintance, but the "ideas of scotch interest" which Fife inspired in him were never to materialize. On the other hand, Boswell became very friendly with Sir Lawrence, until his death in autumn 1781 closed this prospect of advancement.[6]

Boswell's self-proclaimed Toryism would have made it awkward for him to join the Opposition in any case, in spite of his dislike of North's policies; logically, he belonged with the

4. Mem. 2–8 May 1781; Journ. 13, 27, 31 May 1781; to Bute, 3 May (L 339), from Bute [3 May] (C 711), to Bute [6 May] (L 340), from William Stuart, [after 6 May] (C 2592), to Bute, 24 May (L 341), from Bute, [24 May] (C 712), to Bute, 30 May (L 342), 31 May (L 343), from Bute [31 May] 1781 (C 713).

5. *SM, 42* (1780), 495. Not all of these men opposed North consistently (ante, pp. 74–78).

6. For Boswell's relations with Fife, see Journ. 3 Apr. 1775, 25 Mar., 8 May 1787, 16 Mar. 1788, 6 Feb. 1791; Mem. 10 May 1786. Apparently Fife did not take Boswell very seriously (*Lord Fife and his Factor,* p. 222). For Boswell's relations with Sir Lawrence, see Journ. 19–20 Sept., 18, 27 Oct. 1780, 21 Mar., 1 May 1781; Mem. 11 May 1781; from Sir Lawrence Dundas, 8 Feb. 1781 (C 1154).

"independent country gentlemen," a hopeless position for him in practice. North's fall in March 1782 changed the situation sharply, and Boswell immediately thought of his connection to Burke. In spite of their disagreement on political issues, Burke's personal and public eminence had fascinated Boswell for many years. He once told Burke that Burke was the only man he could wish to be, and in return Burke considered him very good-natured, if perhaps not highly endowed intellectually.[7] Boswell cultivated his acquaintance assiduously, approved of his efforts toward administrative reform,[8] and when Burke became Paymaster General of the Forces under the Rockingham–Shelburne ministry, had no inhibitions about asking him for assistance. He wrote to Burke first in general terms of his expectations and then specifically for the vacant office of Judge-Advocate, a legal post in the military establishment in Scotland paying around £180 a year.[9] Boswell's claim, as he told Burke, was based partly on the fact that the office had to be filled by one of the Faculty of Advocates, "of which Society I was the single man who at any of our meetings openly avowed a detestation of the measures of the late Ministry against our Bretheren in America."[1] Burke replied that Boswell much overrated his power of serving his friends, and lamented: "at the decline of my Life there comes to me a temporary office of some emollument, considerable expence, and no power. I have

7. Journ. 12 Apr. 1778; Sir Joshua Reynolds to [Bennet Langton], 12 Sept. (C 2353), from Reynolds, 1 Oct. 1782 (C 2354); *Life,* iii.362 n.2, v.76. Boswell's relationship with Burke is summarized in detail by D. C. Bryant, *Edmund Burke and his Literary Friends,* Washington University Studies, 9 (1939), pp. 99–135; it is interpreted by T. W. Copeland, "Boswell's Portrait of Burke," *Our Eminent Friend, Edmund Burke* (1949).

8. To Burke, 2 Mar. (Fitzwilliam MSS), to Wilkes, 14 Mar. 1780 (L 1296).

9. Boswell told Paoli that the salary was equal to a captain's pay (to Paoli, 19 Apr. 1782, L 1012), and a captain of foot was paid 10s. a day. The Judge-Advocate of the Fleet was paid £182.10s in 1779 (*Parliamentary Register, 1779–80,* xvi.524).

1. To Burke, 18 Mar., 18 Apr. 1782 (Fitzwilliam MSS).

the long arrear of all the obligations and kindnesses that I have received as a charge upon any little Interest I may be able to obtain."[2] Nevertheless, he informed Boswell that he had approached General Conway, the Commander-in-Chief, who had been politely noncommittal. Boswell was to be disappointed again; Mark Pringle, heir to the M.P. from Selkirkshire, was appointed, perhaps through the influence of Dundas and Buccleuch. Burke resigned shortly after Rockingham's death, and Boswell, with intense regret, again saw his prospects for obtaining a place disappear.[3]

Burke was not Boswell's only hope for advancement. In his pursuit of the Judge-Advocate's position, he approached Dempster and C. J. Fox, as well as Lord Pembroke, whom he had rather coyly pressed for years to help advance his career. Dempster and Pembroke were unable to do anything for him in the vigorous scramble for jobs that followed the long Rockingham period out of power; Fox did not bother to reply, though he sent kind regards through Burke.[4] Boswell's irritation at lack of success was not eased by his divided feelings about the Rockingham administration. Shortly after its accession Boswell told Pembroke, "there is indeed now a grand and brilliant assemblage of abilities and genius in Government," but what were more likely his true feelings appear in a letter to Paoli a few

2. From Burke, 23 Apr. 1782 (C 685).

3. Journ. 14, 18, 26, 29–30 Apr., 4 May 1782; Burke to Conway, 23 Apr. (C 686), Conway to Burke, 23 Apr. (C 820), from Burke, 23 Apr. (C 685), to Burke, 30 Apr. (Fitzwilliam MSS), to John Johnston, 9 May (Carlyle MSS), to Burke, 19 July 1782 (Fitzwilliam MSS; L 317); Adam, pp. 315, 320; Alexander Pringle, *The Records of the Pringles* (1933), pp. 175–76, 178.

4. Journ. 18, 26 Apr. 1782; to Paoli, 19 Apr. (L 1012), from Burke, 23 Apr. (C 685), to Burke, 30 Apr. 1782 (Fitzwilliam MSS). For Boswell's hints to Pembroke, see, to Pembroke, 13 Mar. (L 1043), 2 May 1780 (L 1044), from Pembroke, 22 Apr. (C 2211), to Pembroke, 30 Apr. (L 1048), from Pembroke, 18 May 1782 (C 2212), to Pembroke, 3 Feb. (L 1049), from Pembroke, 11 Feb. (C 2213), to Pembroke, 29 June 1783 (L 1050); Reg. Let. 18, 19 Apr. 1782.

months later: "my Tory or monarchical enthusiasm does not perfectly accord with the present majority. I am the Kings friend. I am ambitious of his majestys own protection." Principle conflicted with self-interest, and if self-interest won, it was because, as he told Paoli, "if I could but get a Seat in Parliament with a competency from Government to support the rank I flatter myself I should do well."[5] Where so much was at stake most Scottish, and perhaps most English, office-seekers would never have given such scruples a thought.

Burke advised Boswell to pay his court to Dundas, whom Boswell now believed to be "a strong string" to his bow.[6] He had written a general letter to Dundas (20 April 1782) reviewing the course of Ayrshire politics, and magnanimously forgiving him for his interference in 1774. In recompense for the "injury" he had suffered, however, he expected Dundas to give assistance and advice in his efforts to achieve office. Dundas returned a few mild objections to Boswell's description of their political differences, but declared himself ready to renew their friendship while not committing himself to help Boswell politically.[7]

The two were now on as friendly terms as at any period in their lives. Dundas was in an extremely strong position with the Administration since the support he commanded in Scotland was essential to Shelburne. Boswell pinned him down for a "serious conversation" in July 1782, and Dundas promised his assistance in the sort of vague declaration that he must have made to many people and which his situation required; it was undoubtedly sincere as far as it went, but there were scores of people on his doorstep demanding places, pensions, commissions in the Army, Navy, and East India Company, and every sort of major and minor government job for themselves and

5. To Pembroke, 30 Apr. (L 1048), to Paoli, 4 July 1782 (L 1013).

6. Journ. 16 July 1782; from Burke, 1 Sept. 1782 (C 687).

7. To Dundas, 20 Apr. 1782 (*Letters JB*, ii.523–24; L 448), from Dundas, 12 May 1782 (C 1133).

their relatives. Many of these people were in a position to retaliate if Dundas did not pay attention to their demands. The Shelburne ministry was shaky, and Dundas was anxious to entrench as many of his supporters as possible; he did nothing for Boswell, whose claims were not urgent and whose political interest was negligible.[8]

Dundas retained his place as Lord Advocate when the Coalition ministry was formed in April 1783, but he was not on good terms with Fox and his power declined. His closest political friend was now the young William Pitt, "whose abilities and high virtue were most distinguished," as he told Boswell. Boswell kept after him, but all he got was advice. Dundas warned him not to buy a seat in Parliament, which cost about £3,000 at the current market price, and suggested in view of the uncertain state of political affairs that Boswell practice his profession assiduously; this would establish a claim to a judge's place which Dundas could support.[9] Dundas's dismissal as Lord Advocate in August 1783, however, briefly ended his political usefulness.

8. Relations between Boswell and Dundas during the Rockingham and Shelburne ministries are covered in Journ. 16 July, 5 Aug. 1782, 30 Mar. 1783; to Burke, 19 July (Fitzwilliam MSS; L 317), from Burke, 1 Sept. (C 687), to Dundas, 16 Sept. (L 449), to Burke, 23 (altered to 26) Dec. 1782 (L 319); Reg. Let. 9, 16 Oct. 1782. Boswell spoke of the Shelburne ministry as a "Motley Crew" (to Burke, last Burke ref. above).

9. Journ. 3 Apr. 1783; Namier, *Structure,* p. 317.

4

Dependence and Independence: 1782–1786

The death of Lord Auchinleck in August 1782 freed Boswell from the dependence his father had exacted throughout his lifetime, and made him a figure of some importance in Ayrshire politics: he may well have reflected it was from his class of "barons" that Ayrshire had selected Patrick Craufurd and Sir Adam Fergusson as its representatives in Parliament. He could now strike out on his own, and the role he naturally assumed was that of parliamentary reformer. The mushrooming of nominal and fictitious votes after 1774 had embittered many "real" voters, and Boswell was immediately concerned because of the electoral situation in Ayrshire. When asked once whether the removal of nominal votes from the roll would not be an act of violence, he replied that "it would be an act of violence. But it would be an act of violence like turning thieves out of your house."[1]

Nominal votes were only the focus of his dislike of the electoral system; in a speech at the Ayr Quarter Sessions in October or November 1782,[2] he attacked the whole structure of Scottish

1. *Boswelliana*, p. 327. The anecdote is dated 12 November 1782.

2. Most likely at the regular meeting on 29 October 1782, when Boswell proposed a successful motion that certain votes be declared nominal and fictitious (*Ayrshire*, p. 84). The speech is quoted in the *Caledonian Mercury*, 16 Nov. 1782. Under 18 November 1782 in his "Materials for

politics, asserting that "as that man was esteemed the best sportsman that brought down the most birds, so was he the best representative that brought the best pensions and places to his countrymen"; the representation of the country, he asserted, was "a representation of shadows."[3] This speech, according to a feminine observer, met with loud applause and expressed the concealed sentiments of most of the audience,[4] but like many of Boswell's political actions there was a peculiar lack of logic to it. How could he expect to receive help from Dundas or anyone else when he attacked the methods they used? He was trying to play both sides of the street, to get a job in the conventional fashion while attracting attention as a fine independent country laird, and though he might have sincerely pleaded that under the circumstances he could do little else, it was hardly wise to make his opinions so conspicuous.

Edinburgh newspapers in September and October 1782 published a series of letters signed "An Old Freeholder," which have been tentatively attributed to Boswell.[5] The author of these letters, in his attack on nominal voters, whom he termed "barons of shreds and patches," urged three main points: 1) that freeholders should have a substantial property in their freehold, 2) that they should have only one vote, 3) that qualifications should not be made on the estates of noblemen. Boswell may not have agreed with these specific proposals, but they express the general trend of his thought. He favored trans-

---

Writing the Life of Lord Kames," Boswell mentions having been "today at a Meeting to consider Freehold Qualifications" (M 135). A further meeting was called for 15 Jan. 1783 (from Alexander Montgomerie of Coilsfield, 31 Dec. 1782, C 2046; Reg. Let. 11 Jan. 1783).

3. H. W. Meikle, *Scotland and the French Revolution* (1912), pp. xviii–xix, 16 n.4; P. Hume Brown, *History of Scotland* (1900–09), iii.355 n.2. Quotations in these sources are based on the account in the *Caledonian Mercury,* which I have not seen.

4. *Memoirs of the late Mrs. Elizabeth Hamilton,* ed. [Elizabeth] Benger (1818), i.89.

5. *Lit. Car.,* p. 220. See Meikle, p. 8.

ferring the right to vote from the holders of superiorities to property owners and those who derived revenue from land.[6]

The reform movement, spreading from England, had now become general both in the burghs and counties of Scotland. Though Boswell never joined the group headed by Henry Erskine with which the cause was most closely associated, he did strongly favor reform until 1785. On 7 November 1783, a meeting of the freeholders of Ayrshire was held to press for the abolition of nominal and fictitious votes, and Boswell was elected preses. It was his duty, and undoubtedly his pleasure, to forward a petition to Sir Adam Fergusson from this meeting condemning such votes.[7]

In the practical affairs of the county Boswell was still tied to Eglinton, whom he considered "his Earl." He told Eglinton in January 1783 that he would give him his interest in the next campaign, and asked if he intended to put forward Montgomerie again. When Eglinton replied that he did, Boswell responded in a somewhat illogical way that even if Eglinton did not support Montgomerie Boswell would stand up for him, and if Montgomerie did not want the nomination he intended to offer himself as a candidate. What Eglinton made of these declarations is unknown, but Boswell decided afterwards that he had committed himself to Eglinton's interest.[8]

6. These letters were reprinted in the *Scots Magazine* for January and February 1783. They contain typically Boswellian expressions, such as "ancient Scottish barons," but do not agree exactly with what we know of Boswell's sentiments at the time. Boswell agreed with Kames that if property were to be the basis for voting qualifications, a man should have votes in proportion to the extent of his holdings ("Materials for . . . Kames," 18 Nov. 1782, M 135), and his doubts as to interference of peers in elections seem to have arisen later (Journ. 17 Jan. 1784; Reg. Let. 22 Nov. 1783; *Life,* iv.248–50).

7. Journ. 7 Nov. 1783; to Burke, 20 Nov. 1783 (L 321); Reg. Let. 29 Nov. 1783; *Life,* iv.248. Boswell had also attended an earlier meeting in Edinburgh of "proprietors of land . . . to improve the rights of voting" in the counties (Journ. 24 Feb. 1783).

8. Journ. 3 Jan. 1783, 17 Jan. 1784. See Reg. Let., to [Patrick Douglas of] Garallan, Jan. 1783.

The accession of the Coalition ministry offered to Boswell a new group to petition for a job, though he became even less in sympathy with its personnel and policies than he had been with its predecessor's. He wrote to the Bishop of Killaloe that he was "very seriously concerned to see such a general disregard of all good principles of Government," and he lamented that Burke had "let himself be drawn so far out of . . . his natural sphere" as to take part in this Administration; nevertheless, Boswell must have appreciated the merit of the Bishop's remark that while he trembled for the Constitution he rejoiced that the turn of the wheel had brought some of Boswell's friends to the top, where they might be of use to him.[9] Regarding government in the interim between Shelburne's fall and the formation of the Coalition ministry "as a great dicebox shaken by a faction," Boswell hurried off to London again that spring with Parliament as his maximum goal and a judge's place in Scotland as his minimum.[1]

Mountstuart had meanwhile come back from Turin, and though Boswell had felt neglected since his departure, the news of his patron's return revived his dormant expectations.[2] Boswell informed Lord Mansfield in a confident letter that, though

9. Journ. 22 Mar. 1783; from Thomas Barnard, Bishop of Killaloe, 2 Mar. (C 81), to Barnard, 28 Mar. 1783 (L 37). At Beaconsfield, Boswell told Burke that as a Tory member of a Whig government he was like "a cherrytree among a cluster of pines and other coarser trees" (to John Johnston, 22 Apr. 1783, L 812; see Boswelliana MS, anecdote of the Coalition pudding [?April 1783]). In a later résumé, Boswell told the Bishop of Killaloe that he had good hopes of the Coalition until the cloven foot had shown itself in Fox's East India Bill (8 Mar. 1784, L 38), but other statements show that this remark oversimplified his reaction to the Coalition.

1. Journ. 15 May 1783; Mem. 11 May 1783; to Barnard, 28 Mar. (L 37), to Paoli, 8 Aug. 1783 (L 1016); *Life*, iv.220–21.

2. Journ. 21 Nov. 1780; to Wilkes, 14 Mar. 1780 (L 1296), from Margaret Stuart, 3 July 1781 (C 2620), to Burke, 18 Mar. 1782 (Fitzwilliam MSS), to Paoli, 18 Jan. (L 1014), 18 Feb. 1783 (L 1015); Reg. Let. 4, 17 Feb. 1783.

he recommended another to him, he would never solicit Mansfield's interest for himself; his pretensions, when the time came, would be stated by "a powerful Freind."[3] Actually, when he found himself waiting at Mountstuart's door once more Boswell felt a certain impatience and a desire to assert his independence. Reflection convinced him, however, that he would be foolish to desist in his applications to Mountstuart until he had obtained "some good office." Mountstuart was not particularly cordial, though he and Boswell soon settled down to some of their old political discussions; he emphasized some of the political facts of life to Boswell when, commenting on the Duke of Gordon, he said: "There are but three ways in which a Man can have weight with a Min[iste]r: Talents, Parliamentary interest, or a great deal of Money to buy parliamentary interest." These were facts which Boswell had often refused to take into account, but he was soon to try to claim one of them, talents, in the composition of political pamphlets. Boswell also found himself complaining that Dundas as Scotland's political agent drove the Scots as a salesman drove cattle to market. This, of course, pleased Mountstuart, but he still made no effort to help Boswell to an office, and when Boswell had the indiscretion to tax Dundas with his cattle drover role directly, he received the ingenious reply that it was to the benefit of Scotland to have a "Salesman," as Boswell called him, who distributed offices to the best purpose.[4]

Nothing was done for Boswell, and he had to wait his turn patiently until Dundas's removal from office. This event impelled him to write to Burke at once with a statement of his claims to the posts of Lord Advocate or Solicitor General; he

3. To Mansfield, 14 Feb. 1783 (L 948). "The truth is," Boswell commented on a later visit, "I had no interested view in waiting on Lord Mansfield. I wished only to be with him as a Man of great eminence" (Journ. 3 Apr. 1783).

4. Journ. 23, 25 Mar., 18 May 1783. For Mountstuart's political position at the time, see ante, pp. 76–77.

admitted that he would even accept being joint Solicitor if it was necessary, and promised if given any of these positions that the Ministry would find him sufficiently zealous. He told Burke that he would not apply to Fox, since the latter had returned him no answer to his letter of the previous year, but he hoped that Burke would lay his case before the Duke of Portland. Burke replied frankly that he was assailed by demands from all sides, and that he had totally lost what little credit he possessed with the top men in the Government. He promised to do what he could, but he was very dubious of success, since he would be little consulted about the arrangements in Scotland or in any other place. He ended, "whether you believe this or not I cannot tell. But it is true."[5]

Boswell's solicitation was in vain; the Honorable Henry Erskine, brother to the Earl of Buchan and one of the most prominent members of the anti-Dundas minority in Scotland, became Lord Advocate, and Alexander Wight, an authority on Scots election law, was appointed Solicitor General. Boswell was really angry at being passed over, and he wrote Burke a furious letter:

> The choice of a Solicitor General in Scotland has not only vexed me, as a Gentleman of such connections in every view as give me good reason to think myself ill used, but I can assure you discredits the present ministry more than they are aware. You flattered me with hopes that they were to have no understrapping Manager of affairs on this side of the Tweed. But this appointment is a wretched proof to the contrary. . . . You think it is not easy to sour my temper. But I should think meanly of myself did I entertain no resentment of the total neglect which I have had the mortification to experience, at a time when I had reason to think and when it was generally

5. To Burke, 8 Aug. (L 320), from Burke, 13 Aug. 1783 (C 688). See Journ. 29 May 1783, and *Life,* iv.223.

thought that I could not fail to receive some mark of attention from administration.[6]

At this point Boswell went to Erskine and demanded to know why he had not been appointed Solicitor General; Erskine gave him no satisfactory reply though he asserted his willingness to help him.[7] It was just a month or so later that Fox's East India Bill was defeated in the House of Lords. This determined Boswell to throw in his lot with the new Pitt ministry, and he became just as zealous in their behalf, and with a much clearer conscience, as he had promised to be for the Portland administration if they would reward him. He prepared an Address for the Faculty of Advocates congratulating his Majesty on the happy defeat of the bill, but his fellow lawyers were too cautious to commit themselves in a period of political confusion, and unanimously rejected it. On 23 December 1783, he wrote to Pembroke and Mountstuart asking for their help in becoming Solicitor General under the new Administration,[8] and in four days (26–29 December) he wrote his pamphlet, *A Letter to the People of Scotland On the Present State of the Nation* (1783).[9]

The body of the 1783 *Letter* is an attack on Fox's East India

6. Journ. 10–11 Sept., 12 Nov. 1783; to Burke, 20 Nov. 1783 (L 321). Wight showed his gratitude by dedicating his *Inquiry* (1784) to Portland. Apparently Sir Thomas Dundas served as the Coalition's London manager for Scotland (Fergusson, *The Honourable Henry Erskine,* pp. 238–60); Boswell later complained that as far as Scotland was concerned, the accession of the Coalition ministry involved only a change in Dundases (*LPS 85,* pp. 10–11), and in a deleted section of the MS of *LPS 85,* Boswell described Sir Thomas and Henry Dundas as "the *Castor* and *Pollux* of our political Hemisphere . . . One a fine fellow at Newmarket and tother a capital bruiser in the House of Commons" (p. 2v.).

7. Journ. 21 Nov. 1783.

8. Journ. 20 Dec. 1783; to Pembroke, 23 Dec. 1783 (L 1051); Reg. Let. 23 Dec. 1783. Pembroke had already told him that he lacked sufficient interest to do anything for him (to Boswell, 11 Feb. 1783, C 2213). Henry Dundas's nephew, Robert Dundas, was appointed Solicitor General.

9. A full bibliographical description is given in *Lit. Car.,* pp. 105–08. Quotations here are from the second edition, London, 1784.

Bill based on two contentions: 1) that it violated the property rights of the East India Company; 2) that it violated the Constitution by setting up a Commission with immense power, which in effect diminished the Royal prerogative.[1] These arguments were neither startling nor original, but they were phrased in a lively, vigorous manner. The pamphlet was distinctive, moreover, in the public insistence by a Scot that every administration was sure of support, or at least acquiescence, from Scotland; it also included the usual number of Boswellian personal asides. Boswell praised Oglethorpe and condemned the American war, Dunning's resolution, and the abolition of heritable jurisdictions. The purpose of the *Letter,* Boswell said, was to recommend that the people of Scotland address the King expressing satisfaction that the East India Bill had been rejected by the Lords, and assuring him that they supported the Ministers he had chosen.

Among the flood of pamphlets occasioned by the East India Bill, Boswell's work was one of the most able, being exceeded in reputation perhaps only by William Pulteney's *The Effects to be Expected from the East India Bill.* The public reception of the *Letter* was very favorable; besides the original Edinburgh edition, it appeared in at least one, and probably two, London editions.[2] The *European Magazine* said that the pamphlet was "the most judicious and masterly of any that we have seen on the subject," and the *English Review,* calling it "ingenious and

1. "I had resolved to write and publish a *Letter to the People of Scotland on the State of the Nation,* to endeavour to rouse a spirit for *property* and the *Constitution* in opposition to the East India Bill" (Journ. 26 Dec. 1783).

2. The only known surviving copy of what appears to be the third edition is at Yale, and is entitled *A Letter to the People, on the Present State of the Nation* (P 48). It is a stabbed, unwrapped, octavo pamphlet, 32 pp., marked "London Printed. M,DCC,LXXXIV." An anonymous, cut-down version of the previous editions, it shows three major changes: 1) it is given a national cast by the omission of references to Scotland, and by being addressed generally to the "people"; 2) it eliminates two irrelevant personal passages, the references to Oglethorpe and the Bishop

well written," praised its "pleasantry and good humour." The *Critical Review* commented that Mr. Boswell "has always distinguished himself by an attachment to public liberty." Only the *Monthly Review* was not enthusiastic, objecting particularly to its public call for Addresses and remarking sourly that "the thoughts here communicated are those of Mr. Boswell; Mr. Boswell spurs up their feelings [in Scotland], and whatever may be done in consequence, he has taken sufficient care that Mr. Boswell shall be Alpha and Omega."[3]

Boswell's motives for writing the *Letter* are obvious: though he claimed that the dismissal of the Coalition would cost him his chance of preferment, "an object" he had "most ardently at heart," he knew already that he could hope for little more from Erskine than he had from Dundas, and his proclamation that his principles were "of a Tory cast, that is to say, those of a steady Royalist,"[4] was his public repudiation of the Portland ministry. The pamphlet was hardly the product of reflection; it was the almost instantaneous reaction of a highly irritated man, affected by his emotional attachment to monarchy and a feeling of bad usage, who wrote both with sincerity and with the expectation that what he wrote would help him with the

---

of Salisbury; 3) it eliminates a few lines expressing Boswell's Tory sentiments. The original London edition had been published by 13 Jan. 1784 (Reg. Let.), so presumably Charles Dilly referred to a projected second London edition when he suggested to Boswell in February that the *Letter* be republished (Reg. Let. 14 Feb. 1784). I have been able to discover only one piece of external evidence to show that it was actually sold, Boswell's assertion in a letter to Dundas, 10 July 1786 (L 457): "I hope it will not be forgotten that my Pamphlet against Mr. Fox's India Bill of which there was one edition in Scotland, and two in London, had a considerable effect at a most important crisis."

3. *European Magazine*, 5 (1784) 130–31; *English Review*, 3 (1784), 151; *Critical Review*, 57 (1784), 74–76; *Monthly Review*, 70 (1784), 71–72. All these magazines praised Pulteney's pamphlet highly, though Boswell thought it inferior to his own (to Sir Alexander Dick, 7 Jan. 1784, *Letters JB*, ii.318).

4. Pp. 6, 40.

new Ministry, and "surely" with the King himself. Boswell also hoped that the *Letter* might attract the attention of some other great man, "to whom," he wrote in his journal, "my congenial sentiments and good talents might recommend me, [who] would call me into a respectable employment, and not improbably bring me into parliament."[5] This wish has a terrible irony to it, since the *Letter* may well have attracted the attention of Lord Lonsdale.

The private reaction of the powerful was perhaps even more important to Boswell than his pamphlet's public reception. Mountstuart, who had decided to support Fox, maintained a disquieting silence that Boswell was unable to break with repeated appeals, and which announced the end of their connection.[6] But the new Ministry thought highly of the *Letter*. The Marquess of Graham, an important cohort of Pitt's, wrote Boswell a letter praising it, and Dundas himself quoted it in the House of Commons. Best of all, William Pitt wrote him a short letter commending his "zealous and able Support" of the public cause.[7]

Even before receiving these testimonials, Boswell had started to promote the addresses from Scotland that he had recommended. He persuaded his friend, Sir Charles Preston, to sponsor an address from the burgh of Culross, which Boswell wrote

5. Journ. 1, 10 Jan. 1784.

6. Journ. 10 Jan. 1784, 9 Apr. 1791, 28 Dec. 1793; to Mountstuart, 31 May 1785 (L 347), 15 July 1786 (L 348); Reg. Let. 24 Dec. 1783; *Hist. MSS Comm.*, 10th Report, App. VI, pp. 60–61.

7. Journ. 17, 21 Jan., 9 Feb., 9 Dec. 1784; to Dundas, 2 Jan. (L 450), from Dundas, 27 [Jan.] (C 1134), from Pitt, 5 Feb. (C 2267), to Reynolds, 6 Feb. (*Letters JB*, ii.319–20; L 1099), to Paoli, 9 Feb. (L 1017), to Dundas, 16 Feb. (L 451), to Thomas Percy, Bishop of Dromore, 8 Mar. 1784 (*Letters JB*, ii.322–23; L 1064); Reg. Let. Jan.–Mar. 1784; *Life*, iv.258–60; *Parliamentary Register, 1783–84* [ed. John Debrett], (1781–96), xii.514–15. The reactions of Boswell's friends appear in the following letters: from Robert Preston, 24 Jan. (C 2289), from Temple, 6 Mar. (C 2821), from Barnard, 17 Mar. (C 82), from Temple, 6 May (C 2822), 27 May 1784 (C 2823).

himself,[8] and he also established a tangible claim on Dundas's gratitude, as he was later to remind him, by initiating an address in Midlothian, Dundas's home county, when the Arniston family itself was reluctant to do so. Since Boswell was not a freeholder of this county he had to keep his part in the project hidden, and Sir Alexander Dick, an old friend, ostensibly initiated the meeting. It was successful, and Boswell had the satisfaction of seeing the address carried by "a great Majority."[9]

The undertaking closest to his heart was an address from Ayrshire. A meeting was called for 17 March 1784, and Boswell spent several days beforehand urging his friends to attend. When he arrived in Ayr on the appointed day, he discovered that Fairlie of Fairlie, supposing that Eglinton still adhered to Portland, had rallied Eglinton's followers against Boswell's address. Fairlie must have been unsure of Eglinton's position, however, for his suggested address was, according to Boswell, "a smooth mild composition which could give offence to no party and might have been presented at any time." Boswell's own strong address was eventually adopted by a large majority, as was a vote of thanks to William Pitt. A similar vote of thanks to Sir Adam Fergusson for his conduct in Parliament was opposed by Boswell, who wished to restrict this vote of confidence to Fergusson's "*late* conduct in Parliament or for his conduct *during the present session,*" since he disapproved of Fergusson's support of North and the American War, and this amendment too was carried.[1]

8. To Dundas, 10 July 1786 (L 457); Reg. Let. 1 Jan., 25 Feb. 1784.

9. Journ. 7–11 Mar. 1784; to Dundas, 16 Feb. (L 451), Sir Alexander Dick to Archibald Cockburn, 10 Mar. (C 986), from Dick, 12 Mar. (C 987), to Dundas, 12 Mar. (L 452), from Dick, 19 Mar. 1784 (C 988), to Dundas, 10 July 1786 (L 457). The address was published in the *Scots Magazine, 46* (1784), 162.

1. Journ. 17–18 Mar. 1784; to Barnard, 8 Mar. (L 38), to [Fergusson], 5 Apr. 1784 (L 538), to Dundas, 10 July 1786 (L 457); Reg. Let. 14, 16 Mar. 1784; *EA,* 23 Mar., 26 Mar. 1784. A full account of the meeting, which served as copy for the *Edinburgh Advertiser,* has been preserved (Journ. 17 Mar. 1784; Ayrshire, M 11).

From Ayrshire, Boswell started toward London to press for his political reward, riding on a wave of high spirits, hope, and intense activity. On the way he stopped at York for a meeting of the county freeholders to consider an address; when the chairman was uncertain which side had carried the day, Boswell persuaded him that the pro-Pitt faction was in the majority, and their address was adopted. Hearing at York that the expected dissolution of Parliament had taken place on 25 March, Boswell hesitated but finally turned back to Edinburgh.[2]

The election alignment in Ayrshire was confused as usual, and Boswell's own position was by no means simple. His relations with Eglinton had become strained, partly because Eglinton adhered at first to the Portland party, and also partly because Eglinton offered no encouragement to Boswell's political ambition. The fall of the Coalition ministry in December 1783 had encouraged all possible candidates to prepare for the next election; Boswell himself, intending to be a candidate if Montgomerie withdrew, wrote Montgomerie to that effect (24 December 1783). Montgomerie replied that he was obliged for Boswell's support, and if he did not stand himself he would wish Boswell "the hearty support of all his freinds" (2 January 1784). At the same time, Boswell realized that he had promised his vote to Eglinton, which made him unhappy, not only because he and Eglinton were politically opposed at the moment, but also because he had begun to believe that peers had no right to interfere in county elections. He had asked for Dr. Johnson's opinion on this point, and the oracle, apparently

2. Journ. 20 Mar. 1784; Mem. 22–29 Mar. 1784; to Dundas, 10 July 1786 (L 457); *EA,* 2, 6 Apr. 1784; *Life,* iv.265–66, where Boswell says he wrote to Johnson, "March 28, from York." Actually the date of the letter is 26 March (Life MS); on 28 March, Boswell was in Newcastle (Journ.). Describing William Wilberforce's famous speech at this meeting, Boswell told Dundas on 30 March: "I saw . . . what seemed a mere shrimp mount upon the table; but, as I listened, he grew, and grew, until the shrimp became a whale" (R. I. and Samuel Wilberforce, *Life of William Wilberforce,* 1838, i.54 and n.3).

reversing itself, had replied that the interference of peers was usurpation.[3]

Boswell's confusion was brought to a crisis by a visit from Hamilton of Bargany, an Eglinton henchman, on 17 January 1784. Boswell confessed to him that he felt pledged to Eglinton, regardless of whether Montgomerie was to be the nominee, and that he was sorry for it. Bargany, an "old, sly Politician," told him to say nothing unless his support was directly applied for, and then to insist to Eglinton that whatever administration Eglinton supported should promote Boswell to some official legal post. Then Boswell inveighed against Fox and North, not suspecting at the time that Bargany was a strong partisan of their ministry. Bargany had little to say on this subject, but asked Boswell if he would accept the office of Sheriff-depute of Ayrshire. Boswell replied that he did not much want the job but he would not refuse it, and the conversation ended on this inconclusive note. After Bargany's departure, Boswell took counsel with his conscience. He admitted that he had bound himself to Eglinton's interest, though only in the county. But what if the interest of the State was at stake? Did this not override private interest? Yet this consideration did not set him free from his promise to Eglinton, for a positive promise must be kept; otherwise "any scoundrel might plead *principle* for breaking his word," and "it is exceedingly difficult to have it beleived that a Man is honest in altering a political opinion."[4]

Despite his waverings, Boswell had spread the word among his friends and followers that he intended to stand if Montgomerie for any reason failed to do so, and he went so far as

3. Reg. Let. 22 Nov., 24 Dec. 1783, 2 Jan. 1784; *Life,* iv.248–50. See Mem. 12 Apr. 1784, and ante, pp. 50, 99.

4. Journ. 17 Jan. 1784. Boswell's scruples about breaking his promise were not unusual (see, for example, I. F. Grant, *The MacLeods,* 1959, pp. 522–23). Bargany was accused in the House of Commons of transmitting an offer of a place worth £500 a year to his nephew, Hew Dalrymple, M.P. for Haddingtonshire, to support the Coalition. He denied the charge and the matter was dropped (*SM, 46,* 1784, 23–24; Matheson, p. 101).

to tell John Boswell at Ayr that he might mention this publicly.[5] Others were also hopeful: "Fish" Craufurd, that professional M.P., had gained the backing of Glencairn and Dumfries, while Sir John Whitefoord, an egotistic bumbler, also had ideas of representing the county.[6] Whitefoord was in much the same situation vis-à-vis Fergusson that Boswell was with Montgomerie. Both Whitefoord and Boswell hoped that they could command enough votes to put themselves in a good bargaining position, but Whitefoord had been careful not to commit himself to anyone, and as a free agent with at least eleven votes at his disposal he wrote frankly to Fergusson (25 January 1784): "I am of opinion that altho' I might fail as a principal, I might still, as a party, be an object worth the attention of the other contending powers, and possibly be able to attain what I point at for a few years." This meant he felt that one side or the other might consider him sufficiently important to give him the seat this time in return for his support at the subsequent election. Fergusson, in reply (2 February 1784), made it plain that he intended to be a candidate again, but declared, obviously hoping to conciliate Whitefoord, that he would do nothing relative to Ayrshire without communicating with him.[7]

On 13 February Boswell heard that Montgomerie definitely would be a candidate, and at this time he compromised with reality to the point of telling his relative, Bruce Campbell, that he would support Montgomerie warmly and hope to be supported by him and his friends on another occasion.[8] But there was still just enough confusion among the political groups in Ayrshire to keep Boswell's hopes alive. When Fairlie tried to

5. Reg. Let. 8, 23 Jan., 14 Feb. 1784.

6. Journ. 1 Mar. 1784; Reg. Let. 19 Jan. 1784; *Public Advertiser*, 27 July 1785; Coleridge, *Life of Thomas Coutts*, i.173, 177, 179; Fergusson, "Sir Adam and Sir John," pp. 221–30. For Dumfries's support of Craufurd, see Loudoun MSS 9,136; Craufurd was the first cousin of the Countess of Dumfries.

7. "Sir Adam and Sir John," pp. 223–24.

8. Reg. Let. 13, 17 Feb. 1784.

gather Eglinton's supporters for the March 17th Ayrshire meeting so that they could oppose any pro-Pitt address, Montgomerie refused to appear; he declared he could best show his respect for Eglinton by absenting himself. This faint indication of a split between the two encouraged Boswell to announce in a letter "To the Real Freeholders of the County of Ayr" (19 March) that he would be a candidate if Montgomerie was not.[9] On the 26th he wrote to Montgomerie from York to express the hope that Montgomerie was busy either on his own behalf or Boswell's, now that the dissolution of Parliament was certain. Montgomerie was busy, and for himself; Boswell was forced to face the truth on March 30th when he received final word that Montgomerie was again to stand.[1] Eglinton had transferred his support from the Coalition to Pitt, which meant that Montgomerie and Fergusson divided the pro-Pitt interest, while Craufurd, who intended to stand simultaneously for Ayrshire, Renfrewshire, and the Glasgow burghs for which he sat, gathered what independent backing he could.[2]

Boswell busied himself by recruiting votes for Montgomerie, by holding important conferences with Dundas in Edinburgh, and by publishing in the newspapers a stanza from his *Midlothian Address,* a poem in honor of Dundas and James Hunter-

9. Journ. 17 Mar. 1784; *EA,* 26 Mar. 1784. Boswell had attacked nominal votes at the meeting and again in his letter, which is reprinted in *Ayrshire at the Time of Burns,* pp. 84–85. Another attack on nominal votes appeared in the March and April issues of the *Scots Magazine* (46, 1784, 115–17, 177–79) called "A Serious Address to Freeholders upon Liferents or Wadsets of Superiority," and signed A. B. This article has been tentatively attributed to Boswell (*Lit. Car.,* p. 220); though its sentiments agree with Boswell's, the style does not seem particularly Boswellian to me.

1. Reg. Let. 26, 30 Mar. 1784.

2. Coleridge, i.173, 177. Some of Craufurd's supporters seem to have been lukewarm. William Adam wrote to Thomas Kennedy of Dunure (22 Mar. 1784): "Craufurd . . . is in every way an improper man, except in one respect, that he would vote right. H. Montgomery is an improper man for the only reason that Craufurd is proper, viz. that he would vote wrong" (*Lowland Lairds,* p. 72).

Blair, who was about to be reelected as member for the city of Edinburgh.[3] The real election business was going on behind the scenes, where the three-cornered fight in prospect was little to the pleasure of Dundas, who usually preferred compromise. He wrote to Fergusson on 10 April: "Mr. Hamilton of Sundrum has just been with me. Crawfurd is gone to Ayrshire to offer terms to Bargeny and to support Colonel Montgomery. I do not wish them to have any connexion together, and have told Mr Hamilton to reject them, for I could assure him if upon being rejected by him, Mr. Crawfurd should come to you, and offer from revenge to share his interest, you would decline it." Otherwise, Dundas continued, he could not have asked them to reject an alliance with Craufurd, since his support would put Montgomerie's election out of doubt. He then added: "Upon talking with Mr Hamilton, I find they are all decided that Col. Montgomery must come into Parliament at present. . . . Lord Eglingtoun, when I saw him in London, seemed unwilling to have any engagements as to future elections, but in that I think he is unreasonable, and when he comes down I [?shall] have little difficulty in persuading him to feel so."[4]

On 12 April, Fairlie carried a letter from Fergusson to Montgomerie and a verbal message to Eglinton, which concluded a treaty of mutual assistance. Montgomerie was to be chosen this time, and Eglinton was to support Dundas's candidate at the next election. Dundas had assured Fergusson that he would be brought in for this Parliament for the city of Edinburgh in place of Hunter-Blair, who dutifully resigned in August. Cassillis, on 15 April, also agreed to support Montgomerie though feeling "a little awkward" about it for some

3. Mem. 29 Mar.–6 Apr. 1784. *The Midlothian Address* was sung at a dinner given by the Town Council of Edinburgh for Hunter-Blair on 1 April (Journ. 1 Apr.; *EA,* 2 Apr. 1784; *Lit. Car.,* p. 253; *Arniston Memoirs,* pp. 218–19). Hunter-Blair was returned as M.P. on 5 April (*Official Return*).

4. "Sir Adam and Sir John," pp. 224–25.

unstated reason.[5] Boswell had learned of these arrangements by 18 April, when he wrote Montgomerie from Edinburgh that if all was settled he would not appear at the Ayrshire election but would proceed to Fife instead, where his presence might be necessary "to support the good cause"; but he wrote again to Montgomerie on the same day that "on account of the alarm I have hurried west."[6] Whatever this alarm was, it was a false one, and Montgomerie was elected on 20 April.

The major interests were again taken care of as they had been after the 1781 election, and even Craufurd seemed to bear his disappointment well, but not so Sir John Whitefoord. Fergusson, in informing him of the arrangements (11 and 13 April), presented him with a *fait accompli,* and Whitefoord felt this violated their previous agreement. An extremely cold meeting took place on 17 April, which ended by Whitefoord refusing to shake Fergusson's hand and departing in great anger. Fergusson recorded the whole incident in a memorandum, and added to it that Eglinton had told him that Whitefoord had solicited his aid during the period when Whitefoord and Fergusson were supposed to consult mutually.[7]

Nor had Boswell, despite his friendships with Montgomerie and Dundas, done as well as he had hoped, though he comforted himself with the thought that to have promoted the Ayrshire address was "enough for one Laird to have done." The most damaging possible block to his expectations had been established in the arrangement between Eglinton and Fergusson; it left no room for him. Furthermore, during the excitement of the campaign he had written a complacent and un-

5. Cassillis may well have been anxious about retaining his seat as Representative Peer (Coleridge, i.179). Like many of the Scots Peers, he supported Fox's East India Bill (*Parliamentary Register, 1783–84,* xiv.107–08); unlike them, he remained in opposition to Pitt (Furber, pp. 204, 227).

6. Reg. Let. 18 Apr. 1784.

7. *Public Advertiser,* 27 July 1785; Coleridge, i.184; "Sir Adam and Sir John," pp. 227–30. See also *LPS 85,* p. 56, and *The Whitefoord Papers,* ed. W. A. S. Hewins, 1898, pp. 191–92.

pleasant letter to Fergusson, asking what he had done about presenting the Ayrshire address to the King, and telling Fergusson that after the present election in which he was engaged on Montgomerie's behalf he intended to be a candidate himself on the interest of the real freeholders. He then added: "If I am honoured with your support in that character, I presume you will throw into the same scale your share of those unconstitutional votes which until we obtain relief from the present miserable election law must it seems be employed by the Real Interest in self defence." This letter must have offended Fergusson considerably, and to no purpose. For one so aware of "old hereditary freindship," Boswell's disregard of the close relationship between Fergusson and Dundas seems amazingly insensitive.[8]

Dundas's most authoritative biographer claims that he merely held his own in the General Election of 1784,[9] but this statement, of course, does not take into account the consequences of the election. Pitt's victory fixed Dundas securely in his position as Treasurer of the Navy, and he was soon to become the leading member of the Board of Control for India. The Whig minority (if it may be called that) in Scotland, which included Harry Erskine, Sir Thomas Dundas, Sir John Henderson, Sir William Augustus Cunynghame, William Adam, and others,[1] was to dwindle away for more than a decade. All Scottish posts and sinecures during the remainder of Boswell's life were to be at the almost absolute disposal of Pitt's indispensable Scottish aide.

8. Mem. 12 Apr. 1784; to [Fergusson], 5 Apr. 1784 (L 538). Fergusson replied noncommittally that it was too soon to decide whom to support (*LPS 85*, p. 58).

9. Furber, p. 205.

1. For some account of their connection, see Fergusson, *The Honourable Henry Erskine*, pp. 239–58. The State Counsellors for the Establishment of the Prince of Wales in Scotland seem to have been drawn from the ranks of the Opposition (*Universal Scots Almanack for . . . 1787*, p. 40).

Boswell gained no immediate advantage from his campaign efforts, and even some help which Dundas gave to John Boswell at Ayr at Boswell's request unfortunately miscarried.[2] His career was at a crisis and he knew it. Parliament, though still longed for, was almost out of the question, Scotland was dull, there were no signs of preferment, and the English bar, though it provided wonderful daydreams of eminence and being made "*Baron Boswell of Auchinleck in the County of Ayr,*" was a risky undertaking. The minimum Boswell expected was to follow in his father's path and become a judge, but even this prospect was uncertain. Lord Rockville, one of the Lords of Session, told Mrs. Boswell that although Dundas had thought highly enough of Boswell's East India letter to say that if anything worth two or three hundred pounds at the time had been vacant, Boswell would have got it, his jocularity and open antipathy to many people weighed against his claim to a seat on the Court of Session.[3]

The part that Boswell's personality must have played in his various political ventures is a difficult factor to assess. His admitted good qualities—friendliness, vivacity, and loyalty to his friends—were overbalanced in the eyes of such observers as Horace Walpole, Fanny Burney, and Mrs. Piozzi by his vanity, forwardness, and curiosity. Even his friends warned him against his outspoken honesty, especially since he could never resist telling a malicious joke or retailing to someone what others thought of him; from this habit he may have acquired a reputation for triviality or malevolence.[4] His most constant fault was

2. John Boswell, "Young Knockroon," was attempting to secure the Justice of the Peace clerkship for Ayrshire (to Dundas, 12 Mar. 1784, L 452, from Margaret Boswell, 29 May 1784, C 439; Reg. Let. 27 Apr., 22 May, 10 June 1784).

3. Journ. 9, 12 Dec. 1784; to Temple, 6 July 1784 (L 1236.9); Reg. Let. 26 June 1784.

4. See Journ. 18 Jan., 7 Nov. 1775, 9 Aug., 28 Dec. 1776. Boswell discusses "frankness of behaviour" and "carrying personal reflexions from one company to another" in *Hypochondriack,* no. 23 (Aug. 1779). H. ex-

this childlike indiscretion. Always willing to inform the world of his own virtues, failings, and opinions, he never understood why others were reticent about making similar revelations, and after the publication of the *Tour,* people were sometimes wary of speaking in front of him for fear that their conversations would appear in print.

In politics, Boswell must have been handicapped by his assertion of independence, which some must have interpreted as simple unreliability. Boswell himself was proud of his reputation, and in his *Letter to the People of Scotland* (1785) makes a merit of his failure to gain office through Mountstuart:

> My Friend (my *Maecenas Atavis edite regibus*) Lord *Mountstuart,* flattered me once very highly without intending it.—"I would do any thing for you (said he) but bring you into parliament; for I could not be sure but you might oppose me in something the very next day."—His lordship judged well. Though I should consider, with much attention, the opinion of such a friend—before taking my resolution;—most certainly I should oppose him, in any measure which I was satisfied ought to be opposed. I cannot exist with pleasure, if I have not an honest independence of mind and of conduct.[5]

But apart from the considerable objective difficulties facing Boswell, the root of his political failure perhaps lay in his inability to understand the thought processes of the kind of

---

presses a typical hostile opinion of Boswell when he asserts that Boswell "acquired the character of a giddy flutterer on the stage of life" (*Monthly Magazine, 15,* 1803, 550).

5. Pp. 93–94. Boswell thought highly enough of this passage to quote it in his "Memoirs," in the *European Magazine* (*Lit. Car.,* pp. xlii–xliii); it may have soothed the memory of his relationship with Lonsdale. See Journ. 15 May 1783.

mind which Dundas exemplified: that of the shrewd politician, who did not lack feelings but who allowed emotion very little part in his business.

Boswell turned to Dundas for a confidential conversation on his future in December 1784. Dundas had earlier approved of his coming to the English bar because he believed Boswell had £1,000 or £1,200 a year at his disposal, but when he discovered Boswell had only £500 a year free he was far less certain that the move was advisable. He told Boswell that he would think seriously about it and would speak to Pitt, to Thurlow (the Lord Chancellor), and to Pepper Arden (the Attorney General) to see if Boswell could get a place of some hundreds a year or immediate practice in England, for one of the two was indispensable to his scheme. He also advised Boswell not to press for a seat on the Bench immediately, for if he became a judge he would get no further office; rather he should try to get some sinecure to take to the Bench with him. Impressed by Dundas's manner, Boswell thought him "sincere," but Mrs. Boswell was afraid that Dundas was trying to stall him.[6]

Boswell's innocence, and perhaps his self-esteem, are revealed by his idea that Montgomerie, if given a place, would gladly resign his seat in the Commons in Boswell's favor; but when he sounded Montgomerie in January 1785 about a reward for his efforts in the last campaign Montgomerie was regrettably evasive. When asked directly if he would support Boswell for Parliament, Montgomerie naturally answered that he could not say, which made Boswell realize that he had overestimated Montgomerie's personal regard for him. He then resolved to stand on his own legs, and to attempt to secure "a respectable share of the independent interest of the County, by which in the midst of contending parties," he might be

6. Journ. 12 Dec. 1784; to Temple, 6 July (L 1236.9), from T. D. Boswell, 31 Dec. 1784 (C 506), to Paoli, 14 Feb. 1785 (L 1019).

successful.[7] This resolution marked the end of his dependence on Eglinton in Ayrshire.

Time dragged on, and nothing happened. Boswell wrote a mild letter to the Marquess of Graham hinting that the Government had neglected him, and another letter to Paoli which sounded a plaintive note: "I cannot help thinking it very hard that no place has been found for me in any department of his Majestys Service."[8] Then a glorious opening appeared: James Erskine, who held the position of Knight Marshal of Scotland, died on 27 February 1785. His office, a sinecure worth £400, was one of the most lucrative in the gift of the Crown, and it is not surprising that Boswell wrote to Dundas immediately for it. Dundas replied sensibly that he and Pitt between them had received 37 applications for the job, and since it was a position compatible with a seat in Parliament members of the Commons had first option. "You must be aware," Dundas wrote, "how impossible it is to resist the Claims of Persons so stated and brought forward in competition with others, who however respectable, have certainly not the same Pretensions to bring forward." Dundas ended by saying that he had not forgotten about Boswell, but it would be disingenuous if he said anything which would encourage him to leave Scotland for London. The justice of these remarks was undeniable; Boswell thought the letter "honest and freindly," but he told Dundas, as he had Paoli, that he thought it hard no situation had been found for him. "I have indeed a competency," Boswell added, "though not enough to purchase a ticket in the great Lottery of Parliament. But I do beleive the cravings of ambition are as painful as those of hunger."[9]

For almost twenty-five years Boswell had envisioned himself as a member of Parliament or seated in some lucrative of-

7. Journ. 21 Jan. 1785; to Temple, 20 July 1784 (L 1237).

8. To Paoli, 14 Feb. 1785 (L 1019); Reg. Let. 10 Feb. 1785.

9. From Dundas, 30 Mar. (C 1135), to Dundas, 13 Apr. 1785 (L 453); Reg. Let. 1 Mar. 1785. The disposal of this office illustrates Dundas's shrewdness. It was given to Sir Robert Laurie, M.P. for Dumfriesshire, who was attached to, but not wholly dependent upon, the Duke of Queens-

fice, enjoying *otium cum dignitate,* which would allow him to live in London; for the same length of time he had been using his friends to help him, though without success. Now he was tired of urging and flattering the powerful, tired of working hard in elections and being ignored in the division of the spoils; he was ready to make a drastic move. If he could not advance by serving the government, he might succeed either by being such an annoyance that the government would be forced to give him something, or by putting himself in the forefront of independent opposition.[1]

The honest pretext he needed to focus these years of disappointment was provided on 27 April 1785, when the Lord Advocate, Ilay Campbell, introduced a bill in the Commons to reduce the number of Lords of Session from fifteen to ten and to augment the salaries of the remainder.[2] Boswell reacted to this proposal with the same horror that many a good Republican felt on hearing of F. D. Roosevelt's plan to alter the Supreme Court; he saw red, but he also saw a chance to rouse the country against Dundas and to put himself in the limelight. First he told the people of Scotland through the newspapers not to worry, for he was *"upon the Watch"*;[3] then he published his *Letter to the People of Scotland* (1785).[4]

---

berry ("Old Q"). Dundas's influence was fairly weak in southwestern Scotland, and the appointment strengthened his position there. For Laurie's political position, see *Henry Erskine,* pp. 252–53; Adam, p. 100; Robinson, p. 100; Furber, p. 247.

1. Porritt explained Boswell's general tactics sixty years ago (*Unreformed House of Commons,* ii.137).

2. *JHC* (1784–85) xl.905. The proposal was not new, North having recommended it to the King in 1781 (*Correspondence of George III,* v.301).

3. In a letter first published in the *St. James's Chronicle,* 12 May 1785, and reprinted in the *Edinburgh Advertiser,* 17 May 1785, and in the *Scots Magazine,* 47 (1785), 257. See Journ. 12 May 1785, and *Lit. Car.,* pp. 111, 220, 253.

4. Fully described in *Lit. Car.,* pp. 108–12. It was published on 26 May (Journ.).

Of all Boswell's works, this pamphlet has been the most attacked by later writers. Open, exuberant, an eager bid for notice, it seems evidence that Boswell grasped neither what he was saying nor his audience. Actually, he was well aware of what he was doing; he wrote in 1790: "the *mode* in which it [the *Letter*] was written was intended with a full consciousness of what the event justified that a mixture of argument with a variety of topicks would most effectually excite general attention to a subject not very promising."[5] In consequence, though the Diminishing Bill was its ostensible subject, the *Letter* found room for many digressions: the domination of Dundas, the Ayrshire elections, the position of the advocate in Scottish society, and above all James Boswell, his ambition and his career.

The portion which deals with the Court of Session is well pointed toward its audience. Boswell opens with all the time-honored arguments against change, against "the rage for *innovation,*" and he makes much of the fact that the Bill infringes the Articles of Union. Once allow these Articles to be easily abridged, and next the Scots will suffer from the land tax. Further, the judges of the Court of Session really act as a standing jury in the absence of juries in civil causes, so to cut their number decreases part of the little appeal to his fellow citizens that a Scotsman has. A reduction of judges would also be unfair to that deserving group, the Faculty of Advocates; "it is *unjust,*" Boswell maintains, "to lessen the number of prizes after the lottery has begun drawing, after we, by an expensive education, and much time and labour, have purchased our tickets";[6] only a half-serious argument, but not without some

5. A transcript of this note, written in Lord Binning's presentation copy, is in the Hyde Collection. In presenting the *Letter* to Lord Thurlow at the time of publication, Boswell asked him to forgive the "sallies of vivacity" which had been interjected to hold the reader's attention (to Thurlow, 25 May 1785, Hyde Collection).

6. Pp. 3, 44. 213 advocates were listed as members of the Faculty of Advocates in 1785 (*Edinburgh Almanack for . . . 1785*, pp. 47–48).

effect. On the other hand an augmentation of the judges' salaries might make their places altogether an object of political preferment. Boswell suggests that there are sinister motives behind the bill; the whole political interest of Scotland rests in the hands of these judges who pass on nominal and fictitious votes, and there is danger of a decemvirate being created. He implores his countrymen to petition the King and Parliament against diminishing the number of judges unless Parliament, with the people's approbation, alters judicial procedure in Scotland on some wise plan.

Boswell's remarks about Dundas, "sometimes called *Harry the Ninth,*" and the noble families who allow him to be the minister for Scotland without protest, had some justice to them but were exceedingly indiscreet. A public admonition that "the Stuarts, the Hamiltons, the Erskines, the Craufurds, the Montgomeries, the Douglases, the Grahams, the Somervilles, the Cathcarts, the Kennedies, in short, all the men of blood and of property, who ought to be men of consequence" have allowed the Ministry to appoint a *locum tenens* to drive "the people of Scotland to St. James's and the Treasury as a salesman drives black cattle to Smithfield"[7] had enough sting to it to irritate a great many people. Though Boswell finds, following Johnson, that there is only a slight distinction between a moderate Whig and a spirited Tory, he assails the Whigs for their similar managerial behavior under the Coalition, thus succeeding in alienating almost all possible sources of support. This indiscriminate assault on friend and enemy may have proved him to be independent, but it also assured him the penalties of political isolation.

The conduct of Sir Adam Fergusson and the Earl of Eglinton came in for most particular scrutiny. Fergusson was elected, Boswell asserts, for two parliaments by waving "the standard of *independency,*" and then, according to rumor at least, made overtures to Eglinton; that Fergusson

7. Pp. 6, 9–10. See ante, p. 101.

> was *not elected,* we *know;* that he *voted for his former opponent,* we *know;* and *it is said* he supports the earl's friend for one parliament, and the earl is to make him member next parliament—*if he can.* I have never heard his lordship say this report is true: but if it is, the noble earl must not take it amiss, if some of the best friends of his family should disdain what they think degrading to him, and feel obnoxious to themselves.

Boswell and Fergusson have had troubles over a "paltry money question" (the Corsican subscription), and others in the county dislike Fergusson, so the House of Eglinton can hardly expect Ayrshire to be brought implicitly to heel to vote for Fergusson at the next election. Indeed, Boswell himself intends to stand and has solicited Fergusson's interest. Why should Fergusson have any objection to him, though he has one to the "honourable baronet"?[8]

Dundas was treated much more gently, for apart from attacking his general role as manager of Scotland, Boswell found fault with his conduct in only two particulars: his attempt to displace Sir Lawrence Dundas in Orkney, and his having persuaded Lord Auchinleck to make votes in 1774. Boswell says that he has no more objection "to Mr. Dundas's being sole *Protector* of Scotland, than any other man, if we *must* be so ruled," and adds:

> Nay I have an *interest* that *he* should be the person. For there is an hereditary friendship between our families. We were at college together. We have oft enjoyed
>
> —The "happier hour
> Of social pleasure."—

8. Pp. 52–58.

> And I trust to the generosity of his feelings, that, as he *knows* he once did me a severe injury, which I have from my heart forgiven, he will be anxious to make me full amends, if ever it shall be in his power. The desire of elevation is as keen in me as in himself; though I am not so well fitted for party exploits.[9]

The introduction of Boswell's personal life into the *Letter* resulted in its most startling passages: a long account of his ancestry, and the remarks on his relations with a number of well-known men—Thurlow, Mountstuart, Wilkes, Lord Ossory, Burke, Jack Lee, and others. A political pamphlet in the eighteenth century could be as personal as a campaign speech sometimes is today,[10] and performed many of the same functions, but Boswell's pamphlet was exceptional. He knew it, and gave as his excuse that he wished all this material about himself to be known: "And you who censure it, have read it, and *must* therefore know it."[1] It was the doctrine of publicity at any price.

The reviews of the *Letter* were mainly favorable. The *Critical Review,* noting that Boswell had "on several occasions manifested a zealous regard for the honour and interests of his country," said:

> Whether Mr. Boswell's opposition to the reduction of the Scottish judges operated in any degree towards defeating that proposal, we know not; but it is certain that his arguments are well calculated to excite among the

9. Pp. 61–62. See, to Dundas, 20 Apr. 1782 (*Letters JB,* ii.523–24; L 448).

10. See, for example, the number of personal allusions in John, [5th] Earl of Stair, *The Claims of the Public on the Minister,* 1785.

1. P. 101 n.*

> people of Scotland a disapprobation of such a measure. . . . The Letter contains many sensible observations, and, to use the author's own words, is richly sprinkled with "egotism and vanity;" but these qualities, from the lively and eccentric manner in which they operate, serve only to render it more entertaining.

The *English Review* thought it "the best performance which has proceeded from the pen of Mr. Boswell"; and continued, "it is with a sincere pleasure that we applaud his public virtue and patriotism." But the *Review* deplored the amount of extraneous matter in the pamphlet, and concluded, "if the abilities of the writer had been greater than they are, we should have excused more readily his eternal vanity and egotism." The *Monthly Review* was kinder than it had been to the 1783 *Letter,* saying that "a peculiar vein of humour runs through the whole of this performance, which must please, and cannot offend; and the letter is such, that if it does not universally produce conviction, it will afford instruction and amusement."[2] Ilay Campbell's anonymous reply, *An Explanation of the Bill . . . respecting the Judges in Scotland,* seems to have received no periodical notices at all, and another anonymous pro-reform pamphlet, *Observations on the Jurisprudence of the Court of Session in Scotland,* only a very short notice in the *Critical Review.*[3]

At home the *Scots Magazine,* copying English opinion, was impressed by Boswell's essay and said, "Mr. Boswell, with a patriotic zeal, that claims applause, warns his countrymen of the dangerous innovation that is meditated in the Court of Session; and after paying all the compliments he thinks due to Mr Henry Dundas the late Lord Advocate, for taking the lead

2. *Critical Review,* 59 (1785), 466–67; *English Review,* 5 (1785), 441–44; *Monthly Review,* 72 (1785), 459.

3. 60 (1785), 77–78. I have seen neither of these pamphlets.

in this measure, and to Sir Adam Fergusson for supporting it, he introduces a variety of pointed remarks . . . in which the merits of the alteration are seriously discussed." Extensive quotations from the *Letter* make up the rest of the review.[4]

Even apart from Boswell's intervention, the Diminishing Bill ran into difficulties. It had to be withdrawn on the same day that it was introduced in the House of Commons, since as an abridgment of the Articles of Union it needed the Royal license before action could be taken on it. Consideration of it was postponed thereafter several times, until it was finally ordered to be printed and put over until the next session so that more time could be given to discussion of such an important matter. The Commons, however, sitting as a committee on 3 June 1785, considered some resolutions on the subject. The first, moved by Ilay Campbell, was that the number of judges in Scotland ought to be diminished. After Lord Maitland, a Scottish member of the Opposition, had spoken against this proposal, Dundas argued in its favor that a reduction in the number of judges with an increase in their salaries would attract men of greater talent than at present; under the existing system too much attention was paid to interest and too little to ability. This drew the obvious reply from Maitland that an increase in salary would simply make these positions a greater political gift, and when several others also opposed the resolution it was withdrawn. Augmentation of the judges' salaries was approved in principle, however, and on 10 June the House directed Campbell, Fergusson, and Dundas to prepare a bill for presentation.[5]

Boswell had actively seconded his pamphlet with an address signed by 289 of his Ayrshire tenants, which he presented to

4. 47 (1785), 284–87. This review originally appeared in the *London Chronicle,* 21 June 1785.

5. *JHC* (1784–85) xl.905, 949, 1008, 1047, 1060; *EA,* 24 May, 10, 14, 17 June 1785; *LC,* 4 June 1785; *SM,* 47 (1785), 278–79, 332–33.

the King on 24 June,[6] and eight counties passed resolutions against diminishing the number of judges. Boswell led the fight himself in Ayrshire, at a meeting of the freeholders on 25 October, moving that the attempt to hurry the Bill through Parliament was "unwise, rash, and insolent." On the objection of the Eglinton group and others, this was changed to read, "most improper and disrespectful," and the resolution passed with only four dissenting votes. Debate also arose over improving the procedure of the Court of Session, and it was finally resolved by a majority of one not to petition against the infringement of the Articles of Union as long as juries were introduced in civil causes. A further meeting of the Commissioners of Supply for Ayrshire (the men of property responsible for the land-tax collection) on 6 December resolved to seek concerted action with other counties to support this *quid pro quo;* they also voted to instruct the M.P., Montgomerie, to oppose the Bill unless this bargain was agreed to.[7]

A good deal of feeling had certainly been roused against the Diminishing Bill in Scotland,[8] and much of the credit for this opposition belonged to Boswell. By January 1786, both sides had yielded ground. Campbell declared that he thought the Bill had been abandoned so far as reducing the number of

6. It was printed in the *St. James's Chronicle,* 5 July 1785; *London Chronicle,* 7 July 1785; *Morning Chronicle,* 8 July 1785. See, from Alexander Millar, 4 June (C 2016), to Robert Boswell, 5 July 1785 (*L 202).

7. From Fairlie, 24 Apr. 1786 (C 1226); *EA,* 28 Oct. 1785; *SM,* 47 (1785), 516–18, 569–70, 652–53. Probably Boswell was also concerned with a petition of "Landholders of the Shire of *Ayr*" against nominal votes, presented to the Commons on 28 June 1785, among a series of petitions from Scottish counties (*JHC,* 1784–85, xl.1109–10). A letter from him protesting against such votes appeared in the *Edinburgh Advertiser* on 21 January 1785 (P 25.4).

8. The Faculty of Advocates passed a resolution that the Bill ought to be opposed unless there was "an alteration of the forms of the Court," i.e. presumably to make lawsuits less tedious and expensive (to [Robert Boswell], 26 Aug. 1785, *L 204). See, from Fairlie, 16 Jan. 1786 (C 1224); *EA,* 3 June, 12 Aug. 1785; Omond, *Lord Advocates of Scotland,* ii.175–76.

judges was concerned, while Boswell admitted he was wrong in opposing an increase in salary.[9] Boswell still wished to press for the introduction of juries in civil causes, but Fairlie and Craufurd warned him that to try to raise addresses would be futile. The Bill, limited to providing increased salaries for the members of the Courts of Session and Justiciary, was finally passed in June 1786.[1]

Boswell had achieved his public aim, but at a formidable cost. He knew when he published the *Letter* that it might mean a sharp break with Dundas and his friends; the copy he sent to Dundas was inscribed, "Plato, Amicus Socrates, sed magis Amica Veritas," and when Ilay Campbell asked for a copy of his pamphlet, Boswell promised him one when it was finished with the comment that he was now putting the lead to the end of his taws. Pitt's presentation copy was accompanied by a letter which read in part, "I shall be very glad to attend you, whenever your great occupations allow you time to see me. And indeed I shall be sorry both on your account and my own, if I find myself neglected."[2]

Almost the worst result followed: the great seemed not to

9. Journ. 9, 21 Jan., 5 Mar. 1786; Reg. Let. 9, 11 Jan. 1786; *EA,* 27 Dec. 1785. Boswell's shift on the salary issue, according to Craufurd of Craufurdland, led to suspicions that he had been bought off. Boswell, in denying any such collusion, insisted that the main object was to prevent any reduction in the number of judges unless juries were introduced for civil causes (from Craufurd, 31 Dec. 1785, Hyde Collection, to Craufurd, 10 Jan. 1786, Hyde Collection). Boswell had complained about the lack of such juries as early as 1768 (*LC,* 21 Apr.).

1. From Fairlie, 16 Jan. (C 1224), from Craufurd, 20 Apr. (Hyde Collection), from Fairlie, 24 Apr. (C 1226), from Craufurd, 29 Apr. 1786 (Hyde Collection); *EA,* 11 Apr. 1786; *JHC* (1786) xli.466, 562–63, 737, 814, 875, 904, 907; *Parliamentary Register* (1786) xx.84–87; *SM, 48* (1786), 178, 281, 631–32.

2. Journ. 18 May 1785; to Pitt, 25 May 1785 (L 1074); *R. B. Adam Library* (1929–30), ii. after p. 54. Pitt "took no trouble to attach men to himself—gave no dinners, wasted no time on the small change of politeness, and did not even answer letters" (Pares, *King George III and the Politicians,* p. 78).

react to Boswell's activities at all. Neither Dundas nor Fergusson challenged him to a duel as he had feared, but Jack Lee must have expressed a common opinion when he said that Boswell was "a very odd fellow" to raise so many enemies in Scotland, and in particular Dundas, with whom he was supposedly on terms of friendship. James Stuart remarked to him that in presenting the address from his tenants he was acting like Lord George Gordon.[3] Some of Boswell's friends, of course, praised the *Letter:* Temple and the Bishop of Killaloe were both impressed, though both remarked on the vanity it displayed, and Lord Fife agreed with him in June 1785 that the Bill ought at least to be delayed. Boswell also persuaded Capel Lofft, an English barrister, to let him print his concurring opinion in the newspapers.[4]

In Scotland, too, his friends and adherents rallied around, but significantly their opinions were mixed. John Boswell ("Old Knockroon") praised the *Letter* and thought that Fergusson deserved everything that Boswell had said about him, but admitted that the *Letter* had given offense to several people; James Bruce said cautiously that some had approved of it, and others not. Adam Neill, an Edinburgh printer, reported that some gentlemen there had found many of its observations extremely just, and much of it entertaining. Boswell's protégé, the Rev. Alexander Millar, did not doubt that "those who are united by the strong cement of politicks with the Gentlemen whose characters you have so smartly touched, will feel sore."[5]

As time passed, less favorable reports appeared. Temple wrote from Cornwall in October that he feared Boswell had

3. Journ. 8, 10, 29–30 May, 10, 27 July 1785.

4. From Fife, 1 June (C 1248), from Lofft, 7 June (C 1755), from Temple, 8 June (C 2834), from Barnard, [c. 17 July] (C 85), to [Lofft], 3 Aug. (L 870), from Lofft, [c. 4 Aug.] (C 1756), 17 Aug. (C 1757); *EA,* 6 Sept. 1785.

5. From Neill, 7 June (C 2084), from Millar, 26 June (C 2017), from John Boswell, "Old Knockroon," 16 July (C 391), from Bruce, 23 July 1785 (C 653).

offended Dundas and several others by this pamphlet, "which still people alledge you meant as a managing one." Edmond Malone wrote bluntly in November: "You cannot imagine how much mischief your own pamphlet has done you and how slow people are to allow the praise of good thinking and good writing to one whom they think guilty of such indiscretion in that pamphlet as a man of sound sense (they allege) would not be guilty of." Boswell replied that he would "henceforth *to a certain degree* be more cautious," and he thought it expedient to insert a letter in the newspapers apologizing for any intemperate expressions he might have used.[6]

The publication of the *Tour* in the same year climaxed the dissatisfaction of the Scots with their countryman. Lord Macdonald, Alexander Tytler, and Douglas of Douglas were extremely offended by remarks in the book,[7] and even others not directly concerned, like James Beattie and Sir William Forbes, were agitated by Boswell's injudicious comments. Forbes advised him to insert nothing in the forthcoming *Life* that could give "either pain or offence to any mortal," to which Boswell replied spiritedly that "people must be satisfied to appear as they really did," for otherwise the work would not be authentic. Nevertheless he was discouraged. In December 1785, he wrote to Lord Thurlow, who he hoped would help him if he came to the English Bar, that he was afraid he would be greatly embarrassed if he returned to the bar in Scotland: "His having

6. From Temple, 14 Oct. (C 2836), from Malone, 5 Nov. (C 1900), to Malone, 11 Nov. 1785 (L 926); *EA*, 27 Dec. 1785; *Edinburgh Evening Courant* (P 60).

7. F. A. Pottle has summarized the Macdonald affair (*BP*, xvi.221–59). For Tytler, see Journ. 18, 30 Nov. 1785; from Dugald Stewart, [14 Oct.] (C 2568), to [Tytler], 6 Nov. (L 1250), from Tytler, 7 Nov. (C 3015), to Stewart, 8 Nov. (L 1188), Tytler to Stewart, 9 Nov. (C 3016), from Stewart, [9 Nov.] (C 2569), to Tytler, 18 Nov. (L 1251), to Stewart, 18 Nov. (L 1189), from Tytler, 24 Nov. (C 3017), from Stewart, 25 Nov. (C 2570), to Tytler [1 Dec.] (L 1252), to Stewart, 1 Dec. 1785 (L 1190). For Douglas, see Journ. 22 Mar. 1787; to Douglas, 18 Mar. (L 436), from Douglas, 19 Mar. 1787 (C 1098).

thwarted Mr. Dundas in his job of diminishing the number of the Lords of Session has drawn upon him the displeasure of that provincial despot, and his having had candour enough to speak without prejudice of Scotland in his Tour with Dr. Johnson, had given very general offence to an irritable people."[8]

Scotland did not receive Boswell as badly as he had feared, and the President, who publicly praised his conduct of a lawsuit, even invited him to dinner to the discomfiture of "the narrowminded and timid." One client praised Boswell's "established Reputation for endeavouring to obtain redress" for everything he regarded as a grievance, but compliments did not satisfy ambition and he must have begun to realize that he had destroyed almost every possibility of advancement in Scotland. Finally making the transfer to England that he had contemplated for years, he was called to the English bar on 9 February 1786.[9] This move did not end his efforts to represent Ayrshire in Parliament or to obtain favors from Dundas, but it marked a shift in the focus of his political interests. The tragicomedy of his political career was now to be played out primarily under the auspices of Lord Lonsdale.

8. From Forbes, 6 Dec. (C 1276), to Thurlow, 18 Dec. (L 1244), to [Forbes], 20 Dec. 1785 (L 543), from Hailes, 18 Jan. 1786 (C 1476); Sir William Forbes, *An Account of the Life and Writings of James Beattie* (2d ed. 1807), ii.371–83. See F. A. Pottle's comment on Boswell's "social unpopularity" consequent to publishing the *Tour* and the *Life* (*BP,* xvi.vii–viii), and post, p. 178.

9. Journ. 19 Jan., 9 Feb. 1786; from Fairlie, 23 Jan. (C 1225), to Malone, 24 Jan. (L 930), from Anthony MacHarg, 23 Feb. 1786 (C 1843); Reg. Let. 13 Jan. 1786. Boswell had even talked to the King about his move (to Temple, 6 July 1784, L 1236.9).

5

Lonsdale and the Final Phase: 1786–1795

One of the turning points in Boswell's life came on 21 July 1786, when he received an invitation from the Earl of Lonsdale to dine "to a Turtle."[1] This was to prove the beginning of a connection which brought Boswell closer to a Parliamentary seat than at any other time in his career. It was a chance at which he clutched with the eagerness of despair, and the surprise and pleasure with which he received this invitation only add poignancy to the final failure of his expectations.

Lonsdale was one of the most striking political personalities of his time, and a good deal of material about him survives; but Boswell's description of him provides the most vivid and detailed picture of his personality and methods. Born James Lowther in 1736, he was descended on both sides from one of the most powerful families in Cumberland and Westmorland. His father, Robert Lowther, had once been Governor of Barbados, and his mother, Katherine Pennington, was the granddaughter of John, first Viscount Lonsdale. The eminence of Boswell's patron, however, was based on his inheritance of vast wealth and property from other branches of his family. In 1751 he succeeded to the baronetcy and estates of Henry,

1. Journ. 21 July 1786; from Lonsdale, 21 July 1786 (C 1775). Readers of Creevey will remember his delight at being asked to dine on this delicacy.

third Viscount Lonsdale, and in 1755 and 1756 the deaths of other relatives increased his holdings immensely.

Lowther's career offers an extreme example of the power of great resources supported by equal resolution in contemporary political life. When he succeeded to the baronetcy, his family controlled one seat for Westmorland, one for Cumberland, and one for the borough of Appleby.[2] They seized control of a seat for the borough of Cockermouth from the Earl of Egremont by purchasing, during one week in September 1756, 134 burgages at an estimated cost of £58,060,[3] and acquired the second Westmorland seat in 1759. A sixth seat, for the city of Carlisle, was added at the General Election of 1761.

At this point, opposition to Lowther began to rise, fed by his arrogant disregard for other gentlemen of property and interest in the area; in 1763 it found its leader in the Duke of Portland. Lowther attempted to undermine Portland's position in 1767 by obtaining control of certain of his estates, originally belonging to the Crown, to which Portland's title was not clear. The notorious and expensive contest that followed led to a complex series of lawsuits and eventually a legal victory for the Duke. In the meantime, Lowther's action, widely resented as an attack on private property, increased his unpopularity; in the General Election of 1768 he lost one seat for Carlisle, one for Westmorland, and failed to carry either Cumberland seat. Political compromise became essential, and it was aided by Lowther's drift into opposition to Lord North: though their lawsuits dragged on, Lowther and Portland reached an agreement in 1774 by which Lowther obtained control of one seat for Cumberland and one for Carlisle. He also regained the second West-

2. It is not clear whether Lowther's uncle, Sir John Pennington, who occupied the second Cumberland seat until 1768, was independent of him (Brian Bonsall, *Sir James Lowther and Cumberland & Westmorland Elections, 1754–1775,* 1960, pp. 8 and n.2, 36, 51, 56, 69, 76, 78 and n.2).

3. The second seat for Cockermouth was acquired when its occupant, Sir John Mordaunt, an independent ally of Lowther, retired in 1768 (Bonsall, pp. 12 and n.3, 41, 52, 89 n.2, 106–07).

morland seat in the General Election of 1774, and sometime before 1780 he bought the two seats for the pocket borough of Haslemere, Surrey. As a result Lowther was able to return nine members in the General Elections of 1780 and 1784,[4] and his absolute control over them is suggested by their nickname, "Lowther's Ninepins."[5]

Lowther's ruthlessness made him extremely unpopular among his contemporaries at large. The Rev. Alexander Carlyle remarked about his conflict with Portland that "Lowther went off conqueror, but more detested than any man alive, as a shameless political sharper, a domestic bashaw, and an intolerable tyrant over his tenants and dependents." Horace Walpole thought Lowther "united many odious arbitrary qualities, and was equally unamiable in public and private," while Junius more succinctly called him "the little, contemptible tyrant of the North." Even Sir Nathaniel Wraxall, a less prejudiced observer, said that Lowther's "fiery and overbearing temper combining with a fearless disposition, scarcely under the dominion of reason at all times, led him into perpetual quarrels, terminating frequently in duels; for he never declined giving satisfaction, and frequently demanded it of others."[6] Boswell was to have first-hand experience of this tendency.

4. Two each for Cockermouth, Haslemere, and Westmorland; one each for Appleby, Carlisle, and Cumberland.

5. This sketch of Lowther's early career is based on Bonsall's thorough study, supplemented by R. S. Ferguson, *Cumberland and Westmorland M.P.'s* (1871). For Lowther's quarrel with Portland and his later temporary alliance with the Rockingham Whigs, see also *Letters . . . from the Originals at Welbeck Abbey,* [ed. R. W. Goulding] (1909), pp. 172–84. A. M. W. Stirling gives an interesting account of Lowther's cat-and-mouse tactics with Walter Stanhope, a young, politically aspiring cousin. It anticipates Lowther's treatment of Boswell closely, except that Stanhope was finally given a seat (*Annals of a Yorkshire House,* 1911, i.283–317).

6. Carlyle, *Autobiography,* p. 339; Horace Walpole, *Memoirs of the Reign of King George the Third,* ed. G. F. R. Barker (1894), iii.195; *Letters of Junius,* ed. C. W. Everett (1927), p. 271; Sir Nathaniel Wraxall, *The Historical and the Posthumous Memoirs,* ed. H. B. Wheatley (1884), iii.358.

The disapproval of his age pursued Lowther not only throughout his life, but to the grave and beyond. His high-handed treatment of the colliers of Whitehaven furnished the occasion for Peter Pindar's vigorous attack, *A Commiserating Epistle to James Lowther, Earl of Lonsdale,* and for the *Rolliad's* well-known couplets:

> E'en by the elements his pow'r confess'd,
> Of mines and boroughs *Lonsdale* stands possess'd:
> And one sad servitude alike denotes
> The slave that labours, and the slave that votes.

In its obituary of Lonsdale, the *Gentleman's Magazine* summarized current opinion in remarking upon his "litigious disposition, or rather a determination to oppress, by means of wealth, and under colour of law, all who were obnoxious to him." De Quincey added to the blackness of his portrait by recalling with picturesque detail his character and shabby treatment of the Wordsworth family, and these accounts, spliced together with flourishes of indignant rhetoric in the *Rockingham Memoirs* and Trevelyan's *Early History of Charles James Fox,* fixed Lonsdale's reputation permanently as the "bad Earl," or "Jimmy Gripeall, Earl of Toadstool," as he was called in contemporary pamphlets.[7]

Tyrant, Lonsdale undoubtedly was, cruel or indifferent to the farmer and miner in his power, as well as to the gentlemen satellites who hovered miserably about him; but perhaps something should be said in his favor. Dempster praised him when he heard that he had made Boswell Recorder of Carlisle in

7. *The Rolliad* (1795), p. 173; *GM,* 72 (1802), 587; Thomas De Quincey, *Collected Writings,* ed. David Masson (1889–90), ii.252–55; George Thomas, [6th] Earl of Albemarle, *Memoirs of the Marquis of Rockingham* (1852), ii.68–74; G. O. Trevelyan, *Early History of Charles James Fox* (London, 1880), pp. 411–27; *Early Letters of William and Dorothy Wordsworth,* ed. Ernest de Selincourt (1935), pp. 3–4 and passim; *Cumberland and Westmorland M.P.'s,* p. 205.

1788: "I most sincerely congratulate you," he wrote to Boswell, "not only on your Mr Recordership but on your Lonsdaleship —on your being known to and well with Lord Lonsdale, who has always been[8] a favourite of mine. We sate long beside each other in the House of Commons and I could never discover a spark of sordidness about him—a Homo sui juris—with such a Mass of excentric Force—and rare peculiarities so directly the reverse of a Roman Senator after the fall of the Republic."[9] Lonsdale had plenty of physical courage, and his mental independence is illustrated by his political career. Entering Parliament as M.P. for Cumberland in 1757 under the tutelage of Henry Fox, he turned Tory or rather Bute supporter when he married Bute's eldest daughter, Lady Mary Stuart, in 1761. He supported Lord North's administration at first, but had turned against it by 1775, briefly siding with the Rockingham group. He voted for Dunning's resolution, and in 1781 he was one of the leaders in pressing for the end of the American War. In the same year he brought William Pitt into Parliament at the instigation of the Duke of Rutland, and his adherence to Pitt in the first difficult days of Pitt's ministry earned him his peerage.[1]

Lonsdale's dinner invitation could not have come at a more propitious moment for Boswell. His career at the English bar was proving a failure, and both his personal and political affairs were going badly. An interchange of letters followed by an hospitable welcome from Thurlow, who had strongly discouraged his coming to the English bar, had been unproductive; his friendship with Burke was almost broken off by a

8. Dempster ended one page with "who was always" and started the next one with "who has always been."

9. 22 Mar. 1788 (C 953).

1. *Last Journals of Horace Walpole*, i.424; [Philip Henry, 5th] Earl Stanhope, *Life of the Right Honourable William Pitt* (1861–62), i.46–49, 212–13; *Hist. MSS Comm.*, 13th Report, App. VII (1893), pp. 135–36, 139–41; Christie, *The End of North's Ministry*, pp. 225–26, 271–72. The *Town and Country Magazine* provides tattle about Lonsdale's love life (4, 1772, 625–27).

conversation in which Boswell imprudently mentioned a slander against Burke, and though this was straightened out Boswell lamented that "politicks made a cold separation" between them "which never could be got over."[2] In his widely circulated *Bozzy and Piozzi,* Peter Pindar held up these Johnsonian rivals to such diverting ridicule that even Temple wrote to Boswell, "Pindar is a lying, scrurrilous fellow, yet you must own he has sometimes a fair hit at you." The poem touched one of Boswell's nerve centers, pride of family; he noted in his journal when Mrs. Piozzi's *Letters to and from the late Samuel Johnson* appeared: "I felt degraded from the consequence of an ancient Baron to the state of an humble attendant on an Authour; and what vexed me, thought that my collecting so much of his conversation had made the World shun me as a dangerous companion."[3] Indeed, uneasiness and hostility were added to laughter. His old friend, James Stuart, showed that he was affected by "envious malevolent" reports against Boswell, and some time later George Drummond of Blair-Drummond asked that Boswell submit everything in his contemplated life of Lord Kames, Drummond's father, to him for approval before publication.[4]

In his depression, Boswell had again turned to Dundas. By the summer of 1786, Boswell was willing to return to Scotland

2. For Boswell and Thurlow, see Journ. 26 Feb. 1786; from Thurlow, 5 Jan. (C 2990), to Thurlow, 11 Feb. (L 1245), to Hugh Blair, 21 Apr. 1786 (L 60). For Boswell and Burke, see Journ. 7 Feb., 13 June 1786; to Burke [7 Feb.] (L 328), from Burke, [8 Feb.] (C 691), 9 Feb. (C 692), to [Burke], 10 Feb. (L 329), [10 Feb. 1786] (L 330), from Temple, 7 June (C 2850), from Malone, 14 Sept. 1787 (C 1911), to Forbes, 11 Oct. 1790 (Fett. MSS 1347).

3. Journ. 24 Feb. 1786, 7 Mar. 1788; from [Temple], 21 Apr. 1786 (C 2840). Extracts from Pindar's poem were printed, for example, in the *Scots Magazine, 48* (1786), 197–200. Malone thought Burke's coldness resulted from Boswell's recording conversation (from Malone, 14 Sept. 1787, C 1911).

4. Journ. 7 Mar. 1786; to Drummond, 15 Dec. (L 444), from Drummond, 26 Dec. 1786 (C 1113). See Journ. 22 Mar. 1787.

if he could obtain a judge's seat, and believing that Dundas might be willing to help him, either because of the tradition of friendship between their families or as a politician unwilling to offend an influential voter, he submitted a long "Confidential Case" (10 July 1786) to Dundas, summarizing their dealings with each other, and his claims to attention. Boswell denied that he had written any of the anonymous attacks on Dundas which had appeared in the press,[5] and maintained that his opposition to the Diminishing Bill had been directed against the measure and not against Dundas personally. (He had indeed claimed in the *Letter:* "it is my system to regard, in a publick capacity—measures, and not men; in a private capacity—men, and not measures.") Positively, he urged his services to the Pitt ministry: his first *Letter to the People of Scotland,* his promotion of addresses in Scotland, and his intention of "preparing a popular defence of certain clauses in Mr. Pitt's India Bill," an intention frustrated when these clauses were abandoned. With a mixture of compliments and threats typical of many office seekers, he thanked Dundas for having dissuaded him from trying to purchase a seat in Parliament, but hinted that it would not be "judicious" for Dundas to ignore "a gentleman of respectable family . . . and perhaps produce that sowrness

5. "I beg leave," Boswell wrote, "to vindicate myself from any suspicion of having been the Authour of any of the anonymous virulent attacks upon you. . . . I solemnly protest that not one of them was written by me." This statement seems to rule out any possibility that Boswell wrote the vicious sketch of Dundas that appeared in the *London Magazine, 51* (1782), 498–501, or the mildly unfavorable one in the *European Magazine, 8* (1785), 9. But Boswell seems to have transmitted the sketch that appeared in the *London Magazine.* He wrote to Charles Dilly on 28 September 1782 "Promising Memoirs of Lord Advocate" (Reg. Let.), and this presumably refers to the sketch that appeared in the November issue. This sketch, un-Boswellian in style and viewpoint, was certainly written by a Scot and quite likely by a clergyman of very liberal views.

Others beside Boswell were upset at being suspected of writing these attacks. Caleb Whitefoord, for example, vigorously refuted such a suspicion in a letter (20 Oct. 1786) to Dundas's nephew, William (*Whitefoord Papers,* pp. 198–200).

which is incident to human nature from the feeling of being ill-used." Since a judge's place was not immediately available, Boswell suggested that Dundas might procure something worth £200 or £300 a year that he could take to the Bench with him, and which would help him at the moment to live in London. This eloquent letter received no immediate reply, and by August Boswell regretted ever having written it. Scotland was too narrow a sphere for his activities, and a judge's seat too great a reward for Dundas to bestow on him.[6]

Dundas had good reason to be cautious. Not only was Boswell "independent," i.e. a trouble maker, but he was also now associated personally with prominent Foxites like William Windham and John Courtenay. Nor would Dundas have been pleased to learn that Boswell had written a ballad attacking the Duke of Richmond's Fortifications Bill in February or March 1786: this Bill, an unpopular Ministerial measure, was finally defeated by the casting vote of the Speaker of the House of Commons, Charles Cornwall. The following couplet, among the few manuscript lines preserved, suggests the ballad's tone:

To ballance a straw may suit gentlemen fine,
But to ballance all Europe, great CORNWALL is thine.

While this *jeu d'esprit* was of no importance, it would have offered one more indication of Boswell's unreliability.[7]

For whatever reason, Dundas did not answer Boswell's letter until Boswell prodded him about it in November 1786. Then Dundas, adopting a lofty tone, replied that while he had "not the least disposition to depretiate" Boswell's political services,

6. Journ. 8 July, 2 Aug. 1786; to Dundas, 4 July (L 454), 4 July (L 455), from Dundas, 5 July (C 1136), to Dundas, 6 July (L 456), 10 July 1786 (L 457); *LPS 85*, p. 94.

7. To Malone, [10 Mar.] (L 931), from Malone, 17 Mar. 1786 (C 1905); Reg. Let. 10 Mar. 1786; Articles, or notes for articles intended for publication (M 9:5). Accounts of the debates in the Commons on the Fortifications Bill appear in the *Parliamentary Register, 1786,* xix.83–91, 170–246, and in Wraxall, iv.105–08, 261–71.

he could not admit "that political merit of any kind is the proper Road to Judicial Preferment." He added that while he did not regret Boswell's 1785 *Letter* on his own account, he certainly did on Boswell's. This reply naturally served to make Boswell more dependent on his new acquaintance with Lonsdale.[8]

Boswell acquired his first impression of Lonsdale when Lonsdale was acting as foreman of a grand jury in August 1778:

> It was agreable to see a Man of his great fortune appear doing his duty to his country, both as a Justice and a grand Juryman. . . . There was a swarthy, turklike stateliness in his looks and manner. They speak very differently of him in the County [Cumberland]. It seems to be universally agreed that he is a Humourist. But some say that he is capricious and proud and disobliging, and does not chuse to have interest by making himself agreable, but by compulsion,—by means of his immense wealth. Others say that he is very freindly where he takes a regard.

Apparently Lonsdale's increasing prominence transformed Boswell's attitude of tempered respect, as expressed here, into the feeling of enthusiastic admiration shown in the almost Biblical terms of the 1785 *Letter,* in which Lonsdale is implored to come forward to support the Scots:

> We are his neighbours. *Paries proximus ardet.* We all know what HE can do . . . HE whose soul is all great—whose resentment is terrible; but whose liberality is bound-

8. To Dundas, 9 Nov. (L 458), from Dundas, 26 Nov. 1786 (C 1137). Dundas may well have thought the demand for a judgeship inconsistent with Boswell's announced principles: one of the points in Boswell's attack on the Diminishing Bill was that it could be a way of ensuring complete political dependence of the Court of Session, and thus control of Scottish elections (*LPS 85,* pp. 48–51, 63–64; ante, p. 121). Also, in spite of his assurance that he was personally unaffected by Boswell's attack, Dundas

> less. I know that he is dignified, by having hosts of enemies. But I have fixed his character in my mind upon no slight inquiry. . . . LOWTHER! be kindly intreated!—*"Come over to Macedonia, and help us!"*

Possibly Boswell saw in Lonsdale a realization of his own ambitions: a rich, independent, feudal Tory squire, who lived on a grand scale, and who had attained a peerage. Their political opinions had run fairly parallel: both had supported Bute, had opposed the American War and the North ministry, and were now adherents of Pitt. Boswell's approbation of Lonsdale appeared again in a note to the *Tour,* where, taking advantage of Johnson's reference to the miserly qualities of a previous Sir James Lowther, Boswell proclaimed in a footnote that "a due mixture of severity and kindness, œconomy and munificence" characterized the present representative of this ancient family.[9]

This was still admiration from afar, since Boswell had not met Lonsdale. He had, however, met certain of the members of Lonsdale's little court, and had interested himself in their political affairs. In March 1786, he wrote to a certain James Hatfield, a baker, asking him to make six votes in Lancaster for the Lonsdale choice in the special election, and Hatfield had replied with assurances of help. Also, Boswell attended the meetings of a committee of the House of Commons the following May on the contested election for Carlisle, in which John Lowther, a Lonsdale man, was involved. Boswell records nothing about these sessions except that he "was really sorry" when Lowther was unseated, but he mentions having met John Gar-

---

could not have liked seeing it provide ammunition to his enemies. The *European Magazine* used it when it described Dundas: "by nature indolent, luxurious, and jocular, he is something of a *bon vivant,* and a quondam friend has lately hinted, that he has been by no means unmindful of providing for his family" (*8,* 1785, 9).

9. Journ. 22 Aug. 1778, 3 June 1784; *LPS 85,* p. 28; *Life,* v.113 n.1.

forth, a Lonsdale M.P. there, and he may have met others of the entourage on the same occasion.[1]

The dinner invitation, however, was the first intimation that the great man himself might be interested in Boswell. Both the invitation and Boswell's reception of it were characteristic: Lonsdale ignored the social formalities in tendering it, and Boswell was elated though suspicious:

> This was truly a stirring of my blood. I strutted and said to myself, "Well, it is right to be in this Metropolis. Things at last come forward unexpectedly. The great LOWTHER himself has now taken me up. I may be raised to eminence in the state." Yet as I was not at all acquainted with him, had never called on him, and he had not left a card for me, I suspected that this invitation might be a trick attempted upon me.

In his perplexity, Boswell made roundabout inquiries as to the genuineness of the invitation. It proved to be no trick, but Boswell still hung back. He was already engaged for that night, and the summons was abrupt; finally he took Malone's advice to decline the invitation, and to call with dignity on Lonsdale the following day. Boswell was determined "not to meet him but as an ancient Baron."[2]

Boswell must have pursued Lonsdale's acquaintance assiduously; at least by 9 November 1786, they were friendly enough

1. Journ. 2–3 Apr., 24–30 May, 22 July 1786; to Hatfield, 18 Mar. (L 631), from Hatfield, 21 Mar. 1786 (C 1507). Boswell instructed Hatfield to send his reply "under cover of the Hon. Edward Norton, M.P.," another Lonsdale protégé.

2. Journ. 21–22 July 1786; to Lonsdale, 22 July [1786] (L 873). Perhaps Lonsdale's notice was attracted by the *London Chronicle's* front-page review (21 June 1785) of the *Letter to the People of Scotland* (1785), which quoted Boswell's praise of Lonsdale. "A Westmorland Freeholder" replied with a powerful attack on both Boswell and Lonsdale in a letter to the *Chronicle,* 3 Sept. 1785, which was reprinted as a campaign broadside (P 11.6), presumably for the second Carlisle election of 1786.

so that Boswell, apparently no longer objecting to the interference of peers in elections, could ask Lonsdale to make him Recorder (principal legal officer) of Carlisle. Lonsdale countered by inviting Boswell to be Mayor's Counsel at the forthcoming Carlisle election, an offer which Boswell was happy to accept, and on 25 November he started north.[3]

The electoral situation in Carlisle promised trouble. Lonsdale, who had obtained control of the borough Corporation in the 1760s, was not content with controlling only one of the two borough seats. In 1780, he had had to share the seats with the Earl of Surrey, Carlisle returning Surrey himself and William Lowther, Lonsdale's cousin and heir. Determined to change this situation, Lonsdale had forced his adherents on the Corporation to admit 1,443 nonresident colliers and farmers as honorary freemen between September 1784 and February 1785. The legality of this move was dubious, since the old rules of the borough seemed to provide that all freemen must be members of the eight City Guilds; nevertheless, the point was in dispute, and the identical maneuver had been performed successfully in such towns as Durham, Derby, and Knaresborough. The first test of this action came with the special election of April 1786, which John Lowther had contested as the Yellow candidate against John Christian, backed by Surrey, as the Blue candidate. Lowther had polled only 107 of the old freemen against 422 for Christian, but he had also obtained the votes of 461 honorary freemen, or "mushrooms" as they were called. Lowther was duly returned, but Christian was successful in his appeal to the House, as Boswell had witnessed.[4]

Surrey vacated his seat when he became Duke of Norfolk in November 1786, and Lonsdale decided on a repetition of

3. Journ. 23 Nov. 1786; to Lonsdale, 9 Nov. 1786 (L 874).

4. Ferguson provides an amusing and circumstantial, if not totally accurate, account of the Carlisle election and its background (*Cumberland and Westmorland M.P.'s*, pp. 169–81, 189–204). See also Bonsall, p. 82. Yellows and Blues were the names of local factions.

his recent tactics despite their failure. Edward Knubley was the Yellow candidate, while Norfolk, himself the patron of eleven seats, imported Rowland Stephenson, a rich London banker, to contest the place. Because of the legal technicalities involved, each side hired a lawyer while Boswell stood by to advise the Mayor, Sir Joseph Senhouse, who was also the Returning Officer. The poll, which started on 30 November and continued for fifteen days, was taken up with legal arguments in which Boswell almost invariably sided with Knubley. The crucial question, the right of honorary freemen to vote, arose on 7 December, and Boswell delivered an extended speech "with animation and force," in which he defended the Corporation's right to make as many honorary freemen with voting status as it wished; he asserted that even C. J. Fox, who had been Christian's nominee on the Select Committee of the House the previous May, had not dared to attack this right, and that the Select Committee had not ruled on the question. This point having been decided, Knubley was easily elected, polling 147 "old" votes and 407 "mushroom" votes to Stephenson's 405 "old" votes.[5]

Stephenson immediately petitioned the House of Commons, and a Select Committee examined the question from 15 to 26 February. The debate again revolved around the right of the Corporation to make freemen without the consent of the Guilds, and again the Select Committee refused to rule on the matter, merely deciding that Stephenson had been elected. Boswell attended and made notes on these meetings, but he was not called as a witness.[6]

5. Journ. 7 Dec. 1786; "Carlisle Election, 1786" (Lg 43); Carlisle Election, 1786. Squibs (P 11.6, 11.7); *Cumberland and Westmorland M.P.'s*, pp. 204–06; *A Political History of the City of Carlisle*, ed. Francis Jollie (1820), pp. 16–17.

6. "Carlisle Committee" (Lg 47); *Cumberland and Westmorland M.P.'s*, pp. 206–07; Alexander Luders, *Report of the Proceedings in Committees of the House of Commons, upon Controverted Elections* (1790), iii.506–83; *JHC* (1787) xlii.277, 377, 405–06, 409.

The Carlisle election threw Boswell into really close contact with Lonsdale for the first time, and he was both impressed and disillusioned by what he saw. At first Boswell felt "a certain elevation in being an ally of the great Lowther of Westmorland" and saw in him "an example of an aggregate of grandeur—antiquity of family—immense territory—raised to the nobility by strength of intellect—violence—Parliamentary interest," but this combination of sublime ideas proved difficult to live with at close range. Accompanied on this expedition by four of his Parliamentary members—Garforth, Sir Michael Le Fleming, J. C. Satterthwaite, and Col. James Lowther—Lonsdale, as Boswell noticed, "like Cato gives his little Senate laws," and they retaliated by complaining behind his back of his stinginess, his poor table, and his overbearing manner. Boswell himself soon discovered that Lonsdale "could not bear any obstruction or opposition," and began to believe that he had mostly imagined Lonsdale's greatness unless "his exorbitant tyranny and extreme narrowness may be reckoned great in a bad sense"; he found Lonsdale's company overpowering in the same way that he had found his father's, a bad portent for their future relationship. He was also discouraged by Col. Lowther's remark that Lonsdale wished to keep those around him dependent, and therefore would ask no favors for them, but Boswell felt it necessary to persevere. He even wrote a couple of ballads for the Yellow cause, which he suppressed on reflecting they might jeopardize his impartial position as Counsel. Lonsdale was capable of relaxed moments when an agreeable smile would cross his "black countenance," but these moments were rare, and Boswell escaped from his company whenever he could to the more congenial society of the local pubs.[7]

Matters had gone well, however, on the surface. Lonsdale

7. Journ. 29 Nov., 1–2 Dec., 10–12 Dec. 1786. Some of the remarks quoted are translated from Boswell's rudimentary Italian.

paid Boswell a sizable fee, £157, which was £50 more than had been promised,[8] and once away from Lonsdale's immediate vicinity Boswell's spirits revived; he sent enthusiastic accounts to his friends of his new patron and enhanced prospects, and they encouraged him. Bishop Percy wrote, for example:

> I have heard, with great pleasure of your late Success in the North. I hope it will lead to a lasting Connection with a Nobleman, distinguished for the Zeal and Spirit, with which he Serves his Friends; and I already anticipate the happiest consequences to you from that Connection; especially his bringing you into Parliamt. for one of his numerous Boroughs, an Event which I consider as no less certain than splendid to your Fortunes and Establishmt. in England.[9]

Necessity as well as hope drove Boswell closer to Lonsdale during 1787. His practice at the English bar continued to be negligible, and the expenses of maintaining family and position in London were heavy. His wife and brother, David, continually pressed him to resume his station as Baron of Auchinleck, pointing out the discreditable appearance he made in England without business at the bar, a seat in Parliament, or enough money to keep up a position suitable to his rank. Boswell felt the force of these arguments, but he could not bring himself to abandon his London friends, or the chance to acquire first-hand material for his life of Johnson. Scotland offered only "narrow local topicks"; if in moments of despair he resigned himself to a judge's place in Scotland, even this prospect remained dim, though in his efforts toward reconciliation with

8. To Forbes, 8 May (L 544), to Blair, 2 Aug. 1787 (L 61); "English Fees" (Lg 41).

9. From Percy, 6 Mar. 1787 (C 2233). See, to Barnard, 6 Jan. 1786 (in error for 1787) (L 47), from Barnard, 23 Jan. (C 88), from Temple, 15 Feb. (C 2847), from Blair, 25 Aug. 1787 (C 163).

Dundas, Boswell had finally persuaded him to dine once at his house.[1]

Under these circumstances, it is hardly surprising that Boswell sought for a "more permanent connection" with Lonsdale. Boswell's "ticket in the Lottery" was the Recordership of Carlisle, an important position and a natural stepping stone to a seat in Parliament, Lonsdale having thus elevated the previous Recorder, Edward Norton. Finally in December 1787, Lonsdale offered him the place, and Boswell unexpectedly hesitated; the public friendship or patronage of Lonsdale was a little embarrassing. But the opportunity was too good to be rejected: on 21 December Boswell headed north for his election, and another prolonged taste of Lonsdale's company.[2]

Nothing had changed much. The start from London was delayed for hours by Lonsdale's whim, and the journey was unpleasant. Boswell found himself drawn more and more into

1. Journ. 20, 23 Mar., 11 June, 21 July, 8 Nov. 1787, 20 Feb. 1788; to [Dundas], 19 May (L 460), from Dundas, 22 May (C 1139), from Temple, 7 June (C 2850), to [Dundas], 17 June (L 461), from Dundas, 19 June (C 1140), to [Robert Boswell], 21 July (*L 215), to Dundas [c. 1 Nov.] (L 465), from Dundas, 2 Nov. (C 1143), to Dundas [2 Nov.] (L 466), from Dundas, 4 Nov. (C 1144), to [Dundas], 6 Nov. (L 467), from Temple, 30 Nov. 1787 (C 2852); Reg. Let. 10 Nov. 1787.

Boswell had promised his vote in Fife at the next general election to Sir James Erskine, an opponent of Dundas, but was unwilling to become involved in the by-election of 1787, perhaps for fear of offending Dundas as well as because he took a dislike to Erskine (to [Robert Boswell], 16 June, *L 213, 30 June 1787, *L 214; Reg. Let. 12 June, 3 Aug. 1787). Later he promised the same vote to Col. William Wemyss, if Erskine did not stand (Journ. 2 July 1790; from Henry Erskine, 23 Mar., C 1217, to [Henry Erskine], 13 Apr., L 532, to Veronica Boswell, 2 July 1790, L 263).

2. Journ. 7, 28 Mar., 6 July, 28–29 Nov., 3, 20 Dec. 1787; to Lonsdale, 13 June (L 876), from Lonsdale, 23 June (C 1776), to Lonsdale [1 Dec.] (L 878), from Lonsdale, 20 Dec. 1787 (C 1777). "The Recorders of Parliamentary boroughs, who were usually chosen from among the leading barristers of the circuit, had a considerable influence, especially in corporation boroughs, and often finished by having themselves returned to Parliament" (Namier, *Structure*, p. 44). For the Recorder's official duties, see Giles Jacob, *A New Law-Dictionary* (8th ed. 1762), s.v. Recorder.

the little circle of hangers-on, though he still talked stoutly of independence. Colonel Lowther thought he might be chosen to represent Cockermouth in place of Humphrey Senhouse, who hated Parliament, and soothed Boswell's fears of being without a voice of his own by saying that Lonsdale acted honorably toward his members, and did not require them to utter only his inclinations. Satterthwaite reminded him, however, it was understood in all cases that no member should oppose his patron. Boswell's gloom deepened when the party arrived at Lowther Castle, where "all sat in vile timid restraint." Satterthwaite complained of the Earl's inattention to the happiness of those around him and said, "no man of parts had ever submitted to go along with him." The many difficulties of his future status as Recorder had fully penetrated Boswell's mind by 24 December. Lonsdale would not allow "even decent attention to be paid to his opponents in the Corporation," and his behavior to those to whom he owed election debts was shocking. "I paused," says Boswell, "and asked myself what I had to do with such a Man? . . . I also felt how unworthy it was of the Laird of Auchinleck to hang thus upon a Savage."[3]

By 27 December, Boswell's doubts had hardened into certainties; he resolved to decline the Recordership. His journal for the next day contains a painful review of his predicament: "It was galling to me to find that I was so miserably deceived in the notion which I had formed of the high honour and great advantage of being connected with LOWTHER." But his mistake, he felt, was an understandable one; had he not had the encouragement of Dempster, and the Bishops of Killaloe and Dromore? There remained the problem of telling Lonsdale,

3. Perhaps Boswell remembered what he had written in *The Hypochondriack,* no. 12 (Sept. 1778): "Independency is a truely dignified state, and in proportion as a man recedes from it, he sinks into meanness. He who subjects himself to a servile compliance with the will of another from interested views of obtaining the greatest advantages is justly despised by men of spirit as an abject being."

and here Boswell's heart failed. He packed his bags and stole away to a nearby town the next afternoon, resolving to decline the Recordership by letter "in very smooth, respectful terms." He ran into a fellow courtier here, however, who encouraged his fears that Lonsdale might resent his departure as impertinent, so he returned to give the Earl his decision in person. But Lonsdale was now in a better mood, and with a few kind words persuaded Boswell to change his mind. Boswell summarized his feelings in a sad note on 30 December: "Whelpdale said nobody submitted to keep company with him [Lonsdale], but needy people for the good of their families—or people who had some view of selfinterest. . . . But I thought what does the world *imagine* as to the *consequence* of living intimately with the Great LOWTHER the powerful Proprietor of £50,000 a year. And in the World's estimation one wishes to exist high."[4]

Having paid part of his price for the world's esteem, Boswell received his reward on 11 January 1788, when he was duly elected Recorder; with the prize in his hands, he felt much better: "I was really elated, and could not but inwardly muse how extraordinary it was that I had obtained this promotion." The news spread, and the congratulations poured in with only an occasional warning note. Boswell expressed his own feelings to Percy: "Lord Lonsdale's recommen<ding> me to that office was an honourable proof <of> his Lordship's regard for me, and I may hope that this may lead to further promotion. I have indeed no claim upon his Lordship. But I shall endeavour to deserve his countenance." The common view of Boswell's friends was put succinctly by Lord Rockville, "a man of good understanding, experience, and integrity":

> I take it for granted all these journeys and promotions are the forerunners of your having an M.P. soon annexed to your name—I hope it will happen if you are desirous

4. Journ. 21–30 Dec. 1787.

> of it, and if it does I think Lord Lonsd[al]e is obliged to you equally in accepting of it, as you are to him in Conferring it on you—You know He is not a very Genl favourite of the people either in his own County or indeed Elsewhere. . . . I hope if you are brought in that you will be so on a free liberal footing and without any Important Expence to your Self and family.[5]

Boswell's involvement with Lonsdale did not mean that he had abandoned his plans for contesting the Ayrshire seat at the next election, and the usual maneuvers occupied much of his time and thought. On 3 August 1787 he wrote to John Anderson, a Writer to the Signet and one of Bargany's "votes," that if Bargany would join with him they "should fight together nobly"; on the same day he also wrote to Montgomerie to complain of his "political coldness." Though he found Montgomerie's reply satisfactory, it must have been evident to Boswell that he could not expect support either from him or from Bargany. Both were firmly controlled by Eglinton, who was no longer on cordial terms with Boswell, though he did prefer the Rev. Alexander Millar, Boswell's "Chaplain," to one of the presentations in his gift. Eglinton may have been angry because Boswell revealed his deal with Fergusson in the 1785 *Letter;* Boswell certainly resented Eglinton's neglect of Mrs. Boswell, his relation.[6]

The immediate cause of difficulty lay, of course, in Eglinton's commitment to support Dundas's candidate at the next election.

5. Journ. 10–11 Jan. 1788; from Rockville, 21 Jan. (C 2404), to Percy, 9 Feb. 1788 (*Letters JB,* ii.341). See also, to Forbes, 29 Jan. (Fett. MSS 1337), from Temple, 31 Jan. (C 2854), from Rockville, 4 Feb. (C 2405), from Percy, 29 Feb. (C 2234), from Dempster, 22 Mar. 1788 (C 953); *EA,* 18 Jan. 1788; *LPS 85,* p. 43; *Boswelliana,* pp. 144–45.

6. Journ. 23 July 1786, 9 Apr. 1787, 5 Jan., 13 Apr. 1788; from Millar, 28 Apr. (C 2021), to Forbes, 11 Oct. 1787 (Fett. MSS 1335); Reg. Let. 25 Feb. 1786, 10 Apr., 3 Aug., Sept. 1787; *LPS 85,* pp. 53–56; Adam, p. 29. Boswell may have written some scurrilous verses about the Earl's divorce, called *Too True a Prophesy* (P 77.7; C 3038.4).

One way of gaining Dundas's support would have been to attract Pitt's favorable notice, but this Boswell could not accomplish. He met Pitt with Dundas once, for example, at the Houses of Parliament in March 1788: Dundas was frank and friendly, but Pitt, who paid no attention to him, "looked cold and stiff and proud," which roused Boswell's indignation. As Courtenay reminded him, he had no real claim on either, because he had written against Fox's East India Bill from principle "without regard to party," and he had forfeited Dundas's notice by opposing the Diminishing Bill. Boswell admitted the truth of these arguments, but added in his own defense:

> As I had done the King's Cause essential service, I thought I was entitled to a reward; and as Mr. Dundas had engaged some years ago by letter to assist me in obtaining promotion, and had declared upon his honour, in a conversation with me, that my Court of Session Pamphlet had not been taken ill by him, I trusted that he would keep his word, or rather I was *determined* that by and by he *should*, otherwise he should answer to me.

These were brave words, but they were as futile as Boswell's suddenly conceived notion to attack Pitt's East India Bill; as soon as he thought of it, he realized, as he wrote in his journal: "This was a rash sally of a mind sowred by Pitt's neglect of me, after I had done so much for his cause, (though as the *King's* Cause, to be sure)."[7]

Boswell's desire to support Pitt's national policies kept him from going over to Fox, just as his desire not to make a further enemy of Dundas barred him from openly joining the anti-Dundas faction in Scotland. William Cuninghame of Enterkine came to him in March 1788 with a "foolish application" to vote against the Fergusson–Eglinton alliance in any event. "I told him plainly," Boswell noted, "that I myself was a Candi-

7. Journ. 8, 15 Mar., 19 Apr. 1788.

date for the County; that the only positive resolution I would declare was that I would prefer myself to Sir Adam, but if I had not a majority of the *Real* Freeholders for me, I would not be elected." Boswell went on to say that though he disapproved of Fergusson, he might think it his duty to vote for him against "a professed follower of the Opposition," like "Fish" Craufurd. Cuninghame then suggested that Sir John Whitefoord, a Pitt supporter, might have the best chance of success, but Boswell refused to commit himself to Whitefoord either: "I was positive to come under no engagement whatever. I stood upon the purest independent interest. I never had solicited a Peer. I thought it improper to do it. I asked the votes of the Gentlemen. Whoever should think me worthy of his vote would honour me highly. If he thought another more worthy, I should not take it amiss. It was his duty to vote for him."

In accordance with this attitude of independence, Boswell had informed Dumfries, who was meditating an opposition to the Eglinton–Dundas coalition, that he intended to stand, but added that "His Lordship, knowing this, might dispose of his interest as he pleased." At a London meeting of the Landholders of Scotland, called to discuss county representation, Boswell spoke up boldly against the interference of peers, only to find himself without backing, and opposed by several noblemen, including Hopetoun, Kinnaird, and Sempill. Boswell's motion, however, that the old electoral laws should be clarified in preference to introducing reforms, accorded with the conservative temper of the group, and was passed by a large majority. But the meeting also made Boswell realize that he was unwise to isolate himself as much as he did from Scotsmen of all ranks.[8] It was an old mistake.

8. Journ. 17, 22, 29 Mar., 1788. The reform movement was still connected to the Henry Erskine, anti-Dundas faction (Mathieson, pp. 99–109. See G. S. Veitch, *The Genesis of Parliamentary Reform,* 1913, pp. 103, 243–44, and, for an example, *SM,* 50, 1788, 412). Curiously enough, Kinnaird and Sempill were later active in the burgh reform movement (Mathieson, pp. 120–21).

Having written in April 1788 to his cousin, George Campbell of Treesbank, that he now intended to exert himself as a candidate for Ayrshire, Boswell headed north on 15 May.[9] He knew his chances were slim, but he was determined to campaign vigorously. By 1 July, when he returned to England to go on the Northern Circuit, he found his prospects rather encouraging. He told Malone:

> having been a declared candidate for the County ever since the last election I found such an appearance of stirring, that it was proper for me to begin my canvas directly, in which I tell *you,* not ostentatiously, that I have met with more success than I expected. You know that in the scotch counties there are comparatively speaking few freeholders, I suppose not above 300 in any county; and if the votes which I and many others call *nominal and fictitious votes* be struck off according to the Lord Chancellor's opinion, I suppose there will not be above fourscore in Ayrshire. But the uncertainty as to the *sincerity* of each of those votes (as Lord Thurlow well expressed himself)[1] that is to say being really and true the freehold of the voter, and not a vote *by* the *Grantor through* the voter, will make our county elections curiously dubious if no law be made to ascertain with more precision the legality of our votes. I stand between two parties—the State Coalition interest which is to support one candidate, and a strange coalition between Lord Eglintoune and Sir Adam Fergusson who are both with the present administration, but which has given great offence to many of their friends, who will therefore prefer me who am of the same

9. Journ. 15 May 1788; Reg. Let. 22 Apr. 1788. Another motive for Boswell's journey was his wife's illness (to Forbes, 31 May 1788, Fett. MSS 1338; L 545).

1. See ante, p. 6 n.7. A list in the *Scots Magazine* in 1790 gives the number of real votes in Ayrshire as 86 and nominal votes as 119 (52, 354 n.*), but see ante, p. 59.

political way of thinking, without having the exceptionable circumstance of being in a confederacy to enthral the County. . . . I return to Auchinleck from the Circuit, that I may complete my round of the Freeholders.[2]

Whether many of the freeholders took Boswell as earnestly as he took himself is dubious. On the Circuit, for example, he met an old friend, Keith Stewart, whom Boswell reported as being "dry and rather sarcastical" when he talked of being a candidate: "He said, 'If you mean to be serious I can say nothing (from my connection with Lord Eglintoune) till I know what he is to do.' "[3] Many of Boswell's friends must have given him the same answer.

Boswell returned to Scotland to find that others were active candidates. Whitefoord again wished to stand, and the Eglinton–Dundas group had selected William MacDowall of Garthland (Wigtownshire) to stand. MacDowall's status as an outlander gave Boswell a point of attack, and a meeting of the "real freeholders" of Ayrshire, which was held at Kilmarnock on 25 September, turned into a meeting of partisans that obediently condemned MacDowall and acclaimed Boswell as their candidate. In spite of the brave newspaper account, probably few freeholders attended, since only Sir William Cuningham of Robertland is specifically named beside Boswell and Craufurd of Craufurdland. The great lords of the "State Coalition," Glencairn, Dumfries, and Cassillis, had also fixed on a candidate, Sir Andrew Cathcart, Cassillis's nephew. This formidable combination naturally wished to attach the votes of Boswell and Whitefoord, while each of them nourished the usual hope of squeezing in, if the two large factions were evenly enough divided, by throwing his interest to the highest bidder.[4]

2. To Malone, 12 July 1788 (L 938, a continuation of *Letters JB,* ii.349–51).

3. Journ. 5 July 1788.

4. To Malone, 18 Sept. (L 939), to [Lonsdale, ?28] Sept. (L 882), from Lonsdale, 28 Sept. (C 1778), to [Bruce Campbell], 12 Nov. 1788 (*Letters*

Meanwhile, the King's attack of insanity in November 1788 caused a national crisis, and Boswell once more saw an opportunity for advancement in the overthrow of the Pitt ministry. He confessed that he was carried away by the Prince's cause, and thought of writing one of his "very warm popular pamphlets" for it. "It is said the Chancellor joins the Prince," he wrote to his wife, "and I should think that his Royal Highness will carry it in Parliament. They will be bold or desperate men who will set themselves against the Heir apparrent, whose right of governing may be soon put beyond all question."[5] The attitude of Lord Lonsdale was crucial, however, and though Boswell thought Lonsdale supported the Prince he could not find out definitely because Lonsdale became ill with rheumatic fever. Boswell felt he could not act without Lonsdale's approbation, since they were now closer than ever, and Lonsdale had entrusted him with some highly confidential business which Boswell found very flattering to himself. The nature of this business is unknown, but it is obvious that Boswell thought himself very close to a seat in Parliament. He wrote to Lonsdale:

> I cannot go to sleep without expressing how much I feel myself obliged to your Lordship for the very honourable distinction which your Lordship has now in view for me. Being the representative of an ancient family and possessed of talents which when under able direction may [I] flatter myself be of some consideration in publick Affairs I hope that Ambition which has ever agitated me is not wrong and ought not to be suppressed. I am a zealous freind to our limited Monarchy and wish to support the

---

JB, ii.472), to Temple, 10 Jan. 1789 (*Letters JB,* ii.355); Reg. Let. 12 Nov. 1788; *EA,* 30 Sept. 1788. The four candidates mentioned in Burns's *Fête Champêtre* (apparently written in or shortly after July 1788) are Fergusson, Montgomerie, Boswell, and Whitefoord (see *BP,* xvii.127 n.2).

5. To [Margaret Boswell], 24 Nov. 1788 (L 182). See, to Forbes, 12 Dec. 1788 (Fett. MSS 1339), to Temple, 10 Jan. 1789 (*Letters JB,* ii.355–56).

> Crown against faction but I am attached to no Party but to your Lordship. In the present or any other opening for me I shall most gratefully be, My Lord. . . .[6]

Boswell made notes for a pamphlet on the Regency Bill, but was prudent enough not to publish it.[7] Actually Lonsdale was supporting the Prince,[8] but Boswell does not seem to have been sure of it until early in February 1789, and by that time his enthusiasm for the Prince's cause had cooled. "Considering what myrmidons are about the Prince," he wrote to his wife, "it is certainly right to limit his Regency considerably, at least for some time." He added with great pleasure: "Sir Adam Fergusson's having gone against Pitt is *capital,* as the phrase is. He means to prevent the Regency Ministry from being against him in Ayrshire. But he will find himself mistaken. I shall consider calmly whether to avow Myself against *both* the *Coalition Candidates,* as they both now are."[9]

Politically, it was every man for himself. Thurlow, the Lord Chancellor, had made his rapid and notorious shift to the

6. To [Lonsdale], 23 Nov. 1788 (L 883). See Journ. 27 Mar. 1788; to [Margaret Boswell], 28 Nov. 1788 (L 183), 28 Jan. 1789 (*BP,* xvii.144).

7. To Temple, 10 Jan. 1789 (*Letters JB,* ii.355–56); Regency Bill. Notes for a pamphlet (M 250).

8. To Margaret Boswell, 9 Feb. 1789 (*BP,* xvii.146); *Hist. MSS Comm.,* 13th Report, App. III (1892), p. 389; A. S. Turberville, *The House of Lords in the Age of Reform, 1784–1837* (1958), p. 48 n.4. The courting of Lonsdale by both sides appears in *Hist. MSS Comm.,* 13th Report, App. VII, pp. 141–46.

9. To [Margaret Boswell], 23 Jan. 1789 (L 186). See, to Forbes, 27 Jan. 1789 (Fett. MSS 1340). The compilers of the *View of the Political State of Scotland* remarked about Fergusson: "He is an able man, and of a respectable character; but though he has been long in Parliament, and is a Lawyer, no provision has been made for him by Mr. Pitt" (Adam, p. 19). In spite of this motive for disaffection and Boswell's direct statement, I can find no evidence that Fergusson wavered in his support of Pitt. On the contrary, he voted three times with Pitt and Dundas during the Regency crisis, 16 December 1788, 19 January, and 11 February 1789 (*Parliamentary Register, 1788–89,* xxv.95, 290, 466).

Prince's side and back, and Boswell was swayed by the arguments of the return journey. Confusion led to cynicism; Boswell told Temple, "I begin now to think that whatever Administration should appoint you and me to good places would be the best." And again Boswell's old feeling of resentment against the Government came to the fore: "Pitt (probably influenced by Dundas) has used me very ill. But I yet *cannot* relish the *Coalition,* especially that worthless Minister Lord North. *Nous verrons.*" A further complaint was that Dundas had promised Lord Auchinleck on his deathbed he would look after Boswell's brother, David, and he had not yet done anything for him.[1]

The King's recovery stabilized the general situation, but left Boswell further at a loss how to proceed, and full of repetitious complaints. He reminded Temple again, with a sense of futility and great grievance, that Dundas avoided him even though he had assured Boswell that the 1785 *Letter* had made no difference in their relations. Dundas had further prejudiced Pitt against him, and Pitt had not even answered any of the several letters Boswell had written to him. Bennet Langton had fed Boswell's resentment by saying it was a disgrace that Pitt had not attached Boswell to his administration, "a man of . . . popular and pleasant talents, whose merit, he has acknowledged in a letter under his own hand." Indeed, Boswell admitted to Temple, "Pitt is the ablest and most useful minister" of any of those whom they knew, yet perhaps he would be justified in attacking him, especially since Pitt had behaved insolently toward Lonsdale.[2]

These notions of ill-usage and projected revenge were daydreams in the realistic world of politics, as Boswell must have

1. Journ. 12 Dec. 1784; to Temple, 10 Jan. (*Letters JB,* ii.356), 16 Feb. (*Letters JB,* ii.357–58), to Forbes, 23 May 1789 (Fett. MSS 1341; L 546); Reg. Let. 8 Jan. 1784; Robert Gore-Browne, *Chancellor Thurlow* (1953), pp. 261–78.

2. 31 Mar. 1789 (*Letters JB,* ii.365–67).

occasionally realized. His services to Pitt were ancient history, as was Pitt's letter to him, and Dundas certainly had pretext enough to neglect Boswell if he wished to do so. Temple saw the situation clearly; though he agreed that Dundas had not helped David as he should have, yet David was not immediately useful to him as others were, and David was wise to persevere with patience in this matter. Boswell himself should approach Pitt more calmly: "A person of your family, fortune, and situation appearing so solicitous for office and preferment cannot raise you in the idea of a minister," and Boswell's last letter to Pitt "had a tendency to give offence rather than to obtain the object" of his wishes. Pitt expected to be courted, not threatened; nothing would be gained by opposition.[3]

At this point Boswell thought of a short cut to conspicuousness; he would promote an Address to the Prince of Wales congratulating him on his behavior during the King's illness. This would serve several purposes: it might attract the notice and favor of the Prince; it would bring Boswell prominently to the attention of his county; and it would show Pitt and Dundas that it was dangerous to ignore him. A Quarter Sessions meeting of the Justices of the Peace for Ayrshire was held on 5 May 1789; only six Justices were present, a disappointingly small number, but Boswell was elected preses, and his motion for an address was carried. Written by Boswell, the Address read in part:

> While your Royal Father, our beloved Sovereign, was afflicted by an awful visitation of Divine providence, We, Sir, were none of those who pressed forward to worship the appearance of a rising Sun. But now that Almighty God has been graciously pleased to restore His Majesty to perfect health and the full exercise of his Government, we humbly beg leave, from the purest disinterested motives, to assure your Royal Highness of the grateful sense

3. 26 Apr. 1789 (C 2870).

> which we entertain of your admirable moderation and truly patriotic conduct.

The Address was then triumphantly circulated among the absent Justices for signature, and sent off to the Earl of Eglinton to be presented by him and any other J.P.'s who happened to be in London. Boswell himself failed to be on hand for the presentation, as he had hoped; Eglinton promised to introduce him to the Prince the next winter, but the promise was never fulfilled.[4]

This was a successful move for public attention, though the reaction was not entirely favorable. John Kennedy of Greenan, to whom Boswell had sent the Address, approved of its content but regretted that it had not been proposed at a fuller meeting, and an anonymous J.P. remarked in a letter to the *Edinburgh Evening Courant* that under the circumstances it could hardly be said to express the will of the majority of Ayrshire Justices. Nor did Temple think it a wise step:

> I cannot say I much approve your Country politicks. To oppose Dundas can never answer any good purpose and as to the Prince of Wales, you might as well have left others to address him. . . . It is to be feared that this instance of your *Conspicuousness* will neither recommend you to the King nor the Minister. . . . You shew every one how eager you are for office and preferment, and yet by your own rashness throw obstacles in your way.[5]

4. To [Robert Boswell], 21 May (*L 223), to Eglinton, 23 May (L 495), to Forbes, 23 May (Fett. MSS 1341; L 546), from John Boswell, "Old Knockroon," 23 May (C 392), from Eglinton, 31 May (C 1183), to Eglinton, 13 July (L 496), from Eglinton, 13 July (C 1184), to Temple, 2 Aug. (*Letters JB,* ii.376), to Eglinton, 26 Aug. 1789 (L 497). The Address was printed in full in the *Edinburgh Evening Courant,* 21 May 1789 (P 4), and in Percy Fitzgerald, *Life of James Boswell* (1891), ii.61–63. Both a rough draft and a fair copy of the Address survive (M 12).

5. From Kennedy, 16 May (C 1658), to Temple, 22 May (*Letters JB,* ii.371), from Temple, 28 May (C 2871), to Robert Boswell, 27 June 1789

That May, Lonsdale peremptorily summoned Boswell to accompany him to London on legal business for Carlisle. Boswell had recently informed Temple that he hoped Lonsdale would become more and more his patron, and that he was making the trip, despite his wife's serious illness, because "to be *zealous* is with justice a strong recommendation; and such is his great Parliamentary influence, that be minister who will, he may when he pleases, get almost any thing for a friend. I have no right to expect that he will give me a Seat in Parliament, but I shall not be surprised if he does." Boswell then summarized again the outlook in Ayrshire and his opinion of Pitt:

> *Entre nous* my chance for representing my own County is very small. . . . Against [MacDowall] there are three Candidates: One who has a large number of votes, and two of us who have each such a number that he cannot succeed unless we both join him. It is possible, that by remaining firm, there may [be] such a throw of the dice or such a junction that I may be member at least for a part of the Parliament. Mean time *knowing my small chance*, I spend almost nothing in electioneering—yet keep up a spirited appearance. . . . As to Pitt, he is an insolent fellow, but so able that I *must* upon the whole support him, against the *Coalition.* But I will *work* him; for he has behaved very ill to me. Can he wonder at my wishing for preferment, when Men of the first family and fortune in Great Britain struggle for it?[6]

(*L 224); *Edinburgh Evening Courant,* 21 May 1789 (P 4). Col. Craufurd of Craufurdland replied vigorously to this attack in the same newspaper on 1 June (P 4 and C 851). A list of "Justices of the Peace" (C 53) and an Extract from the Records of the Justices of the Peace (C 52) indicate that eventually about 35 of approximately 140 Justices signed the Address.

6. To Temple, 5 Mar. (*Letters JB,* ii.361), to [Robert Boswell], 21 May (*L 223), to Temple, 22 May (*Letters JB,* ii.370–71), to Forbes, 23 May 1789 (Fett. MSS 1341; L 546).

When in London, Boswell received the dreaded news that his wife was worse, and he set off at once for Ayrshire. She was dead when he arrived. This was a terrible blow, and Boswell reproached himself for having left her; his remorse was not lessened by Lonsdale's temporary neglect of him. But mourning gave way to the exigencies of politics: Montgomerie was appointed Baggage Master and Inspector of the Roads in North Britain on 27 June at a salary of £500 a year, and the special election was set for 3 August. The compilers of the *View of the Political State of Scotland* thought the race would be fairly close, estimating the voting strength as follows:[7]

	Certain or Probable	*Doubtful*
MacDowall	61	21
Cathcart	50	7
Whitefoord	10	4
Boswell	4	2
	64	13

Boswell, on the scene, was not hopeful, even though he and Whitefoord had definitely joined Cathcart; however, they would make an "admirable figure," he told Temple, and he hoped to negotiate for part of a Parliament at the next general election. MacDowall won by the large majority of 21 votes, and his success, as David Boswell observed, was "a good omen

7. To Temple, 4 June (L 1238), to Lonsdale, 8 June (L 887), to Richard Penn, 3 July (L 1058), from Penn [10 July] (C 2220), from Fairlie, 11 July (C 1232), to Forbes, 15 July (L 547), from Lonsdale, 20 July (C 1780), to George Wood, 29 July 1789 (*L 1305.4); *BP*, xvii.117; *SM*, *51* (1789), 311–12. I have drawn these very tentative estimates from the figures and comments supplied in Adam, pp. 18–42. It should be remembered that these figures were compiled some time in advance, probably in the winter of 1789, and that the compilers supported Cathcart. They had no doubt that Boswell would vote for him (Adam, p. 30).

for Sir Adam Fergusson at the general election, unless something extraordinary should happen in the mean time."[8]

Boswell fell back on his last and strongest hope, Lonsdale. He spent part of the summer with him in the North, and was in attendance during the fall in London, where Richard Penn, another Lonsdale dependent, encouraged him by saying that Lonsdale had noted Boswell's desire to be in Parliament. Boswell thought to himself that he would not wish to be in Parliament unless he were given a good deal of independence, but his public language was of a different cast. Congratulating Lonsdale on a victory over the Duke of Norfolk in Wigton, Boswell wrote: "And now, My Lord, allow me humbly to press upon your Lordship the *use,* as old fashioned sermons say, of this recent proof of the great power of Lowther. May it be increased more and more, and may your steady friends be made to shine arround you in their several orbits."[9] Boswell assisted at Lonsdale's victory (temporary as it proved) to make freemen in Carlisle without restraint in December 1789; and he dined a number of times at his London house during the early months of 1790, always conscious that he lived much "with a Great Man who upon any day that his fancy shall be so inclined may obtain for me an office which would make me independent."[1]

Instead of his prospects becoming brighter, they began to dim. It was not possible for Boswell to live in enduring harmony with his patron; he would endure much of what Penn

8. To Temple, 2 Aug. (*Letters JB,* ii.375–76), from T. D. Boswell, 17 Aug. 1789 (C 516); *EA,* 7 Aug. 1789. See *Letters of George Dempster,* p. 196. The three certain Boswell votes, apart from his own, were nominal votes made by his father.

9. Journ. 14 Nov. 1789; to Temple, 23 Aug. (*Letters JB,* ii.376–78), to [Robert Boswell], 12 Sept. (*L 225), to Temple, 13 Oct. (*Letters JB,* ii.379), to Lonsdale, 26 Oct. 1789 (L 889). See Journ. 10 Nov.–20 Dec. 1789.

1. Journ. 7 Dec. 1789, 20 Jan., 11, 15 Feb. 1790; to Temple, 28 Nov. 1789 (*Letters JB,* ii.384), 13 Feb. 1790 (*Letters JB,* ii.390); *St. James's Chronicle,* 15 Dec. 1789 (P 60.1); *BP,* xviii.29.

called Lonsdale's "shocking ferocity" for the sake of advancement, but he had too much pride to be entirely reduced to the state of a "dog," as he termed the more servile of Lonsdale's retainers. The first in a series of crises arose in May 1790, when Lonsdale behaved so inconsiderately that Boswell "inwardly resolved to withdraw . . . from all connection with him"; he did not carry out this resolution, perhaps because of the approaching general election, which, as Temple remarked, would serve as a crucial test of Lonsdale's intentions.[2] A further intimation of disaster came from Col. Lowther, who said when he had suggested to Lonsdale that he bring in Boswell for Carlisle, Lonsdale had disapproved because Boswell "would get drunk and make a foolish speech." Boswell noted in his journal: "this, if fairly reported, was an absolute proof that his Lordship had no confidence in me, and indeed his not employing me in Westminster Hall might shew this. I could not bear the thoughts of being engaged by him in some of his political jobs."

On 14 June, Lonsdale precipitated another crisis by demanding that Boswell go north with him to fulfill his duties as Recorder and to attend the Carlisle election. Penn and Col. Lowther hinted that he should not hang back now; David and Temple urged him to resign his office; Malone suggested that he temporize. Boswell definitely decided to resign, but there was no immediate escape, for Lonsdale, furious, first told him that he had never had any intention of bringing him into Parliament, and then insisted that Boswell fulfill his immediate duties as Recorder: he had solicited the position, and there was no time to elect a successor.[3]

The catastrophe came during the trip north. Boswell further irritated Lonsdale by talking of his "liberal and independent views, and of their inconsistency with being brought in by him

2. Journ. 16 Dec. 1789, 4, 10–11 Apr., 15–16, 22 May 1790.

3. Journ. 14–17 June, 14 July 1790; to [Lonsdale], 15 June (L 890), to Temple, 21 June 1790 (*Letters JB,* ii.396–97).

unless special terms were granted." Lonsdale used "shocking words" in reply and offered to give him satisfaction. Boswell's account continues:

> "My Lord," said I, "you have said enough." I was in a stunned state of mind, but calm and determined. He went on with insult: "You have kept low company all your life. What are *you,* Sir?" "A gentleman, My Lord, a man of honour; and I hope to shew myself such." He brutally said, "You will be settled when you have a bullet in your belly."

But Boswell staunchly maintained his dignity and his courage, and the quarrel was patched up.[4]

Having left Lonsdale at Lancaster to attend to election business, Boswell proceeded to Carlisle in a wretched state of mind. His letter of resignation is dated 23 June 1790, but he was forced to remain for the election poll, and to carry out other duties. "Never again," he wrote to his daughter, Veronica, on 2 July, "shall I make myself dependent upon any great man. . . . I shrink from the noise and tumult of the election. Should the Earl be *diabolical* he may continue it till Monday 19 July." Boswell was, in fact, in "irksome captivity," deeply and unwillingly involved in "low, dirty politicks," though he refused to go to the lengths that Lonsdale demanded. Once he thought himself in danger from a mob, and he was continually subjected to Lonsdale's "ferocious caprice." Though ill with a venereal disease and often "in such a state of spirits that the grashoper is a burthen," he "played the game all through" until Lonsdale released him on 15 July. "I parted from the Northern Tyrant in a strange equivocal state; for he was half irritated,

4. Journ. 17–20 June 1790; to Temple, 21 June (*Letters JB,* ii.396–98), to Forbes, 2 July 1790 (Fett. MSS 1346); Memorandum. On JB's quarrel with Lord Lonsdale, 17 July (in error for June) 1790 (M 196). Boswell was asking for terms which Lonsdale had not even granted to Pitt (Pares, *King George III and the Politicians,* pp. 36–37).

half reconciled," Boswell told Temple: "But I promise you I shall keep myself quite independent of him," and this promise he kept.[5]

Boswell now felt that his situation was desperate: he had no chance to win the seat for Ayrshire or money to purchase one somewhere else; certain of his failure at the English bar, he was unable to bear the idea of returning to an advocate's life in Edinburgh or a laird's life at Auchinleck. He was ready, he maintained, to go to the East Indies, the West Indies, anywhere. Perhaps a friend or two in London could help, but even this possibility seemed slight. Yet life had to go on, and amid the commiseration of his friends Boswell looked to see what could be salvaged of his hopes.[6] As early as December 1789, he had been interested in publishing a pamphlet on the "Loyalty of Ayrshire," which was to contain the Ayrshire addresses of 1784 and 1789. The pamphlet was to include as well an attack on Pitt's Regency Bill with a defense of the Duke of Queens-

5. Journ. 21 June–15 July, 1790; to the Mayor, Aldermen, Baliffs, and Capital Citizens of Carlisle, 23 June (*Letters JB,* ii.398), to Robert Boswell, 24 June (*L 234), to Penn, 26 June (L 1059), to Robert Boswell, 28 June (*L 235), from Penn, 28 June (C 2222), to Malone, 30 June (L 942), from Temple, 30 June (C 2887), to Forbes, 2 July (Fett. MSS 1346), to Veronica Boswell, 2 July (L 263), to Temple, 21 July 1790 (*Letters JB,* ii.399–400).

Boswell remained on rather distant terms with Lonsdale, though he dined with him in the summer of 1794 (to Le Fleming, 3 Mar. 1795, *R. B. Adam Library,* i.second p. 10).

6. Journ. 2 July 1790; to Forbes, 2 July (Fett. MSS 1346), from Forbes, 9 July (C 1292), from Temple, 16 Aug. 1790 (C 2889), from Dempster, 8 May 1791 (C 954). Dempster's letter must have been delightful consolation: "It is in vain you assign the selfish and wise reason that nothing was to be expected from such a Patron. . . . Your real motive was, I am confident, some whiggish independant spirit of Peccant humour, hereditary I own and therefore the more excuseable, but also the more dangerous. Our Edition of the Story, was that his Lordship intended bringing you into Parliament, That Lord Loughbro' had got the Prince to ask the Seat for Anstruther, and altho' it was obvious this favour when so asked could not be refused, yet you had taken Pet and as Aphra says in the play *dissolved the Connection.*"

berry and the Marquess of Lothian, who had gone over to the Prince during the Regency crisis and had been stranded there, much assailed by public ridicule, when the King recovered. Boswell communicated this plan to Queensberry, but the project came to nothing, either because of Queensberry's lack of interest or because the subject was no longer timely.[7]

Otherwise, Ayrshire promised little. One of the reasons Boswell had not wanted to go to Carlisle in June 1790 was its proximity to Ayrshire, where the general election was being held on 19 July; his neighbors might expect that a candidate could make it the rest of the way, but Boswell had finally resolved not to stand this time. He wrote to Veronica:

> As I myself have no chance in Ayrshire, my standing would do me no good but the contrary; and as I believe a union between Sir A. Cathcart, Sir J. Whitefoord and myself would not be sufficient to defeat the coalition between Lord E. and Sir A. Fr aided by ministerial influence, I think the triumph will be smaller, if victory can be ascribed to our separate interests not agreeing, and I may decline with a good grace, declaring that I hope for effectual support on a future occasion.

He thought that he might address the real freeholders, mentioning that he would stand once nominal and fictitious votes were outlawed; in this way he could keep up his candidacy, which gave him consequence.[8] This was also the official version he presented to the world in the autobiographical sketch pub-

7. To Robert Boswell, 4 Feb. (*L 230), to Queensberry, 9 Mar. (L 1093), from Queensberry, 12 Mar. (C 2339), to [Robert Boswell], 3 Apr. (*L 232), 17 Sept. 1790 (*L 238); Reg. Let. 18 Dec. 1789, 13 Apr. 1790; "Loyalty of Ayr<shi>re, with a fair State of the conduct of the Duke of Queensberry and The Marquis of Lothian" (M 13). Queensberry lost his place at Court and Lothian his regiment after the King's recovery (*Correspondence of Charles, First Marquis Cornwallis,* ed. Charles Ross, 1859, ii.27–28).

8. Journ. 14, 30 June, 5, 9 July 1790; to [Robert Boswell], 3 Apr. (*L 232), to [Lonsdale], 15 June (L 890), to Robert Boswell, 24 June

lished in the *European Magazine,* where Boswell stated that he had declined the poll because "the power of the Minister for Scotland was exerted for another person, and some of those whose support he might reasonably have expected could not withstand its influence; he therefore declined giving his friends the trouble of appearing for him; but has declared his resolution to persevere on the next vacancy."[9]

Fergusson was chosen unanimously,[1] as Boswell had expected, but in November 1790 the rumor spread that he was to get a place and vacate his seat. This occasioned a strong letter from Boswell to Dundas:

> I assure you *solemnly upon my honour* that in the year 1784 when I was of no inconsiderable service to the present administration, you gave me your *word* and *hand,* after dinner at Hillhead, that you would give me your interest to be member for my own County, which has ever been and ever will be the fond object of my ambition. I have never claimed that *promise,* because it was made, after we had participated largely of your generous wines, and *I wish to do as I would be done by.* . . . Mr. Pitt (I am utterly at a loss to know for what) has treated me arrogantly and ungratefully, as I can state to you, at our leisure. Mean time, I nevertheless am compelled for my own interest as Laird of Auchinleck, and as a sincere lover of my Country, to support him. Colonel Fullarton is a candidate for Ayrshire. *That great County must not go into opposition.*

Boswell never mentions this promise elsewhere, and it is obvious that Dundas, perhaps because of the generous wines, had

---

(*L 234), to Veronica Boswell, 2 July (L 263), to Temple, 21 July 1790 (*Letters JB,* ii.400).

9. *Lit. Car.,* p. xliii.

1. *EA,* 23 July 1790; *View of the Political State of Scotland,* attributed to Alexander Mackenzie, pp. 51–60. See Furber, pp. 217, 227.

forgotten any such commitment. His reply has not been recovered, but it is evident from Boswell's next letter that he informed Boswell he had engaged for two Parliaments with Lord Eglinton, and insinuated or stated flatly that Boswell had invented the whole incident. This stung Boswell into a sharp reply. He admitted that the arrangement was contingent on Montgomerie's vacating the seat during his term in office and the matter being settled with Eglinton, but said he had been previously unaware that Dundas's agreement with Eglinton covered more than one Parliament, and continued sarcastically: "As to your compliment on my lively fancy, it has never yet exerted itself in inventing facts; nor am I one of those who are blessed with an accommodating memory which can recollect or invent facts as it may suit self-interest for the time." Boswell concluded: "As my services to the present administration are admitted, and my attachment to it, upon independent principles still continues . . . will you or will you not give me what interest you may have in Ayrshire, that I may represent it."[2] The answer was as obvious to him as to Dundas, who had

2. To Dundas, 16 Nov. (*Letters JB*, ii.524–25), [21–23 Nov. 1790] (*Letters JB*, ii.525–26). Boswell seems to have been disingenuous in pleading ignorance of the Eglinton–Dundas two-term agreement. In his reply to "An Ayrshireman" (*Public Advertiser*, 27 July 1785), he wrote: "I *ask* if he [Fergusson] did not *bind* himself by an *agreement* to support for the whole of this Parliament *any* candidate whom that *Peer* [Eglinton] should name, upon *condition* that that *Peer* should support him for the next Parliament?" And see ante, pp. 121–22. The agreement seems to have been common knowledge (see Adam, p. 18). The range of Boswell's attitudes toward, or approaches to, Dundas in 1790 is indicated by two surviving manuscript fragments: in one, Boswell called him, "Dundas that worshiper of the powers that be—be who they may—that *Valet de* PLACE ready for every minister" (M 84); in the other, apparently intended for a newspaper squib, Boswell emphasized the personal friendship between them in spite of their being "very opposite to each other in the politicks of Scotland." It concludes: "Dundas and Boswell are more alike than is generally supposed. They are both excellent bottle companions. They are both roaring boys! They have both a large stock of *impudence*. The difference is Dundas wisely carries it to market. Boswell *gives* it to his friends" (M 9:5).

no reason to do Boswell so great a favor; also, Boswell was still on distant terms with Eglinton, the other half of the coalition.[3] Ironically, the whole discussion was idle in any case, since Fergusson did not resign his seat.[4]

Boswell did manage to score a few points, however, in his unending battle with Dundas and Fergusson. He brought his relentlessly pursued suit against the "impostor" Fergusson for his Corsican subscription successfully to a close in 1790.[5] And on 4 October 1791 at the Michaelmas head-court, he triumphed over Fergusson in a debate on nominal and fictitious votes. One hundred six of these votes were expunged from the roll by a vote of 25–6, and Boswell's sentiment and perhaps his hand may be seen in the sentence which concludes the account of the meeting in the *Edinburgh Advertiser:* "Thus the great County of Ayr has set a noble example of public spirit and patriotism, in securing the freedom of election, and destroying the *Parchment Barons* of Scotland."[6]

3. Journ. 8 Apr. 1791; from Fairlie, 12 Jan. (C 1234), to Eglinton, 20 Mar. 1793 (L 498), to James Boswell, the younger, 24 Sept. 1794 (L 143).

4. Pitt later proposed Fergusson, "a steady supporter and . . . capable of being a very useful man of business," as Surveyor-General of Crown Lands, to George III (29 Jan. 1791). The King approved, but Fergusson was never appointed (*Later Correspondence of George III,* ed. A. Aspinall, 1962, i.516–17). Appointment to this office would not have required Fergusson to vacate his seat (Robinson, p. 10).

5. Ante, pp. 42–43; to Robert Boswell, 18 July 1785 (*L 203), 4 May (*L 222), 27 June (*L 224), 13 Oct. (*L 226), 8 Dec. (*L 228), 29 Dec. 1789 (*L 229), 4 Feb. (*L 230), 24 June (*L 234), 28 June (*L 235), 17 Sept. 1790 (*L 238), from Robert Boswell, 20 Jan. (C 460), to Robert Boswell, 10 Feb. (*L 244), 15 Mar. 1791 (*L 246); Reg. Let. 20 Oct. 1782, 13 Mar. 1789, 13 Apr. 1790; *Whitehall Evening Post,* 2 Feb. 1790 (P 60.2); *LC,* 6 Feb. 1790.

6. *EA,* 7 Oct. 1791. See Coleridge, *Life of Thomas Coutts,* i.303; *Letters of George Dempster,* pp. 205, 209. There were 221 voters on the roll at the election meeting of 1790, 110 on the roll at the Michaelmas head-court of 1791, and 112 on the head-court roll of 1794 (*Ayrshire,* p. 102). It is ironic that the elimination of these nominal votes may have assured the election in 1796 of Col. William Fullarton, whose projected candidacy

Dundas, too, finally gave David Boswell a position in the Navy Pay-Office, which settled that old obligation. Boswell described to Lady Auchinleck how he had pressed Dundas closely on the matter

> till he gave me his hand and word of honour that David should have the first place that should be vacant in his Office. "Well" said I "remember it, for I would fain think you ane honest fellow." He smiled[7] and said in his manner—"There can be na doubt of that." He accordingly kept his word and he has since without solicitation, but from perceiving his merit given him a promotion though four Members of Parliament solicited him for another person. This is much to his honour so let him flourish.[8]

Just before his exchange of letters with Dundas in 1790, Boswell made another attempt to touch the heart of William Pitt. He composed a ballad, *William Pitt, the Grocer of London,* which he sang no less than six times at the Lord Mayor's feast at the Guildhall, which Pitt attended. Boswell followed this with a lively if diffuse poem on the Slave Trade Bill, *No Abolition of Slavery; or the Universal Empire of Love,* in which he attacked the Abolitionists, Wilberforce, and Fox, and in a more good-humored way his friends, Windham and Courtenay;

Boswell had violently opposed in 1790 (to Dundas, 16 Nov., *Letters JB,* ii.525).

7. MS, smilled.

8. Journ. 5 Feb. 1791; from David Boswell, 30 June 1789 (C 511), to Temple, 13 Feb. 1790 (*Letters JB,* ii.390), to Malone, 25 Feb. (*Letters JB,* ii.423), to Dundas, 11 Apr. (L 468), to Lady Auchinleck, 4 June (L 126), to Dundas, 10 Aug. 1791 (L 470). David's position after promotion in 1792 was as clerk in the Inspector's Branch at a salary of £162.3s a year (*London Calendar . . . for the Year 1792,* p. 132). In 1793, Temple and Boswell were similarly successful after three years of effort in prevailing upon Dundas to help Temple's son, Frank, in his naval career (from Temple, 5 Nov. 1793, C 2944). Both the Temple–Boswell and the Boswell–Dundas correspondences after 1790 are full of references to this project.

he also tried to justify slavery by arguing that the Negroes were better off in civilized hands as slaves than they were as free savages in Africa. To support this point Boswell described the lot of the London poor:

> Hear the shrill piteous cry of *sweep,*
> See wretches riddling an ash heap. . . .
> Some share with dogs the half-eat bones,
> From dunghills pick'd with weary groans.
> (ll.203–09)

In contrast, the lives of the slaves were a parade of carefree contentment:

> Ev'n at their labour hear them sing,
> While time flies quick on downy wing;
> Finish'd the bus'ness of the day,
> No human beings are more gay:
> Of food, clothes, cleanly lodging sure,
> Each has his property secure. (ll.245–50)

Boswell also worked in praise for Thurlow and Pitt, but the portrait of the latter includes a reminder of those of Pitt's measures which Boswell had opposed:

> Thus, like a witch, you raise a storm,
> Whether the *Parliament's Reform,*
> A set of *Irish Propositions,*
> *Impeachment*—on your *own conditions,*
> Or RICHMOND'S wild *fortifications,*
> Enough to ruin twenty nations. (ll.127–32)

Boswell's last, distant bid to attract Pitt's notice met with the same indifferent silence which had greeted his previous overtures.[9]

9. *William Pitt, the Grocer of London* (P 81); *No Abolition of Slavery; or the Universal Empire of Love,* 1791; Newspaper clippings (P 60.2); *BP,* xviii.96–99; *Lit. Car.,* pp. 141–48. An account of the Guildhall dinner and

After this final rejection, which was softened by the enthusiastic reception of the *Life,* Boswell practically abandoned for some time his efforts for preferment or a Parliamentary seat. This is not to say that ambition had left him, or that he did not complain to his friends. But Temple put the case to him fairly:

> Ever dissatisfied, ever repining. People think you too independent, too volatile for business. Wedderburn and Dundas had no manour, no old castle, were not ambitious of the reputation of wit and authorship. . . . You want high place and office. But can you be useful, can you go all lengths with your party? I fear there is no other way of succeeding, and is it worth while at such a price? You have had experience of one patron (it is true you made an ill choice) but where are better to be found? You must afford them inducement to seek you, and I fear they will not think your virtues and talents fit for their use. They are too refined, too conscientious. Disdain them all then, be the Baron, the wit, the philosopher, do not appear to court them, and it may be, they will court you.[1]

Though he could do nothing for himself, Boswell was able to help others less fortunate, since he was prominent in the

---

newspaper reaction to it appears in Lucyle Werkmeister, "Jemmie Boswell and the London Daily Press, 1785–1795," *Bulletin of the New York Public Library,* 67 (1963), 97–101. Pitt left the dinner before Boswell sang (Newspaper clippings, P 60.1).

1. 6 Dec. 1791 (C 2915). See Journ. 21 Feb. 1791; 9 Sept. 1792; from Langton, 2 Oct. 1790 (C 1693), to Alexander Boswell, 10 Feb. (L 93), to [Paoli], 10 Dec. 1791 (L 1023), from Temple, [21 Apr.] (C 2965), 3 Nov. 1794 (C 2976). Perhaps Boswell's last flicker of hope for representing Ayrshire appears in a letter to James Neill of Barnweill (11 July 1792): "Whatever your *caution* may suggest, I shall *myself* stand for Ayrshire, and at least *shame* the *Majority* and *honour* the *chosen few*" (*R. B. Adam Library,* i.second p. 37).

literary world and at least conspicuous in the public eye. Much of his energy went into such activities as his successful fight for Mary Broad and the other Botany Bay convicts,[2] but he was equally diligent in more prosaic matters, like helping an old school friend, Alexander Dawson, obtain a post as a tide-waiter,[3] or rescuing a poor relation who had been pressed into the Navy.[4] It was the same sympathy for those whom he considered unjustifiably oppressed, combined with the admiration Boswell felt for the "Great Man" in any field, that led him to support the cause of Warren Hastings and even to disagree with Burke in person on that delicate subject.[5] Even the dead were not beyond his notice; it is not surprising that a mind sensitive both to public executions at Tyburn and to the martyrdom of Charles I should have been deeply moved by the death of Louis XVI. Boswell started to collect subscriptions for a monument to his memory, but when he tried to enlist official aid Dundas told him that Pitt disapproved, which brought the project to an abrupt conclusion.[6] Boswell also dabbled in London politics, and the last few months of his life found him

2. *BP,* xviii.125–28; F. A. Pottle, *Boswell and the Girl from Botany Bay* (1937). There is a great deal of material about this affair among the Yale MSS.

3. From Dawson, 25 Nov. (C 910), to Dawson, 21 Dec. 1790 (L 405), from Dawson, 24 May (C 911), to [Dawson, c. end of May] (L 406), from Welbore Ellis Agar, 31 May (C 21), from Dawson, 2 June (C 912), from Agar, 3 June (C 22), from Dawson, 11 June (C 913), to Agar, 13 June (L 10), 29 June (L 11), from Agar, 30 June 1791 (C 23), from Dawson, 13 June (C 914), to [Dawson, 16 Aug. 1792] (L 407), from Dawson, 4 Jan. (C 915), to Agar, 16 Feb. (L 12), from Agar, 17 Feb. 1795 (C 24).

4. From David Boswell of Leith, 26 July (C 314), from Edmund Antrobus, 2 Aug. 1791 (C 38).

5. Journ. 20 Mar. 1787, 24 Feb. 1788; Mem. 23 Jan. 1790; to Hastings, 27 Feb. 1790 (L 626), 17 June 1794 (L 630), 24 Apr. 1795 (*Letters JB,* ii.466–67); *Life,* iv.66; *BP,* xviii.273–76.

6. From Coutts, 30 Jan. (C 847), to Dundas, 2 Feb. (L 476), from T. D. Boswell, 3 Feb. (C 521), from Dundas, 5 Feb. 1793 (C 1148); Louis XVI of France (M 171), with French translation (M 170).

canvassing the city for a friend who was campaigning for Alderman.[7]

The one comfort, or rather the one illusion, that Boswell had always retained was that if his situation in London became unbearable he could return to Scotland to become a judge of the Court of Session. Whenever he was momentarily content with life, no prospect appealed to him less. After one party, for example, he noted in his journal: "The *tout ensemble* operated upon me and revived my spirits so much that as I was walking home, I said to myself, 'A Lord of Session? I would not be the Lord President.' So much did I at the moment look down on a narrow, provincial situation. But surely in *solid reason* I was wrong." A few days later his whole future looked hopeless:

> I was now not only disappointed in any views of ambition in the wide sphere of London, but from my having addicted myself almost entirely to English Society, and my aversion to Scotch manners and contempt of provincial consequence being known, I had too much reason to apprehend that should I apply for the office of Lord of Session, I should not be able to obtain it. I was in truth in a woeful state of depression in every respect. The animating delusion that I might get practice in Westminster Hall had vanished; for I saw plainly that all my habits and appearances in publick were, as Malone well observed, against me as a Lawyer; and I was conscious that I had

7. To Alexander Boswell, 23 Feb. (L 122), 18 Mar. 1795 (L 123). The successful candidate was Sheriff Eamer (*The Aldermen of the City of London,* ed. A. B. Beaven, 1908–13, i.172). Boswell campaigned some years earlier for Alderman Curtis (from George Macaulay, 2 July 1791, C 1816, 24 June 1792, C 1817; Song, for the glorious 26th of June, P 76; Newspaper clippings, P 59.6, P 60.1, P 60.2, P 62.3). Miss Werkmeister describes Curtis's anniversary dinner and the newspaper reaction to Boswell's song and behavior (pp. 169–77), and also documents the newspapers' steady ridicule of Boswell from 1785 to 1795, but her inferences about his motives and his authorship of various pamphlets, etc. are not reliable.

> never applied seriously to English Law, and could not bear the confinement and formal course of life which Practice at the bar required. I yet shrunk from the thought of retiring to my seat in the country, and considered that as my profession was *Jurisconsultus,* it would be a sad thing to abandon it.[8]

A life of long and constant disappointment went into this disconsolate review, and it also made Boswell cautious about any prospects. For years he had kept up as much acquaintance as possible with Lord Thurlow, but now he began to wonder if this acquaintance would ever prove valuable.[9] When his friend, William Windham, became Secretary at War in July 1794, Boswell wrote to his son, James: "I hope Windham will make a good Secretary at War. . . . Whether he will have the power and inclination to do any thing for me I know not. I must let him first be well established in office before I try."[1] There is no record that he ever did.

Time told on Boswell in other ways; like most men, he grew more conservative with age. Though approving of the States General, he was opposed to the Revolutionists in France from the beginning, and wrote to Temple in the fall of 1789: "The present state of that country is an intellectual earthquake, a Whirlwind, a mad insurrection without any immediate cause, and therefore we see to what a terrible anarchy it tends. I do not mean that the french ought not to have a *Habeas Corpus* Act. But I know nothing more they wanted." In 1790, he

8. Journ. 21 Dec. 1792, 16, 24–26 Sept. 1793; to Euphemia Boswell, 5 Apr. 1790 (National Library of Scotland MS 2,521 ff. 18–19), to Barnard, 16 Aug. 1792 (L 49), from Temple, 18 July (C 2938), 7 Sept. 1793 (C 2940), 14 June (C 2974), to James Boswell, the younger, 12 Sept. (L 142), 27 Oct. 1794 (L 148).

9. Journ. 7 July 1790, 24 Dec. 1793; from Temple, 21 Feb. 1790 (C 2880), 14 Jan. (C 2899), to Thurlow, 13 May 1791 (L 1246), from [Temple, May or early June] (C 2935), 18 July 1793 (C 2938).

1. To James Boswell, the younger, 21 July 1794 (L 133). See, to Alexander Boswell, 7 Feb. 1794 (L 108).

sketched a play called "Favras," in which Dumont "who has his head full of the fiery modern writings about the rights of man raves like Rousseau" against Favras, the loyal monarchist. Favras "shews that subordination and right of any sort are coeval and coexistent." At home, the Revolutionary Societies aroused strong feelings: "I really look with contempt as well as indignation on these ridiculous and mischievous *Societies* who attempted to disturb nay to overthrow our excellent Constitution under which they as well as all the rest of His Majesty's subjects have such advantages." Uniting action to words, he joined an Association which opposed these Societies.[2]

Though Boswell consistently advocated the abolition of nominal and fictitious votes, he regarded this step as a restoration of the electoral laws rather than as a reform. He had undergone a sudden change of heart on the general subject of Parliamentary reform at the time of writing the second *Letter to the People of Scotland;* from a zealous partisan of the reform cause, he became an opponent of all innovation, having been "fairly converted," he told the Bishop of Killaloe, "by observing that Reformers can agree upon no one Plan, and that all of them have an inordinate spirit of resistance to their Superiors coupled with a desire of power over their inferiors."[3] In consequence he had refused an invitation in 1785 to be a delegate

2. Journ. 4, 14 Nov. 1792; to Temple, 28 Nov. 1789 (*Letters JB,* ii.386), to Andrew Kippis, 11 July 1791 (L 831), to Blair, 3 Nov. 1792 (L 62.2), from Temple, 11 Jan. (C 2931), to Andrew Erskine, 6 Mar. 1793 (L 531), to Forbes, 29 May (Fett. MSS 1359; L 551), to James Boswell, the younger, 29 Nov. 1794 (L 153); Reg. Let. 15 Apr. 1790; "Favras" (M 84); "Let those who abhor all Kings and Priests" (M 328); "Fox's Opposition, 1793" (M 337). The name of the organization which Boswell joined was the "Association for Preserving Liberty and Property against Republicans and Levellers" (P 2).

3. From Fife, 1 June (C 1248), from Temple, 8 June (C 2834), to Barnard, 1 July (L 42), from Temple, 31 Aug. 1785 (C 2835), from Fife, 3 July 1793 (C 1250); *LPS 85,* pp. 29–31, 74, 79. In the MS of *LPS 85,* Boswell deleted a remark that he rejoiced at the recent defeat of a motion to reform Parliament (p. 19).

from Edinburgh to a Reform Convention.[4] Boswell's increasing conservatism even elicited a solemn plea from his son, Alexander, in 1791 that the forthcoming *Life* might not contain any sentiments on liberty different from those expressed in *Corsica:* "I have several times heard you speak quite different in conversation from the Noble sentiment which your Book conveys to the mind."[5] Boswell undoubtedly felt in his later years more admiration for that "subordination of rank, by which all the elegance of life is produced,"[6] than he did for the nebulous concepts of liberty which he had praised in his youth, and which had now materialized in such terrifying form.

One last disappointment was in store for Boswell. He had thought in his early days of becoming an envoy to a foreign court, and more recently had considered going as private secretary to the ambassador on diplomatic missions to the United States and China.[7] Now a big opportunity seemed available for foreign service. The Corsicans had revolted against France, and had almost driven the French from their country in 1793; they announced that they were willing to be annexed to Great Britain, and British troops landed on the island in February

4. From Thomas McGrugar, 15 Oct. (C 1842), to [McGrugar], 20 Oct. 1785 (L 905). Surprisingly enough, Boswell later thought burgh reform in Scotland was necessary (to Alexander Boswell, 19 Nov. 1792, L 104).

5. [c. 20 Mar. 1791] (C 248). Boswell replied, 22 March 1791 (L 96), that he would attend to the subject of liberty in summing up Johnson's character, but he does not seem to have touched on it except for the remark that Johnson "had, perhaps, at an early period, narrowed his mind somewhat too much, both as to religion and politicks" (*Life,* iv.426). Boswell's sentiments had certainly started to shift as early as 18 March 1775, when he wrote to Temple: "That I am a Tory, a lover of power in Monarchy, and a discourager of much liberty in the people I avow" (*Letters JB,* i.213). In *Hypochondriack,* no. 19 (Apr. 1779), he attacks over-zealous "*lovers of liberty,*" and speaks of the misguided "animation of resistance" of his youth. See also *Hypochondriack,* no. 64 (Jan. 1783).

6. Journ. 8 Sept. 1792.

7. Ante, p. 22; Journ. 3 Dec. 1789; to [Lady Mary Lindsay-Crawford], 16 Dec. 1789 (L 865), to Andrew Erskine, 6 Mar. 1793 (L 531).

1794.[8] Boswell's connection with Corsica and Paoli was well remembered, and he sincerely felt himself to be as well qualified as anyone to serve as Minister to Corsica or as its Royal Commissioner. He wrote to Dundas on 17 March 1794 asking for such a post and reminding him of his long and unsuccessful pursuit of preferment, but a "cold Ministerial letter" informed him that Sir Gilbert Elliot had full charge of dealings with Corsica, and that his services could not be used.[9] Elliot indeed had great claims: along with Windham, one of the Whigs who had abandoned Fox for the Ministry in 1793, he was Civil Commissioner at Toulon, and had visited Corsica in January. Boswell complained of his disappointment to his friends, but admitted to himself that he was not sorry this particular application for employment had failed: "I had begun to shrink from the thoughts of quitting London and going among foreigners, etc. etc. But it hurt me to think that Dundas, after his apparrently cordial professions, was minded to neglect me totally. However, I thought of pressing him resolutely."[1]

Whether Boswell actually did secure an interview with Dundas as he proposed is unknown; if he did, the interview could not have been very encouraging, for after the rebuff over Corsica he alternately indulged only "a visionary, pleasing hope" of preferment, or pined at his lack of prospects.[2] But he could never quite reconcile himself to having no political future, and only a few months before his death he thought he

8. J. H. Rose, "British Rule in Corsica," *Pitt and Napoleon* (1912); *Life and Letters of Sir Gilbert Elliot, First Earl of Minto*, ed. [Emma Eleanor Elizabeth], Countess of Minto (1874), ii.211–41.

9. Journ. 17, 26 Mar. 1794; to Dundas, 17 Mar. (*L 478.1; L 478), to Alexander Boswell, 17 Mar. (L 112), from Dundas, 23 Mar. 1794 (C 1151).

1. Journ. 26 Mar. 1794; to [Paoli], 31 Mar. (L 1025), from Temple, 18 Apr. (C 2964), to James Boswell, the younger, 11 Aug. 1794 (L 137), to Paoli [?Mar. 1795] (L 1027); Minto, ii.209–22; *Hist. MSS Comm.*, 12th Report, App. VII (1890), p. 362.

2. To Alexander Boswell, 26 Apr. (L 114), from Temple, 4 May (C 2966), 16 May (C 2967), to James Boswell, the younger, 12 Sept. (L 142), 6 Oct. 1794 (L 145).

saw signs that Dundas might be better disposed toward him. A truer illustration of their relationship was that even small matters miscarried: an office which Dundas had promised eleven years previously to his kinsman, "Young Knockroon," had still not been secured at the time of Boswell's death, 19 May 1795.[3]

"You complain of your ill success in life and so do all who do not succeed," Temple told him, "but perhaps our disappointments are owing to ourselves. You affected a character incompatible with assiduity and business." Boswell was only too aware of this and other defects. He advised his heir, Alexander: "You must be very cautious of letting other people know that you are such an *Observer* and such a *censor morum,* as they may be apt to misunderstand and form a wrong notion of you. I speak from experience, because I am certain that there is not in reality a more benevolent man than myself in the World; and yet, from my having indulged myself without reserve in discriminative delineations of a variety of people, I know I am thought by many to be ill natured."[4]

Boswell's increasing self-awareness made him more bitterly and intensely conscious of his lack of political success. A tone of somber lamentation appears in the comments of his last years on his achievements: "Unluckily I have all my life indulged fond hopes of raising myself and of consequence my family, by obtaining some preferment which would be both honourable and profitable"; on "finding no prospect of attaining my ambitious objects, I tried to soothe myself with the consideration of my fame as a Writer, and that by the good management of my Estate, and saving, I might in time pay my debts." In November 1794, he assured his favorite son, James:

3. To Dundas, 14 June (L 479), from Dundas, 19 June 1794 (C 1152), from Temple, 5 Mar. (C 2979), from John Boswell, "Young Knockroon," 24 Mar. 1795 (C 400); ante, p. 115.

4. To Alexander Boswell, 7 Feb. (L 108), from Temple, 3 Nov. 1794 (C 2976).

"I will try to avoid repining. Yet at the same time, I cannot be contented merely with literary fame, and social enjoyments. I must still hope for some creditable employment; and perhaps I may yet attain to it."[5]

This was not to be, of course; nothing was to satisfy that ambition, which Boswell said, "has ever raged in my veins like a fever."[6] His political career, begun in high and shaky hopes, turned into a series of delays and disappointments, and ended in frustration. Born into the governing class of Great Britain, and possessed of a good estate and fortune, Boswell reached no higher office than the Recordership of Carlisle, which was much inferior to his father's position as Lord of Session and Justiciary. His political influence was restricted to promoting the Corsican cause unsuccessfully in his youth, and to the temporary effects of his later pamphlets. Since Boswell considered his political career as the central purpose of his life, there is little doubt that he saw himself essentially as a failure, a verdict which time has reversed too late to comfort him. "How has Dundas overtopt us all?" Temple once asked him.[7] In his wildest visions of fame, Boswell could hardly have foreseen the day when his journals would be read by hundreds of thousands to whom Dundas was no more than a name in a footnote.

5. Journ. 13 Feb. 1794; to James Boswell, the younger, 27 Oct. (**L 148**), 21 Nov. 1794 (L 152).

6. To Temple, 10 Jan. 1789 (*Letters JB,* ii.353).

7. From Temple, 7 Sept. 1793 (C 2940).

Index

In general, this is an index of proper names, but Part I of the article, Boswell, James, collects and digests under general headings references to his traits of character, opinions, feelings, etc. Observations on specified persons are ordinarily entered under the person in question; for example, Boswell's opinions of Lord Auchinleck will be found under Lord Auchinleck and not under Boswell. Letters to and from Boswell are entered under his correspondent, but letters between other persons are entered under the writer. Place names are entered only when the references have political significance; where Boswell is involved, they are entered under Boswell as well as under the place. Emperors, kings, and British princes of the blood are entered under their Christian names; noblemen and lords of session and their wives are entered under their titles. Ordinarily the styles chosen are those contemporary to the reference (e.g. Mountstuart, John Stuart, *styled* Lord, *not* Bute, John Stuart, 4th E. and 1st M. of), though occasionally further information is provided to avoid confusion. Persons who "flourished" after 1800 are not indexed. Ordinarily the only sources indexed are those published in the eighteenth century or earlier which are mentioned in the text or quoted in the text or footnotes. Along with certain standard abbreviations, the following are used: D. (Duke), M. (Marquess), E. (Earl), V. (Viscount), B. (Baron), L. (Lord, when the Scottish equivalent of Baron), JB (James Boswell), HD (Henry Dundas), AF (Sir Adam Fergusson).